**INDIA BOOKVARSITY**

**LOTUS CHOICES**

**Editor: Mahendra Kulasrestha**

# The Golden Book of ISLAM

## Religion of Equality, Duties and Peace

Lotus
PRESS

# THE GOLDEN BOOK OF ISLAM

Dr. (Mrs.) Nilofer Ahmad
and
Dr. Majdood Ahmad

**The Golden of Islam**

by Dr. (Mrs.) Nilofer Ahmad
and Dr. Majdood Ahmad


ISBN: 81-8382-199-5 (p/B)

**Lotus Press : Publishers & Distributors**
Unit No. 220, 2nd Floor, 4735/22, Prakash Deep Building,
Ansari Road, Darya Ganj, New Delhi- 110002
Ph.: 32903912, 23280047 • E-mail : lotus_press@sify.com
www.lotuspress.co.in



*Published by* : **Lotus Press,** New Delhi-110002
*Printed at* : Concept Imprint, Delhi

## Peace Is Supreme

The root word of 'Islam' in Arabic connotes peace. The word for belief is 'Iman', which is derived from 'Amn', which also means peace. Then, while greeting one another, the Muslim says, 'Assalam-o-Alaikum' which means 'Peace be upon you', to which the other replies in the same manner.

The opening verse of each chapter in the Holy Qur'an describes the main attributes of Allah as Merciful and Compassionate, which is repeated at the start of every work.

All these clearly and unambiguously underline the character of a Muslim and the Islamic society.

Editorspeak

# The Good Points

Although now at age 80, I do not think twice at saying that "I'm not a religious person", when young, my interest in religion was intense, and as editor of a weekly published from Lucknow, which gave me the unique opportunity of writing down as well as publishing my views on various subjects, I used it to explore in this area also in a variety of interesting ways. I met religious leaders and discussed with them, and even formulated an 'Adhyatmic Jiwan Vyavastha' (Life System Based on Spiritualism), which covered every aspect, including the political and economic, of human life. I read as much as I could about other religions also, Christianity and Islam in particular, and later on, when I started contributing to the leading magazines of those times, Sarita, Mukta and Caravan, while critically examining the Hindu systems, I occasionally praised the Islamic values and ethos of equality, which my editor cheerfully published.

As my studies and experience grew, and as I started dabbling more in philosophy than in religion, changing places from Lucknow to Bombay to Delhi via Hoshiarpur in Punjab - with an interlude in Japan – and now when I'm carefully compiling and editing this Golden Books series on religions, my views on Islam, though terribly disturbed by its present-day behaviour, do not seem to have changed in its essentials. In fact, a few more positives have been added to it. Like, the mandatory Zakaat – which, after the grand failure of Communism, I've come to regard as the viable solution to the problem of poverty –, Islamic jurisprudence and economics. My regard for the unlettered Prophet has vastly grown; and I sometimes comment that had he been born in India – or in China for that matter – his mission would have been more successful. I agree with some Western analysts that Arab ethnicity overpowered this great mission for total human welfare, perhaps from day one, after the rather early demise of the great Prophet.

This reminds me of the venerable Gandhian litterateur, Jainendra Kumar, who, when once I told him that I had acquired a biography of Prophet Muhammad, asked me to give it to him post haste, after reading which he gave an inspiring talk at a meeting of social workers and intellectuals held at the NCERT in Delhi. And, he never returned the book to me.

I once met a retired Muslim police chief of Bihar, a scholar of Islam, and a preacher now that he was free, who I thought could write a good book on Islam for non-Muslim readers, to which he agreed, but because he had never written something on the book-scale, he wanted me to collaborate. A well-wishing Muslim friend of mine came to know about it, and he strictly forbade me to do any such thing; he was so afraid of the fanatics! I was not surprised. I'm not surprised that one single problem of a group is so frightening that it is leading so many good things to waste, a few of which are rare. Objective discussions are not possible. Redemption does not seem to be in sight.

I did want to publish a book in this series of religions, but, to be honest, was not keen. Then, as if from the skies, dear Nurin, the only child of the present authors, descended on me, riding a motorbike – yes, that was so. Soon I found that her parents could do the job. I ate a fine vegetarian meal at their home not very far from mine, and was duly impressed. And I was thoroughly satisfied when the manuscript finally arrived; their treatment of the subject was most unique and authentic. I hope readers will welcome it.

I will close this note with a thrilling saying of the Prophet - which I heard for the first time while watching the special TV programme on his birthday: 'The wage-earner must be paid his dues before his sweat is dried'. My wife was running a social work organisation in Delhi at that time, and had a fairly large office. I immediately asked her to have it written in large letters and hang it prominently in her office. Amen!

Authors-speak

# A Religion of Peace, Justice and Brotherhood

*"We begin in the name of Allah, the most Gracious and the most Merciful."*

Our objectives in writing this book are:

1. to clarify that Islam is a religion of peace and is totally against terrorism.
2. to communicate to as many people as possible the guidance of the Almighty Allah and apprise them of the real duties and responsibilities.

In this book, efforts have been made to explain the following points in the light of the Holy Qur'an and Sunnat:

a. Allah commands affirmation in:

   i) Oneness of Allah;

   ii) Allah's angels (Peace be upon them);

   iii) Holy Books of Allah;

   iv) Prophets (Anbiyaas) and Messengers (Rasools) (Peace be upon them);

   v) To believe in the day of Doom, Resurrection and Judgement;

   vi) Individual's Fate - good or bad.

b. There are five fundamental principles of Islam: Imaan, Salaat, Saum, Zakaat, and Hajj.

c. There are three types of rights: Rights of Allah (Haquooqul Allah), Rights of self (Haquooqun Nafs), Rights of people (Haquooqul Ibaad).

d. Allah the Almighty commands establishment of peace, justice, human brotherhood, dignity, amity, equality, love for all and hatred for none. Hence all our brothers and sisters deserve supportive and sympathetic treatment.

e. Islam has streamlined the principles for the professionals engaged in households, business communities, cultivators, factories and science and technology as stated in the Qur'anic verses.

f. The Islamic laws (Shariat) are universal and can be followed for all times to come.

g. Qur'an clarifies various theories on various principles related to astrology, geology, medical sciences, plant and animal kingdom, etc.

This book may Insha-Allah clarify certain general and basic principles of Islam.

The encouragement and support given by our daughter Nurin Ahmad has initially helped us in planning and compilation of this book.

Finally, we would like to sincerely thank the readers of this book and advance thanks to those who would take the trouble of making valuable suggestions regarding it.

# Title Verses on Islam

"There is no compulsion in religion."

(Al Baqara : 2.256)

"'O people of the book! Let us get together on what is common between us and you: that we shall worship none but Allah; that we shall not associate any partners with Him; that we shall not take from among ourselves any lords besides Allah.' If they reject your invitation then tell them: 'Bear witness that we are Muslims (who have surrendered to Allah).'"

(Al-i'Imran: 3.64)

"Verily, this brotherhood of yours is a single brotherhood and I am your only Rabb, therefore, worship Me Alone. But the people have divided their religion into sects betwen them–to Us they shall all return."

(Al-Anbiyaa: 21.92-93)

"O believers! Believe in Allah, His Rasool, the Book which He has revealed to His Rasool, and every Book which He previously revealed. He who denies Allah, His angels, His Books, His Rasools and the Last Day has gone far astray."

(An-Nisaa: 4.136)

"Allah commands doing justice, doing good to others, and giving to near relatives, and He forbids indecency, wickedness, and rebellion. He admonishes you so that you may take heed."

(An-Nahl: 16.90)

"Allah invites you to the Home of Peace and guides whom He pleases to the Right Way."

(Yunus: 10.25)

"If two parties among the believers fall into mutual fighting, make peace between them."

(Al-Hujurat: 49.9)

"Terrorists are to be dealt with severely under the Islamic law, once it is proved that they have really terrorised innocent people... They are the pests of which the society has to be cleared... The 33rd verse of Al Maidah in the Qur'an suggests that the rioters, if captured before repentance, should be either put to sword or finished."

– Dr. Abdul Moghni

## ABBREVIATIONS USED

1. **a.s. – Alaihis Salaam (Peace be upon him)**
2. **s.a.w. –Sallallahu Alaihi Wasallam (May Allah bestow salaah and salaam on him)**
3. **r.a.a – Razi Allahu Anhu/Anha (May Allah be pleased with him/her)**
4. **p.b.u.t. – Peace Be Upon Them**
5. **p.b.u.h. – Peace Be Upon Him / Her**

# Contents

# 1. The Basics

*"In the name of Allah, the Compassionate, the Merciful. All praise is for Allah, the 'Rabb' of the Worlds. The Compassionate, the Merciful. Master of the Day of Judgment. O'Allah! You alone we worship and You alone we call on for help. O'Allah! Guide us to the right way. The way of those whom You have favored; not of those who have earned Your wrath, or of those who have lost the way."*

*(Al-Fathiha: 1.1-7)*

Allah is one and the greatest of all. He is self sufficient master, whom all creatures need. He gave no birth nor was He born. He has given the life and will take it back one day. He is sustainer of all. He is maker of the whole universe. No one is His partner or His companion. None but Allah is worthy of worship. He is for ever and will remain for ever. He is omnipresent and nothing is out of His knowledge. Islam is a religion which teaches total acceptance and submission to Allah - the Almighty. The word 'Islam' is derived from the Arabic verb 'Aslama' which means to accept, surrender or submit. The follower of Islam is known as 'Muslim'. All Muslims believe that 'none is worthy of worship but Allah; Muhammad (Sallallaahu Alaihi Wasallam) is the messenger of Allah.

The Muslims have fundamental faith in Imaan. It means to believe in someone's words and relying solely on His authority. In religious terms, it implies belief in the unseen and relying solely on the authority of the messenger of Allah.

Muslims demonstrate Islam by worshiping Allah, following His commands and strictly avoiding polytheism. Thus Islam is a monotheistic religion. Muslims believe in the doctrine that there is only one God that is Allah - the Almighty.

Monotheism has three aspects: -

a. Oneness of Allah: to believe that there is only one 'Ilah' (God) for the entire universe Who is its Creator, Organizer, Sustainer and Giver of Security, etc.

b. Oneness of the worship of Allah: to believe that none has the right to be worshiped (e.g. –praying, invoking, asking from help, swearing, offering sacrifice, fasting, pilgrimage) but Allah.

c. Oneness of the names and the qualities of Allah: to believe in the following;

   - ✓ We must not name or qualify Allah except by what He or His messenger (S.A.W) has named or qualified Him.
   - ✓ None can be named or qualified with the names or qualifications of Allah.
   - ✓ We must believe in all the qualities of Allah which Allah has stated in His book – The Holy Qur'an and mentioned through His messengers.

●●●

# 2.
# Making of the Universe for Mankind

Universe is defined as all existing things, including the earth and its creatures and all the heavenly bodies.

1) Qur'anic verses referring to the story of the creation of earth, mountains, seasons, skies and heavens are given below.

   a. "Ask them: "Do you really deny the One Who created the earth in two periods and do you set up rivals in worship with Him while He is the Rabb of the worlds. He set upon it mountains towering high above its surface, He bestowed blessings upon it and in four periods provided it with sustenance according to the needs of all those who live in and ask for it. Then He turned towards the sky, which was but smoke, He said to it and to the earth: 'Come forward both of you, willingly or unwillingly,' and they submitted: 'We shall come willing'. So, from this creation, He formed the seven heavens in two periods and to each heaven He ordained its laws. He adorned the lowest heaven with brilliant lamps and made it secure. Such is the design of the All-Mighty, the All-Knowing." (Ha-Mim: 41.9-12)

   b. "Surely your Rabb is Allah Who created the heavens and the earth in six Yome (time periods) and is firmly established on the throne of authority. He makes the night cover the day and the day follows the night automatically. He created the sun, the moon and the stars; and made them subservient to His will. Take note: His is the creation, and His is the command. Blessed is Allah, the Rabb of the worlds! Call on your Rabb with humility and in private; for He does not love the transgressors." (Al-A'raf: 7.54-55)

2) Qur'anic verses referring to that there was universe before mankind are given below:

"Has there not passed over man a period of time when he was nothing – not even mentioned?" (Ad-Dahr: 76.1)

3) Qur'anic verses referring to Adam's creation are as follows:

a. "Note that occasion, when your Rabb said to the angels: I am going to place a vicegerent on earth. The angels said: "Will You place there one who will make mischief and shed blood while we sing Your praises and glorify Your name?" Allah said: "I know what you know not." (Al-Baqara: 2.30)

b. "To Adam We said: "Dwell with your wife in Paradise and eat anything you want from its bountiful food from wherever you wish, but do not approach this tree, or you shall both become transgressors." " (Al-Baqara: 2.35)

c. Shaitan vowed to mislead Adam and his descendants:

"Indeed We created you, then We fashioned you, then We asked the angels: "Prostrate yourselves before Adam." They all prostrated accordingly except Iblees (Shaitan) who did not join those who prostrated. Allah said: "What prevented you from prostrating when I commanded you?" He replied:

"I am better than he; you created me from fire and him from clay." Allah said: "Get down from here. You have no right to brag here of your superiority. Get out; henceforth you are of the petty ones." Shaitan requested: "Give me respite till the Day of Resurrection." Allah said: "The respite you requested is hereby granted." Shaitan declared: "Since You let me deviate, now I will lie in ambush for mankind on Your right way. I will come upon them from the front, from the rear, from the right, and from the left, and You will not find most of them to be grateful." Allah said: "Get out from here, you despicable outcast; I will certainly fill hell with you and all of them who follow you." " (Al-A'raf: 7.11-18)

d. Shaitan caused Adam to lose paradise:

   "But Shaitan tempted them with the tree to disobey Allah's commandment and caused them to be expelled from Paradise, and We said: "Get out from here, some of you being enemies to others, and there is for you in the earth an abode and provisions for a specified period." " (Al-Baqara: 2.36)

e. Need of Allah's revelations for guidance:

   "Get out from here all of you," We said at the time of Adam's departure from Paradise. There will come to you a guidance from Me, those who accept and follow it shall have nothing to fear or to regret. But those who reject and defy Our revelations will be inmates of Hellfire wherein they shall live forever." (Al-Baqara: 2.38-39)

f. "O Prophet, remind mankind about incident when your Rabb brought into existence the offspring from the loins of Adam and his descendants (virtually each single individual of mankind) and made them testify about themselves. Allah asked them: "Am I not your Rabb?" They all replied: "Yes! We bear witness that You are." This We did, lest you mankind should say on the Day of Resurrection: "We were not aware of this fact that You are our Rabb and that there will be a Day of Judgement." " (Al-A'raf: 7.172)

g. "O mankind! We created you from a single pair of a male and a female, and made you into nations and tribes that you might get to know one another. Surely the noblest of you in the sight of Allah is he who is the most righteous. Allah is All-Knowledgeable, All-Aware." (Al-Hujurat: 49.13)

4) Qur'anic verses referring to that there was one nation having one religion for mankind are as below:

   a. "Mankind was one nation having one religion. Later when people invented other religions, Allah appointed Prophets as bearers of good news and warnings; and revealed to them the Book with the True Guidance to settle the matters of dispute between mankind. But the very people to whom it was given, started disputes after the clear arguments had come to them, because of rivalry between one another. Allah has guided the believers by His will to the truth in those matters in which they had differences. Allah guides whom He pleases towards the right way." (Al-Baqara: 2.213)

   b. Creation of jinns and mankind for Allah's worship:

      i. "He created man from sounding clay similar to pottery, and created jinns from smokeless fire." (Ar-Rahman: 55.14-15)

      ii. "We have not created jinns and mankind except to worship Me." (Az-Zariat: 51.56)

5) Qur'anic verse referring to the human life cycle is as below:

"We have created you from the earth, into it We shall return you and from it We shall bring you back to life once again." (Ta-ha: 20.55)

## Not a New Religion

Islam is not a new religion but a divinely executed combination of all the old inspired ones and provides the via-media, the golden means. On the one hand, its comprehensively high code of ethics which is unique for many reasons equips its votary for his journey towards the ultimate goal of a sincere seeker after truth and, on the other, directs its followers to foster and maintain fraternal relations with all the human beings and achieve the utmost progress in all the spheres of arts, commerce, science and material walks of life. Islam absolutely discards: narrow-mindedness, arrogance, false pride, avarice, injustice, tyranny, oppression and self aggrandizement.

1) Qur'anic verses referring to that no religion is acceptable to Allah other than Islam are as below:

   a. "Are they looking for a religion other than the Deen (religion and Way of Life) of Allah knowing well that everything in the heavens and in the earth, willingly or unwillingly, has submitted to Him? And to Him they shall all return." (Al-i'Imran: 3.83)

   b. "If anyone is looking for a religion other than Islam, then let it be known that it will not be accepted from him; and in the Hereafter he will be among the losers." (Al-i'Imran: 3.85)

   c. "O Prophet, say: "We believe in Allah and what is revealed to us and what was revealed to Ibrahim (Abraham), Isma`il (Ishmael), Ishaq (Isaac), Ya'qoob (Jacob) and their descendants; and in that which was given to Musa (Moses), Isa (Jesus) and other Prophets from their Rabb; we do not discriminate any one of them, and to Allah do we submit in Islam". " (Al-i'Imran: 3.84)

2) Qur'anic verses referring to that Allah named the believers as Muslims is as below:

   "Strive in the Way of Allah as you ought to strive with sincerity and discipline; He has chosen you and has not laid upon you any hardship in the observance of your faith - the faith of your father Ibrahim (Abraham). He named you Muslims before in prior scriptures and in this (The Qur'an), so that His Rasool may testify against you and you yourselves may testify against the rest of mankind. Therefore, establish Salah, pay Zakah and hold fast to Allah; Who is your Protector - so what an excellent Protector and what a splendid Supporter!" (Al-Haj: 22.78)

3) Qur'anic verses referring to that Muslims are the best nation as below:

   "You are the best nation which has ever been raised for the guidance of mankind. You enjoin good, forbid evil, and believe in Allah. Had the People of the Book (Jews and Christians) believed, it would surely have been better for them; among them some are believers but most of them are transgressors." (Al-i'Imran: 3.110)

4) Qur'anic verses referring to that Islam was declared to be the complete and perfect Deen (way of life) after the last and final code; the holy Qur'an was revealed on Muhammad (S.A.W) are stated as below:

   a. "Today I have perfected your religion for you, completed my favor upon you and approved Al-Islam as a Deen (way of life) for you." (Al-Maida: 5.3)

b. Prophecy and Risalat concluded on Muhammad (S.A.W.):

   "Muhammad is not the father of any of your men (he is not going to leave any male heirs). He is the Rasool of Allah and the Seal of the Prophets." (Al-Ahzab: 33.40)

5) Qur'anic verses referring to the call towards the way of Allah with wisdom, advice and reason in a courteous manner:

   a. "Call people to the way of your Rabb with wisdom and best advice, and reason with them, if you have to, in the most courteous manner: for your Rabb knows best who strays from His Way and He knows best who is rightly guided. If you have to retaliate, let your retaliation be commensurate with the wrong which was done to you; but if you endure with patience, the best reward indeed is for those who endure with patience. Be patient - for your patience is not but with the help of Allah - do not grieve over them and do not distress yourself because of their plots, for Allah is with those who fear Him and adopt the righteous attitude." (An-Nahl: 16.125-128)

   b. "Let there arise from among you a band of people who should invite to righteousness, enjoin good and forbid evil; such are the ones who shall be successful." (Al-i'Imran: 3.104)

## A Religion of Non-Violence

Islam is humanity's very old and universal religion of non-violence to which people after people are attracted by its inherent, magnetic force.

1) Qur'anic verses referring to that all Rasools preached against Terrorism:

a. "It was said: "O Nuh! Disembark (from the ark) with Our peace and blessings on you and on the peoples who are with you. As for other people, We shall grant them the provisions of life for some time, and if they do not behave righteously, then they shall have a painful punishment from Us."" (Al-Hud: 11.48)

b. Prophet Saleh's address to his people:

   i. ""Have fear of Allah and obey me. Do not follow the bidding of extravagant, who create corruption in the land and reform nothing." " (Ash-Shu'araa: 26.150-152)

   ii. "For the people of Thamud We selected their brother Saleh, who said: "O my people! Worship Allah; you have no other god but Him. Now a clear proof has come to you from your Rabb; here is Allah's she-camel as a sign for you, therefore leave her alone to pasture on Allah's land and do not touch her with bad intentions, lest you incur a painful punishment. Remember how you were made the heirs of 'Ad and settled on the land, capable of building mansions in the valleys and carving out homes in the mountains. Therefore, remember the favors of Allah and do not spread mischief in the land." " (Al-A'raf: 7.73-74)

c. Prophet Shu'aib's address to his people, their disbelief and their fate:

   i. "For Madyan We selected their brother Shuaib, who said: "O my people! Worship Allah, you have no other god but Him. A clear guidance has come to you from your Rabb. Give just measure and weight, do not undersell others in their goods, and do not create mischief in the land after it has been set in order; this is better for you if you are true believers." " (Al-A'raf:7.85)

ii. "Give full measure and be not of those who cause losses to others by fraud. Weigh with even scales and do not cheat your fellow men of what is rightly theirs: nor spread evil in the land. Fear Him Who has created you and the generations before you." (Ash-Shu'araa:26.181-184)

d. Allah chose Musa as His Rasool and assigned him towards Fir'on (Pharaoh):

   i. "You and your brother should go with My Signs and do not neglect to mention Me. Go both of you to Fir'on, for he has indeed transgressed all bounds." (Ta-ha: 20.42-43)

   ii Israelites deliverance from Pharaoh's persecution:

   ""Remember how We delivered you from the people of Fir'on (Pharaoh): they had subjected you to severe torment, killing your sons and sparing your daughters; you were facing a tremendous trial from your Rabb. And We parted the Red Sea for you, taking you to safety, and drowned Fir'on's people before your very eyes."" (Al-Baqara: 2.49-50)

   iii. Qarun (a rich man) was from the people of Musa but he rebelled against the guidance of Allah:

   "The fact is that Qarun (Korah) was one of Musa's people, but he rebelled against them. We had given him such treasures that their very keys were a heavy burden to a band of strong men. When his people said to him: "Do not exult, for Allah does not love the exultant.

Rather seek, by means of what Allah has given you, to attain the abode of the hereafter, while not neglecting your share in this world. Be good to others as Allah has been good to you, and do not seek mischief in the land, for Allah does not love the mischief-makers." Then We caused the earth to swallow him, together with his dwelling, and he had no host to help him against Allah; nor was he able to defend himself." (Al-Qasas: 28.76-77, 81)

2) Qur'anic verses referring to that Allah invites you to the Home of Peace:

   a. "Allah invites you to the Home of Peace and guides whom He pleases to the right way. Those who do good deeds shall have a good reward and even more than they deserve! Neither blackness nor disgrace shall cover their faces. They will be the inhabitants of paradise; they will live therein forever. As for those who have done evil deeds, they will be rewarded with like evil: disgrace will cover them - they shall have none to protect them from Allah - as if their faces have been covered with patches of the dense darkness of night. They will become the inmates of the Fire; they will live therein forever." (Yunus: 10.25-27)

   b. "Verily this brotherhood of yours is a single brotherhood and I am your only Rabb, therefore worship Me Alone. But the people have divided their religion into sects between them - to Us they shall all return." (Al-Anbiyaa: 21.92-93)

   c. "If two parties among the believers fall into mutual fighting, make peace between them. Then if one of them transgresses against the other, fight the one who has transgressed until he returns to the commands of Allah. Then, if he returns, make peace between them with justice and be fair; for Allah loves those who are fair and just." (Al-Hujurat: 49.9)

3) Qur'anic verses referring to that the children of Adam are directed to follow the guidance of Allah, provided to them through His Rasools and to avoid violence as stated below:

   a. "O children of Adam! Whenever there come to you Rasools from among you and recite to you My revelations, those who will become righteous and mend their ways will have nothing to fear or to regret; but those who deny Our revelations and treat them with arrogance, shall be the inmates of hellfire to live therein forever." (Al-A'raf: 7.35-36)

   b. Believers' actions and their rewards:

      "The true believers, both men and women, are protectors of one another. They enjoin what is just and forbid what is evil; they establish Salah, pay Zakah, and obey Allah and His Rasool. It is they on whom Allah will have His mercy; surely Allah is Mighty, Wise. Allah has promised to the believers, both men and women, gardens beneath which rivers flow, to live therein forever, and they will have beautiful mansions in these gardens of everlasting bliss. Best of all, they will have the good pleasure of Allah. Now that is the highest achievement." (At-Tauba: 9.71-72)

   c. Virtues remove evils; Allah does not let the reward of the righteous be wasted:

      "Establish Salah (prayers) at the two ends of the day and in the early part of the night. Indeed virtues remove evils. This is a reminder for the mindful. Be patient; for sure Allah does not let the reward of the righteous be wasted. Why were there not among the generations before you, good persons who could forbid the people from making mischief in the land, except a few of those whom We delivered from among them? The wrongdoers, however, pursued the worldly pleasures they were provided, and became confirmed criminals. It is not possible that your Rabb would destroy the towns unjustly while their habitants were to mend their ways." (Hud: 11.114-117)

d. Formula for the way to salvation:

"By the time through the ages! Surely mankind is in loss, except those who believe and do good deeds; exhort one another to the truth and exhort one another to patience." (Al-Asr: 103.1-3)

e. "Besides this, he should be of those who believe, enjoin fortitude, encourage kindness and compassion. Such are the people of the right hand (going towards paradise)." (Al-Balad: 90.17-18)

f. Make peace between the believers if they fell into fighting among themselves:

"If two parties among the believers fall into mutual fighting, make peace between them. Then if one of them transgresses against the other, fight the one who has transgressed until he returns to the commands of Allah. Then, if he returns, make peace between them with justice and be fair; for Allah loves those who are fair and just. The believers are brothers to one another, therefore, make reconciliation between your brothers and fear Allah, so that you may be shown mercy." (Al-Hujurat: 49.9-10)

4) There is no compulsion in Islam:

a. "There is no compulsion in religion. True guidance has been made clearly distinct from error. Therefore, whoever renounce 'Taghut' (forces of Shaitan) and believes in Allah has grasped the firm hand-hold that will never break. Allah, Whose hand-hold you have grasped, hears all and knows all." (Al-Baqara: 2.256)

b. "If it had been the will of your Rabb that all the people of the world should be believers, all the people of the earth would have believed! Would you then compel mankind against their will to believe? It is not possible for anyone to believe except by the permission of Allah, and He throws filth on those who do not use their common sense. Say: "Look at whatever exists in the heavens and the earth." Signs and warnings do not benefit those people who do not believe. Now are they waiting for evil days like the ones that befell the people who passed away before them? Say: "Wait if you will; I too will wait with you." When such a time comes, We rescue Our Rasools and those who believe - this is Our way; it is but right that We rescue the believers." (Yunus: 10.99-103)

c. "O people of the Book! Let us get together on what is common between us and you: that we shall worship none but Allah; that we shall not associate any partners with Him; that we shall not take from among ourselves any lords beside Allah." If they reject your invitation then tell them: "Bear witness that we are Muslim (who have surrendered to Allah)." (Al-i'Imran: 3.64)

5) Behavior of the wrongdoers towards Allah:

   a. "We have destroyed generations before your time when they adopted unjust attitudes: their Rasools came to them with clear signs but they would not believe! Thus, do We requite the criminals." (Yunus: 10.13)

b. Misguided people are like animals or even worse:

   "Certainly, We have destined many Jinns and human beings for hell; those are the ones who have hearts with which they do not understand, they have eyes with which they do not see, they have ears with which they do not hear. They are like animals - or even worse than them, because they are those who are heedless." (Al-A'raf: 7.179)

c. Non-believers' actions and their punishment:

   "And those who have done evil deeds, shall be flung upon their faces in the hellfire. Should you not be rewarded according to your deeds?" (An-Naml: 27.90)

d. "As for those who break their covenant with Allah after confirming it and cut asunder what Allah has commanded to be joined and create mischief in the land, they are the ones on whom there shall be a curse and they are the ones who will have a terrible home." (Ar-Ra'd: 13.25)

6) Those who divide the religion into sects are not Muslims:

   a. "Surely those who divide the religion into sects and identify themselves as a sect, O Muhammad, you have nothing to do with them. Their case will be called to account by Allah Himself, He will inform them as to what they did." (Al-Anam: 6.159)

   b. "Do not create mischief in the land after it has been set in order. Pray to Him with fear and hope. Surely the mercy of Allah is always close to those who do good to others." (Al-A'raf: 7.56)

   c. "When it is said to them: "Do not make mischief on earth," they say: "We make peace." Be aware! They are the ones who make mischief but they do not realize it." (Al-Baqara: 2.11-12)

d. Punishment for killing a believer and laws of blood wit:

"It is not befitting for a believer to kill a believer except by accident, and whoever accidentally kills a believer, he is commanded to free a believing slave and pay blood wit to the family of the victim, unless they forgo it as a charity. If the victim is from a hostile nation, then the freeing of a believing slave is enough, but if he belonged to a nation with whom you have a treaty, then blood wit must be paid to his family along with the freeing of a believing slave. Those who do not have the means (blood wit and or a slave) must fast two consecutive months: a method of repentance provided by Allah. Allah is the Knowledgeable, Wise." (An-Nisaa: 4.92)

7) Permission is granted to the believers to fight in self defence, and for the cause of Allah:

a. "Permission to fight back is hereby granted to the believers against whom war is waged and because they are oppressed (before this revelation, Muslims were not allowed to fight even for self defence); certainly Allah has power to grant them victory - those who have been unjustly expelled from their homes only because they said, "Our Lord is Allah." Had not Allah repelled some people by the might of others, the monasteries, churches, synagogues, and mosques in which Allah's praise is daily celebrated, would have been utterly demolished. Allah will certainly help those who help His cause; most surely Allah is Mighty, Powerful. These are the people who, if We establish them in the land, will establish Salah and pay Zakah, enjoin justice and forbid evil; the final decision of all affairs is in the hands of Allah." (Al-Hajj: 22.39-41)

b. "O believers! Be patient, excel in patience during confrontation, hold yourselves ready for battle and have fear of Allah so that you may succeed." (Al-i'Imran: 3.200)

●●●

# 3.
# Cardinal Articles of Faith in Islam

The cardinal articles of faith in Islam are as follows:

1) To believe in the oneness of Allah. (Tauheed)
2) To believe in Allah's angels.
3) To believe in the holy books of Allah.
4) To believe in all His prophets and messengers.
5) To believe in the day of Doom, Resurrection and Judgement.
6) To believe in fate, good or bad.

Allah commands affirmation in the following:

## 1) Oneness of Allah - the almighty and his attributes (adjectives) by depth of the heart

All Muslims (followers of Islam) believe that "none is worthy of worship but Allah; Muhammad (Sallallaahu Alaihi Wasallam) is the messenger of Allah." Muslims have fundamental faith in Imaan. The literal meaning of Imaan is to believe in someone's words and relying solely on his authority. In religious terms, it implies belief in the unseen and relying solely on the authority of the messenger of Allah.

a. "O believers! Believe in Allah, His Rasool, the Book which He has revealed to His Rasool, and every Book which He previously revealed. He who denies Allah,

His angels, His Books, His Rasools and the Last Day has gone far astray." (An-Nisaa: 4.136)

b. Allah's attributes and "Ayat-al-Kursi":

"Allah! There is no god but Him: the Living, the Eternal. He neither slumbers nor sleeps. To Him belongs all that is in the Heavens and the Earth. Who can intercede with Him without His permission? He knows what is before them and what is behind them. They cannot gain access to anything out of His knowledge except what He pleases. His throne is more vast than the heavens and the earth, and guarding of these both does not fatigue Him. He is the Exalted, the Supreme." (Al-Baqara: 2.255)

c. Testimony of Allah about Himself and that the True Religion in the sight of Allah is Al-Islam:

"Allah Himself has testified to the fact that there is no god but Him and so do the angels and those who are well grounded in knowledge standing firm on justice. There is no Ilah (God) except Him, the Mighty, the Wise. Surely the only Deen (true religion and the Right Way of life) in the sight of Allah is Al-Islam: Those to whom the Book was given did not adopt ways different than this except out of envy among themselves, and after the true knowledge had come to them. They should know that Allah is swift in calling to account those who deny His revelations. So if they argue with you (O Muhammad), tell them: "I have submitted myself entirely to Allah and so have those who follow me." Then ask those who are given the Book and those who are illiterates: "Will you also submit yourselves to Allah?" If they become Muslims they shall be rightly guided but if they turn back, you need not worry, because your sole responsibility is to convey the Message. Allah is watching all His servants very closely." (Al-i'Imran: 3.18-20)

d. "Allah has done a great favor to the believers that He raised among them a Rasool from among themselves, reciting to them the Revelations of Allah, sanctifying them and teaching them the Book and Wisdom, although before this they were in manifest error." (Al-i'Imram: 3.164)

e. Muhammad (pbuh) is the Prophet for the whole of mankind:

   "O Muhammad, say: "O mankind! I am the Rasool of Allah towards all of you from He to whom belongs the kingdom of the heavens and the earth. There is no deity but Him. He brings to life and causes to die. Therefore, believe in Allah and His Rasool, the unlettered Prophet (Muhammad) who believes in Allah and His Word. Follow him so that you may be rightly guided." " (Al-A'raf: 7.158)

## 2) Allah's angels (Peace be upon them)

Angels are called as 'malaika' in Arabic, 'malakh' in Hebrew, 'Angelos' in Greek while 'Farishte' in Persian and Urdu. Allah created angels which are quite different to mankind. They are spiritual creatures of Allah, made by Noor (light). They do not have the capacity to think but simply obey the commands of Allah. They are invisible to us but everything is visible to them. They do not have any gender thus they do not marry nor have any offspring. They neither feel hungry nor sleepy as their bodies are immaterial but they can resume in any form by the command of Allah. They have two or more wings without muscles and feathers unlike birds. They are assigned separate duties related to the heavenly bodies and the universe.

The Qur'anic verses referring to the creation of angels (P.B.U.T):

a. "Praise be to Allah, the Creator of the heavens and the earth! Who appoint the angels having two, three and four pairs of wings as His messengers. He adds to His creation as He pleases; for Allah has power over all things." (Fatir: 35.1)

b. "The angels in fact say: "We each have our appointed place. We range ourselves in ranks for His service and we are surely those who declare His glory!" " (As-Saffat: 37.164-166)

c. "He sends down His angels with inspiration of His command to whom He pleases of His servants, saying: "Warn the people that there is no one else worthy of worship except Me, therefore fear Me."" (An-Nahl: 16.2)

d. Angels show respect to Adam:

"When We ordered the angels: "Prostrate before Adam in respect," they all prostrated except Iblees (Shaitan) who refused in his arrogance and became a disbeliever." (Al-Baqara: 2.34)

There are four arch angels of Allah which are superior to others which includes Jibraeel, Mikaeel, Izraeel, Israfeel. (P.B.U.T.)

1) **Jibraeel** – His task is to bring Allah's messages, commands and books to the prophets. The message is called as Wahi (revelation). Jibraeel conveyed the Holy Qur'an to Hazrat Muhammad (S.A.W) bit by bit. He used to console and guide the prophets in their sorrows on behalf of Allah.

Qur'anic verses referring to the duties of Jibraeel (Gabriel):

a. "Surely this word (The Qur'an) is brought by a noble Messenger (Gabriel), possessor of mighty power, having very high rank with the Owner of the Throne (Allah), who is obeyed in heaven, and is trustworthy." (At-Takwir: 81.19-21)

b. Their animosity for Gabriel and other angels:

"Say O Muhammad: "Whoever is the enemy of Jibra'el (Gabriel) should know that he revealed this Qur'an to your heart by Allah's command, which confirms previous scriptures, and is a guidance and good news for the believers." Let them know that whoever is an enemy to Allah, His angels, His Rasools, Jibra'el (Gabriel) and Mika'el (Michael); Allah is an enemy to such unbelievers." (Al-Baqara: 2.97-98)

c. "You should know that guardian angels have indeed been appointed over you, who are noble writers, they know all that you do." (Al-Infitar: 82.10-12)

2) **Mikaeel** - His responsibilities include sending rains and provisions to Allah's all creatures. Countless angels work under him to control winds and all water bodies (e.g, mountains, oceans, lakes and rivers).

Qur'anic verses referring to the duties of Mikaeel:

a. "And We send down from the sky Rain charged with blessing and We produce therewith Gardens and Grain for harvests." (Al-Qaf: 50.9)

b. "Each person has been assigned guardian angels before him and behind him, who watch him by the command of Allah. The fact is that Allah never changes the condition of a people until they intend to change it themselves. If Allah wants to afflict a people with misfortune, none can ward it off, nor they can find any protector besides Him." (Ar-Ra'd: 13.11)

c. "None can withhold the blessings which He bestows on people and none can award besides Him what He withholds. He is the Mighty, the Wise. O mankind!

Call to mind the favors of Allah on you; is there any other creator than Allah who provides for you from the heavens and the earth? There is no god but Him. How then are you being deceived?" (Fatir: 35.2-3)

3) **Izraeel** - His task is to draw souls from the bodies of all the living creatures. Innumerable angels coordinate under his supervision to draw souls of the righteous and evil-doers.

Qur'anic verses referring to the duties of Izraeel:

a) "Say: "The angel of death (Izra'il) is assigned for you will carry off your souls and bring you back to your Rabb."" (As-Sajda: 32.11)

b) "By those angels who violently pull out the souls of the wrongdoers, and those who gently draw out the souls of the righteous, and those who glide about swiftly through space, then speed headlong to carry out the commands of Allah, and those who regulate the affairs of the world! (An-Nazia't: 79.1-5)

4) **Israfeel** - His task is to blow the trumpet after which the universe will perish and then again at the time of resurrection.

Qur'anic verses referring to the duties of Israfeel:

a) "On that Day, the Trumpet shall be sounded and you shall come forth in multitude." (An-Nabaa: 78.18)

b) "On that Day when the heavens shall burst asunder with clouds and the angels will be sent down ranks after ranks." (Al-Furqan: 25.25)

c) "The angels will stand all around and eight of them will be carrying the Throne of your Rabb above them." (Al-Haqqa: 69.17)

d) "And the Trumpet shall be blown; that will be the Day of which you were threatened! Each soul will come forth; with it there will be an angel to drive and an angel to bear witness. It will be said: "You were heedless of this, but now We have removed your veil, so your eyesight is sharp today!" His companion will say: "Here is my testimony ready with me."" (Al-Qaf: 50.20-23)

e) "It is guarded by nineteen guards. We have appointed none but angels as wardens of the fire; and We have made their number a trial for the unbelievers, so that the People of the Book may be convinced and the faith of the true believers may be increased, and that no doubts will be left for the People of the Book and the believers, and that those in whose hearts there is a disease and the disbelievers may say: "What could Allah mean by this parable?" Thus, Allah leaves to stray whom He wills and guides whom He pleases. No one knows the forces of your Rabb except Himself, and this (Qur'an) is nothing but a reminder to mankind. " (Al-Muddaththir: 74.30-31)

f) " - those whom the angels cause to die while they were still engaged in doing injustice to their own souls. At the time of death they offer submission, saying: "We were not doing anything wrong." The angels will reply: "O Yea! How dare you deny! Certainly Allah is aware of what you were doing. Now go ahead and enter the gates of Hell, there you will abide forever." In fact, very awful will be the abode of the arrogant." (An-Nahl: 16.28-29)

g) "On the other hand when the righteous people are asked: "What is it that your Rabb has revealed?" They say: "That which is the best." Good is the reward for such righteous people in this world and the home of the hereafter will be even better. How splendid will be the home for the righteous Gardens of Eden will they enter, beneath which rivers flow, having therein all that they wish to have. Thus shall Allah reward the righteous, - such pious people the angels cause to die, saying: "Peace be upon you! Enter the paradise because of the good deeds you have done."" (An-Nahl: 16.30-32)

## 3) Holy books of Allah

Allah has sent His messages to prophets which were memorized by some of His selected disciples. They were revealed through the angel Jibraeel (p.b.u.h). These books were called the divine books or scriptures: the four big ones are called the holy books while the small ones are called scrolls (Sahifas). The four famous holy books are as following:

a. Zabur (Psalm) or old testament revealed on Dawud (Alaihis Salaam),

b. Taurat (Torah) or new testament revealed on Musa (A.S.),

c. Injil (The Bible) revealed on Isa (Jesus) (A.S.); the son of Mariyam (Mary),

d. Qur'an revealed on Hazrat Muhammad (S.A.W.),

### a) ZABUR (PSALM):

i. This Qur'an carries the same message as was sent to Noah, Abraham, Moses and Jesus and Al-Quran's authenticity is verified by Allah Himself:

"O Muhammad, We have sent revelations to you just as We sent to Nuh (Noah) and the Prophets who came after him; We also sent revelations to Ibrahim (Abraham), Isma`il (Ishmael), Ishaq (Isaac), Ya'qoob (Jacob), his descendants, Isa (Jesus), Ayub (Job), Yunus

(Jonah), Haroon (Aaron) and Sulaiman (Solomon), and to Dawood (David) We gave the Psalms. Revelations were also sent to those Rasools whom We have already mentioned to you and to those whose name We have not mentioned; to Musa Allah spoke directly. All these Rasools conveyed good news to mankind and admonished them so that, after conveying the message through the Rasools, people should have no excuse to plead against Allah. Allah is Mighty, Wise. People may or may not believe it, but Allah bears witness that what He has sent to you, O Muhammad, He has sent with His own Knowledge and so do the angels; though only Allah's testimony is sufficient." (An-Nisaa: 4.163-166)

ii. "Surely We sent Our Rasools with clear signs, and sent down with them the Book and the Scales of Justice, so that men may conduct themselves with fairness. We also sent down Iron, with its mighty strength and diverse uses for mankind, so that Allah may know those who will help Him, though unseen, and help His Rasools. Surely Allah is All-Powerful, All-Mighty." (Al-Hadid: 57.25)

## b) TAURAT (TORAH):

i. Allah is the One Who revealed the Taurat and Al-Quran:

"Those people have not valued the attributes of Allah, the way His attributes should be valued, who say: "Allah has never revealed anything to a human being." Ask them: "Who then sent down the Book (Torah) which Musa brought, a light and guidance for mankind? You have transcribed it on separate sheets, publishing some and suppressing much of that given knowledge, which neither you nor your forefathers previously possessed." If they do not answer, then just say: "Allah" and leave them alone with the discourse of their useless arguments." (Al-An'am: 6.91)

ii. "Moreover, He said, We gave Musa (Moses) the Book to complete Our favor on those who would do good to others; it contained details of all things, and was a guide and a mercy, so that they should believe in the ultimate meeting with their Rabb." We have revealed this Book, similar to the Book given to Musa, as a blessing; therefore, follow it and adopt a God-fearing attitude so that you may receive mercy. Lest you say: "The Book was revealed only to two parties before us and we were unaware of what they read," or lest you say: "If the Book had been revealed to us, we could have followed its guidance better than them," a veritable sign has now come to you from your Rabb as a guidance and mercy. Who then is more unjust than the one who denies the revelations of Allah and turns away from them? Very soon those who turn away from Our revelations will face dreadful punishment for their aversion." (Al-An'am: 6.154-157)

iii. Musa (A.S.) was given the written tablets of Taurat (Torah) and arrogant people cannot get guidance:

"We inscribed for him upon tablets all kind of instructions and details of everything, concerning all branches of life, and said: "Observe these with firmness and enjoin your people to follow them according to the best of their abilities. Soon I shall show you the homes of the transgressors. I will turn away from My signs the eyes of those who are unjustly arrogant in the land, so that even if they see each and every sign they will not believe in it. If they see the Right Way before them they will not follow it; but if they see a crooked way they will follow it; this is because they denied Our revelations and were heedless of them. Those who deny Our signs and the meeting of the Hereafter, their deeds are null. Should they be rewarded except for what they have done ?." (Al-A'raf: 7.145-147)

iv. Musa was given Al-Furqan (the criterion of right and wrong):

"Certainly, We granted to Musa (Moses) and Haroon (Aaron) the Criterion of Right and Wrong, a light and a reminder for those righteous people who fear their Rabb though they have not seen Him, and dread the Day of Judgment. And now We have revealed this blessed Reminder (The Qur'an). Will you then deny it?" (Al-Anbiyaa: 21.48-50)

v. It is Allah Who has revealed Torah, Gospel and Al-Quran:

"Allah! There is no god but Him; the Living, the Eternal. He has revealed to you this Book with the Truth, confirming the scripture which preceded it, as He revealed the Taurat (Torah) and Injeel (Gospel)." (Al-iImaran: 3.2-3)

vi. "O Prophet, say: "We believe in Allah and what is revealed to us and what was revealed to Ibrahim (Abraham), Isma`il (Ishmael), Ishaq (Isaac), Ya'qoob (Jacob) and their descendants; and in that which was given to Musa (Moses), Isa (Jesus) and other Prophets from their Rabb; we do not discriminate any one of them, and to Allah do we submit in Islam."" (Al-i'Imran: 3.84)

vii. Laws of Taurat (Torah) and those who do not judge by the laws of Allah they are unbelievers and they are wrongdoers:

"Indeed We revealed the Taurat to Moses, in which there is guidance and light: By its laws, all the Prophets, who were Muslims, judged those who call themselves Jews and so did the rabbis and jurists of law. They were entrusted the protection of Allah's Book and they themselves were witnesses. Have no fear of people; fear Me, and do not sell My revelations for a petty price: those who do not judge by the law which Allah has revealed, are indeed kafirs (unbelievers). We ordained in Taurat for them: "A life for a life, an eye for an eye, a nose for a nose, an ear for an ear, a tooth for a tooth and for a wound an equal retaliation." But if anyone remits the retaliation by way of charity it will be an act of atonement for him; those who do not judge by the law which Allah has revealed, they are the wrongdoers." (Al-Maida: 5.44-45)

**c) INJIL (The BIBLE):**

i. They are transgressors:

"Then in the footsteps of those Prophets, We sent Isa (Jesus) the son of Maryam (Mary) confirming whatever remained intact from the Taurat in his time, and gave him the Injeel (Gospel) wherein was guidance and light, corroborating what was revealed in the Taurat; a guidance and an admonition to those who fear Allah." (Al-Maida: 5.46)

ii. Birth of Isa (Jesus) son of Maryam and Miracles given to Isa (Jesus):

"Hearing this, Maryem said, "O my Rabb! How can I have a son when no man has ever touched me?" He replied, "Even so, Allah creates however He wants; whenever He decides to do anything, He only says it to 'Be' and it is! Allah will teach your son the Book, the Wisdom, the Taurat (Torah), and the Injeel (Gospel) and send him forth as a Rasool to the Children of Israel with this message: 'I have brought you signs of my appointment from your Rabb. I will make for you the likeness of a bird from clay; I will breathe into it and, with Allah's leave, it will become a living bird. I will heal the blind and the lepers, and raise the dead to life, by Allah's leave. Furthermore, I will tell you what you have eaten and what you have stored in your houses. Surely these are the signs to convince you if you are believers. I am appointed to confirm that which is before me from the Taurat (Torah) and to make lawful to you some of the things forbidden to you. Now I have brought you the signs from your Rabb, therefore fear Allah and obey me. In fact, Allah is my Rabb as well as your Rabb, therefore, worship Him; this is the right way."" (Al-i'Imran: 3.47-51)

## d) THE HOLY QUR'AN:

i. The Quran was revealed during the month of Ramazaan:

"Surely We have revealed this (Qur'an) in the night of Qadr. And what will make you understand, what the night of Qadr is! The night of Qadr is better than one thousand months. The angels and the Spirit (Gabriel) come down with every decree, by the leave of their Rabb, that night is the night of Peace, till the break of dawn!. " (Al-Qadr: 97.1-5)

ii. Al-Qur'an is revealed in the Arabic language:

"We have revealed this Qur'an in the Arabic language so that you (Arabs) may understand. We relate to you the best of stories through this Qur'an by Our revelation to you (O Muhammad), though before this you were one of those who did not know." (Yusuf: 12.2-3)

iii. "On that Day you shall see that every nursing mother will forget her nursing-babe and every pregnant female will miscarry, and you will see people as if they are intoxicated, though they will not be drunk: such will be the horror of Allah's chastisement." (Al-Sajda: 32.2)

iv. This Quran is the revelation of Allah:

"This Qur'an is not such as could be produced by anyone other than Allah; in fact it is the confirmation of prior revelations (Psalms, Torah, and Gospel) and fully explains the Holy Book (prior scriptures); there is no doubt in this fact that it is (revealed) from the Rabb of the Worlds. Do they say: "He (the Prophet) has forged it?" Tell them: "If what you say be true; then produce one Surah like this, you may even call to your aid anyone you want other than Allah." Nay! They do not believe that which they cannot grasp, for they have not yet seen its prophecy fulfilled. The same way those who passed before them disbelieved. But see what was the end of the wrongdoers! Of these people there are some who will believe in it and some will not; and your Rabb best knows the troublemakers." (Yunus: 10.37-40)

v. Al-Qur'an is a guide for those who are God-conscious:

"This is The Book in which there is no doubt. (Since its Author, Allah, the Creator of this universe, possesses complete knowledge, there is no room for doubt about its contents.) It is a guide for those who are God-conscious, who believe in the Unseen, who establish Salah (five regular daily prayers) and spend in charity out of what We have provided for their sustenance; who believe in this Revelation (The Qur'an) which is sent to you (O Muhammad) and the Revelations which were sent before you (Torah, Psalms, Gospel...) and firmly believe in the Hereafter. They are on True Guidance from their Rabb and they are the ones who will attain salvation." (Al-Baqara: 2.2-5)

vi. Al-Qur'an is revealed to admonish and to declare that there is Only One God, Allah:

"Ask them: "Whose testimony is the most reliable?" When they say Allah, then tell them: "Let Allah be Witness between me and you (that I am the Rasool of Allah) and this Qur'an has been revealed to me by Him so that I may warn you thereby and all those whom it may reach. Can you really testify that there are other gods besides Allah?" Tell them: "As far as I am concerned I will never testify to this!" Say: "Indeed He is the One and the Only God and I am absolutely disgusted with the Shirk you commit. Those to whom We have given the Book know this fact as they know their own sons. In fact those who have lost their souls, will not believe." (Al-An'am: 6.19-20)

vii. "This Qur'an is not such as could be produced by anyone other than Allah; in fact it is the confirmation of prior revelations (Psalms, Torah, and Gospel) and fully explains the Holy Book (prior scriptures); there is no doubt in this fact that it is (revealed) from the Rabb of the Worlds." (Yunus: 10.37)

viii. Al-Qur'an is a mercy, blessing, and cure for the problems of mankind:

"O mankind! There has come to you an instruction from your Rabb, a cure for whatever (disease) is in your hearts, a guidance and a blessing for the true believers. Say: "It is the grace and mercy of Allah (that He has sent this Qur'an), so let the people rejoice over it, for it is better than (the worldly riches) they are collecting." O Prophet, ask them: "Have you ever considered that out of the sustenance which Allah has given you, you yourselves have made some things Halal (lawful) and others Haram (unlawful)? Ask them: "Did Allah permit you to do so, or do you ascribe a false thing to Allah?" What treatment do they think those people will get, who ascribe false things to Allah, on the Day of Resurrection?

Indeed Allah is full of grace to mankind, but most of them are not grateful." (Yunus: 10.57-60)

ix. The Book of Allah has come to you for your guidance so that there may be no excuse about the true Word of Allah:

"Lest you say: "The Book was revealed only to two parties before us and we were unaware of what they read," or lest you say: "If the Book had been revealed to us, we could have followed its guidance better than them," a veritable sign has now come to you from your Rabb as a guidance and mercy. Who then is more unjust than the one who denies the revelations of Allah and turns away from them? Very soon those who turn away from Our revelations will face dreadful punishment for their aversion. Are they waiting for the angels or your Rabb to come down to them or are they waiting to be given a certain sign of your Rabb! On the Day when that certain sign of your Rabb appears, the belief will not profit that soul which did not believe before, or who, while professing to believe did not do good deeds.

Say to them: "Wait if you will; we too are waiting."" (Al-An'am: 6.156-158)

x. Righteous Jews and Christians can recognize the truth of Al-Quran and feel that they were Muslims even before hearing it:

"We have conveyed Our Word to them over and over again in order that they may take heed. Those to whom the scriptures were given before this (Jews and Christians), they do recognize the Truth and believe in this (Qur'an). When it is recited to them they say: "We believe in it, surely this is the Truth from our Rabb: indeed we were Muslims even before this." They are the ones who will be given their reward twice, because they have endured with fortitude, repelling evil with good and giving in charity out of what We have given them. When they hear vain talk, they withdraw from it saying: "Our deeds are for us and yours for you; peace be on to you: we do not desire the way of ignorant."" (Al-Qasas: 28.51-55)

## 4) Prophets (Anbiyaas) and Messengers (Rasools) (Peace be upon them):

Allah has sent His prophets and messengers to show the path of religion to all the people in different countries at different times. More than a lakh of messengers were sent among which the first was Adam (A.S.) – the father of mankind and the last was Muhammad (S.A.W.).

1) "Allah chooses His messengers from among the angels and from among the human beings, for surely Allah is All-Hearing, All-Seeing." (Al-Hajj: 22.75)

   a. Every nation was sent a Rasool for their guidance:

   "Every nation was sent a Rasool. Once their Rasool came, judgement was passed between them with all fairness and they were not wronged in the least. They ask: "When will this promise be fulfilled, tell us if what you say be true?" Say: "I have no control over any harm or benefit to myself, except what Allah wills. For every nation there is a deadline: when their deadline comes, it can neither be delayed for even a moment, nor it can be advanced. Say: "Have you ever considered that if his scourge fall upon you by night or by day you can do nothing to avert it? What then is there that the criminals wish to hasten? Would you believe it when it actually overtakes you? Then you would beg it to be removed although it had been your own wish to hurry it on." Then it will be said to the wrongdoers: "Taste the everlasting punishment! Should you not be rewarded according to your deeds?". " (Yunus: 10.47-52)

b. All Rasools speak the language of their own people:

"We have not sent any Rasool except that he speaks the language of his own people, so that he could explain to them clearly. Then Allah leaves in error whom He will and guides whom He pleases: He is the Mighty, the Wise." (Ibrahim: 14.4)

c. All prophets of Allah were Divinely Guided and chosen:

"These are some of the Prophets on whom Allah bestowed His favors from among the descendants of Adam and of those whom We carried in the Ark with Nuh, and of the descendants of Ibrahim and Israel, and of those whom We guided and chose. Whenever the Revelations of the Compassionate (Allah) were recited to them, they fell to prostrate and weep." (Maryam: 19.58)

d. All Rasools were sent with the same Message, there is no god but Allah, so worship Him alone:

"The fact is that to every Rasool whom We sent before you, We revealed the same Message: "There is no god but Me, so worship Me Alone." Inspite of receiving that message, they still say: "The Beneficent (Allah) has offspring!" Glory be to Him! The angels are but His honored servants. They do not precede Him in speaking and they act according to His commandment. He knows what is before them and what is behind them and they do not intercede except for the one whom He approves, and for fear of Him they tremble. If any of them were to say: "I am also a deity besides Him," We would send him to hell, thus shall We reward the wrongdoers." (Al-Anbiyaa: 21.25-29)

e. Children of Adam (A.S.) are directed to follow the Guidance of Allah provided to them through His Rasools:

"O children of Adam! Whenever there come to you Rasools from among you and recite to you My revelations, those who will become righteous and mend their ways will have nothing to fear or to regret; but those who deny Our revelations and treat them with arrogance, shall be the inmates of hellfire to live therein forever. Who can be more unjust than the one who invents a lie against Allah or rejects His revelations? Such people will have their destined portion from the Book (what was written for them to receive during their life on earth); until when Our messengers (angels of death) arrive to take away their souls, they will ask: "Where are those gods whom you used to invoke besides Allah?" They will reply: "They have forsaken us" and they will bear witness against themselves (admit) that they were indeed *kuffar* (unbelievers). Allah will say: "Enter the fire and join the nations of Jinns and men who have gone before you." "As each nation will enter hell, it will curse its preceding sisters till all are gathered there, the last of them will say about the first one: "Our Rabb! These have led us astray; therefore, give them double punishment of the fire." He will answer: "There will be double for all, although you may not know because of being predecessor or successor in sin and aggression." Then the first will say to the last: "If we were to blame, you too, were no better than us; now taste the punishment of your misdeeds"." (Al-A'raf: 7.35-39)

f. Rasools have no power to show any miracle without the sanction of Allah and When Allah commands, there is none to reverse it and that Allah is the Master of all planning:

"We have sent forth other Rasools before you and given them wives and children and it was never in the power of a Rasool to show any miracle without the sanction of Allah. For each period there was a Book: Allah abrogates and confirms what He pleases - with Him is the Master Copy of the Book. O Muhammad! Whether We let you see, within your lifetime, a part of what We threaten them with or cause you to die before We smite them, your mission is only to deliver the Message and it is for Us to take accountability. Do they not see that We are gradually reducing the land in their control through curtailing its borders? When Allah commands, there is none to reverse His command and He is swift in taking accountability." (Ar-Ra'd: 13.38-41)

g. True belief on the preaching of Prophets:

   i. "Allah does not burden any human being with more than he can bear. Everyone will enjoy the credit of his deeds and suffer the debit of his evil-doings. The believers say: "Our Rabb! Do not punish us if we forget or make a mistake. Our Rabb! Do not place on us a burden as You placed on those before us. Our Rabb! Lay not on us the kind of burden that we have no strength to bear. Pardon us, Forgive us, Have mercy on us. You are our Protector, help us against the unbelievers."" (Al-Baqara: 2.286)

   ii. "They say: "Our Rabb, Do not cause our hearts to deviate now after you have guided us. Grant us Your own mercy; You are the Grantor of bounties without measure. Our Rabb, You will surely gather all mankind before You on the Day about which there is no doubt; surly Allah does not break His promise." " (Al-i'Imran: 3.8-9)

iii. "Their only words were, "Our Rabb! Forgive our sins and our excesses; establish our feet firmly and give us victory over the unbelievers." Therefore, Allah gave them the reward in this world and also an excellent reward awaits them in the Hereafter. Allah loves the righteous who are good to others." (Al-i'Imran: 3.147-148)

h. Signs from nature and supplication of the believers:

"For sure, in the creation of the heavens and the earth and the alternation of the night and the day there are signs for men of understanding. Those who remember Allah while standing, sitting, and lying on their sides, and meditate on the creation of the heavens and the earth. Then cry out:" Our Rabb! You have not created this in vain. Glory to You! Save us from the punishment of Fire. Our Rabb! Those to whom You will cast into the Fire will be in eternal shame: and there shall be no helper for such wrongdoers. Our Rabb! We have heard someone calling to the true faith saying; 'Believe in your Rabb,' so we have believed. Our Rabb! Forgive us our sins, remove from us our evil deeds and make us die with the righteous. Our Rabb! Grant us what You have promised through Your Rasools and save us from the shame on the Day of Resurrection; for You never break Your promise"." (Al-i'Imran: 3.190-194)

i. Do not deny the Prophet's preaching as those who opposed the Prophets will be treated with heavy fetters and blazing fire:

"Narrate to them the example of the people of a certain town to whom the Rasools came. At first We sent to them two Rasools, but when they rejected both We strengthened them with a third and they all said: "Surely we have been sent to you as Rasools." But the people replied: "You are but humans like us. The Compassionate (Allah) has revealed nothing; you are surely lying." They said: "Our Rabb knows that we have indeed been sent as Rasools towards you and our only duty is to convey His message plainly." The people replied: "We regard you as an evil omen for us. Desist, or we will either stone you or you will receive from us a painful punishment." They said: "Your evil omens lie within yourselves. Do you say this because you are being admonished? Indeed you are a nation of transgressors." In the meantime a man came running from the remote part of the city and said: "O my people! Follow these Rasools. Follow the ones who ask no reward of you and are rightly guided". " (Ya-Sin: 36.13-21)

j. High-ranking Prophets:

"Indeed Allah exalted Adam, Nuh (Noah), the family of Ibrahim (Abraham) and the family of Imran above all the worlds. They were the offsprings of one another. Allah hears all and knows all." (Al-i'Imran: 3.33-34)

2) The story of Adam's (A.S.) creation:

"When We said to the angels "Prostrate yourselves before Adam", they all prostrated themselves except Iblees (Shaitan), who refused. Then We said: "O Adam! This Shaitan is a real enemy to you and to your wife. Do not let him get you both out of Paradise and get you in trouble. Here in Paradise you shall go neither hungry nor naked; you shall neither suffer from thirst nor from the scorching heat. - But Shaitan seduced him saying: "O Adam! Should I show you the Tree of Immortality and an everlasting kingdom?" They both end up eating the fruit of the forbidden tree. As a result their private parts became apparent to them and they both began to cover themselves with the leaves from the Garden. Thus did Adam disobey His Rabb and go astray. Later on Adam repented and his Rabb chose him, accepted his repentance and gave him guidance, saying: "Get down from here all of you (Adam, Eve and Iblees); you will remain enemies to one another, whenever there comes to you guidance from Me and whosoever will follow My guidance will neither go astray nor get into trouble; but the one who will turn away from My reminder shall live a meager life and We shall raise him back to life as a blind person on the Day of Resurrection." " (Ta-ha: 20.116-124)

3) Story of Prophet Nuh (A.S.) and his people:

   a) "Quote to them the story of Nuh (Noah) when he said to his people: "O my people! If it offends you that I should live among you and preach to you the revelations of Allah, then you should know that I have put my trust in Allah. Go ahead and muster all your Shoraka' (deities you worship) and come up with your united decision. Plan it well so that you may not have any doubt about its being foolproof. Then execute it against me and give me no respite. If you have turned away from my message, I did not lose anything, for I did not ask any reward from you for my services: my reward is only with Allah, I have been commanded to become a Muslim!." " (Yunus: 10.71-72)

b) Prophet Nuh's address to his people, their disbelief and their fate:

"Indeed We selected Nuh for the guidance of his people, and he said: "O my people! Worship Allah, you have no god but Him. If you do not listen to what I say, I fear for you the punishment of a Mighty Day." The chiefs of his nation said: "Surely we see that you are in evident error." He replied: "O my people! I am not in error; on the contrary, I am a Rasool from the Rabb of the worlds. I am appointed to deliver the message of my Rabb and give you friendly advice for I know from Allah something that you do not know. Do you wonder that there has come to you a message from your Rabb through a man from among yourselves to warn you, so that you may fear Allah in order to receive His mercy?" But they denied him, as a result We saved him and all who were with him in the ark, and drowned those who denied Our revelations. Surely they were a blind nation!. " (Al-A'raf: 7.59-64)

c) Prophet Nuh prayed and Allah responded to his prayers:

" Nuh prayed to Us; see how excellent was Our response to his prayer! We delivered him and his people from the mighty distress, and made his progeny to be the only survivors, and We left his good name among the later generations. Salutation to Nuh among the people of the worlds. Thus do We reward the righteous. Surely he was one of Our believing devotees. Then the rest We drowned in the great flood." (As-Saffat: 37.75-82)

4) Prophet Hud's address to his people, their disbelief and their fate:

For the people of 'Ad We selected their brother Hud, who said: "O my people! Worship Allah! You have no god but Him. Will you not fear Him?" The chiefs of his nation who denied his message said: "We can see that you are crazy and we think that you are lying." He replied: "O my people! I am not crazy, on the contrary I am a Rasool from the Rabb of the worlds. I am conveying the message of my Rabb to you, and I am an honest adviser to you. O you wonder that a reminder from your Rabb has come to you through one of your own men to warn you? Remember that He made you successors after the people of Nuh and gave you a tall stature as compared to other people. Therefore, remember the favors that you have received from Allah, so that you may prosper." They replied: "Have you come to us with the demand that we should worship Allah alone and give up those whom our forefathers used to worship? Well, bring us what you are threatening us with if what you say is true!" Hud said: "You have already incurred the blight and wrath of your Rabb. Would you dispute with me about mere names which you and your forefathers have invented, and for which Allah has revealed no sanction? If so then wait for the decision of Allah, I too will wait with you." We saved him and his companions by Our mercy and We cut off the roots of (annihilated) those who denied Our revelations and did not become believers." (Al-A'raf: 7.65-72)

5) Prophet Saleh's (A.S.) address to his people, their disbelief and their fate:

"For the people of Thamud We selected their brother Saleh, who said: "O my people! Worship Allah; you have no other god but Him. Now a clear proof has come to you from your Rabb; here is Allah's she-camel as a sign for you, therefore leave her alone to pasture on Allah's land and do not touch her with bad intentions, lest you incur a painful punishment. Remember how you were made the heirs of 'Ad and settled in the land, capable of building mansions in the valleys and carving out homes in the mountains. Therefore, remember the favors of Allah and do not spread mischief in the land." The arrogant leaders from his nation asked the oppressed among them who have believed: "Do you really believe that Saleh is a Rasool from his Rabb?" They replied: "We do indeed believe in the revelation which he has been sent." The arrogant, who considered themselves superior, said: "We deny all that you believe in." Then they hamstrung the she-camel, defied the commandment of their Rabb and challenged Saleh saying: "Bring down the scourge you have threatened us with, if you truly are one of the Rasools." Thereupon an earthquake overtook them and they became lifeless bodies in their homes with their faces down. Saleh left them saying: "O my people! I did indeed convey to you the message of my Rabb and gave you good advice but you did not love the good advisers."" (Al-A'raf: 7.73-79)

6) Prophets Nuh (A.S.), Ibrahim (A.S.) and Isa (Jesus)(A. S.) were sent for the guidance to the Right Path, as for the monasticism, people instituted it themselves:

"We sent Nuh (Noah) and Ibrahim (Abraham), and bestowed among their descendants Prophethood and the Book. Some of them adopted the right guidance, but most of them were transgressors. After them We sent other Rasools, one after the other, and followed them with Isa (Jesus) the son of Maryam. We gave him The Injeel (Gospel), and put compassion and mercy into the hearts of his followers. As for monasticism, they instituted it themselves - for We did not enjoin it on them - in order to seek the good pleasure of Allah, but they did not observe it as it should have been observed. Yet We rewarded those among them who were true believers, but most of them are transgressors. O believers! Fear Allah and believe in His Rasool (Muhammad, peace be upon him). He will grant you a double share of His mercy, provide for you a light to walk with and forgive you your sins. Allah is Oft-Forgiving, Most Merciful. You should adopt this way so that the people of the Book may know that they do not have the sole right to the grace of Allah, and that His grace is entirely in His own hands, which He bestows on whomever He wills: and Allah is the Owner of mighty grace." (Al-Hadid: 57.26-29)

7) Story of Prophet Ibrahim (A.S.), 'The Friend of Allah':

   a. "Surely Ibrahim belonged to the first group (who followed Nuh's way), when he came to his Rabb with a pure heart. Behold, he said to his father and to his people: "What are these that you worship? Would you serve false gods instead of Allah? What is your idea about the Rabb of the worlds? Then he looked at the stars one time and said "I am feeling sick." So his people left him behind and went away to their national fair. He sneaked into the temple of their gods and addressed them: "Why don't you eat from these offerings before you? What is the matter with you that you don't even speak?" Then he fell upon them, smiting them with his right hand. The people came running to the scene. "Would you worship that which you have carved with your own hands," he said, "when Allah is the One Who created you and that which you have made?" They said to one another: "Prepare for him a furnace and throw him into the blazing flames." Thus did they scheme against him: but We humiliated them in their scheme." (As-Saffat: 37.83-98)

b. The prayer of Prophet Ibrahim(A.S.) which is made a part of five daily prayers:

"Remember when Ibrahim (Abraham) said: "My Rabb! Make this city a city of peace and save me and my sons from the worship of idols. O Rabb! They have indeed led many people astray (and they might led my descendants astray as well). Therefore, only those who follow my ways belong to me and I leave those to You who disobey me; surely You are Forgiving, Merciful. Our Rabb! I have settled some of my offspring in a barren valley near Your Sacred House. Our Rabb! I have done this in the hope that they would establish Salah, therefore, turn the hearts of the people toward them and provide them with fruits so that they may give thanks. Our Rabb! Certainly You know what we conceal and what we reveal. In fact, nothing on the earth or in heaven is hidden from Allah. Praise be to Allah who has given me Isma`il (Ishmael) and Ishaq (Isaac) in my old age. Indeed my Rabb hears all prayers. O Rabb! Make me and my descendants establish Salah. Our Rabb! Accept my prayer. Our Rabb! Forgive me and my parents and all believers on the Day when the accountability will take place."" (Ibrahim: 14.35-41)

8) Lut (A.S.) was also a Rasool of Allah:

a. "Thus do We reward the righteous. He was surely one of Our believing devotees. Lut was one of Our Rasools. Behold, We delivered him and his whole family except an old woman who was among those who remained behind, and We destroyed the others. Surely you pass by their ruins by day and by night. Will you not use your common sense?" (As-saffat: 37.131-138)

b. Prophet Lut's (A.S.) address to his people, their disbelief and their fate:

"We also selected Lut, who said to his people: "Will you do such indecent acts as no one else in the world has committed before you? You satisfy your lust with men (homosexual) instead of women. Indeed you are a nation who has transgressed beyond bounds." His people had no answer but to say: "Drive them out of your town, they pose to be very pious!" So We saved him and his family except his wife, who was of those who lagged behind. We let loose rain of brimstone and every one of them was killed; see what was the outcome for such criminals!" (Al-A'raf: 7.80-84)

9) Prophet Shu'aib's (A.S.) address to his people:

"For Madyan We selected their brother Shuaib, who said: "O my people! Worship Allah, you have no other god but Him. A clear guidance has come to you from your Rabb. Give just measure and weight, do not undersell others in their goods, and do not create mischief in the land after it has been set in order; this is better for you if you are true believers. Do not sit in ambush on every road to threaten people and hinder from the Way of Allah those who believe in Him, seeking to make His Way crooked. Remember how He multiplied you when you were a few in number and see what was the end of the mischief-makers of prior nations. If there are some among you who believe in the message with which I have been sent and others who disbelieve it, then be patient until Allah judges between us, for He is the best of all judges."" (Al-A'raf: 7.85-87)

10) Allah blessed Ibrahim (A.S.) with son (Ishaq, A.S.) and then a grandson (Ya'qoob, A.S.) and made each of them Prophets:

"We gave him a son Ishaq (Isaac) and then a grandson Ya'qoob (Jacob); and We made each of them a righteous man. We made them leaders who guided other people by Our command and We sent them revelations to do good deeds, establish Salah and pay Zakah. To Us Alone did they serve. To Lut (Lot) We gave wisdom and knowledge, and We delivered him from the town which practiced abominations - surely its inhabitants were very wicked transgressors - and We admitted him to Our mercy: for he was of the righteous people." (Al-Anbiyaa: 21.72-75)

11) Allah blessed Prophets Dawood (A.S.) and Sulaiman (A.S.) with wisdom, knowledge and kingdoms:

a. "We also bestowed favors upon Dawood (David) and Sulaiman (Solomon): when the two were judging a case regarding the field into which the sheep of certain people had strayed by night, and We were watching them to arrive at judgment, at that time We gave Sulaiman insight to arrive at the right decision, although We had given wisdom and knowledge to both of them. We caused the mountains and the birds to celebrate Our praises with Dawood; it was We Who made this happen. We taught him the armor's craft, so that they might protect you in your wars: yet are you ever grateful? We made the raging winds subservient to Sulaiman, pursuing its course by his command to the land which We had blessed; and We have knowledge of everything. And We had subjected to him many of the shaitans who dived for him into the sea and performed other duties besides this; and We were the One Who had control over them for him." (Al-Anbiyaa: 21.78-82)

b. Story of Prophet Sulaiman (A.S.), to whom Allah gave rule over jinns, men, birds and winds:

"We bestowed knowledge on Dawood (David,) and Sulaiman (Solomon). They both said: "Praise be to Allah Who has exalted us above many of His believing servants." Sulaiman succeeded Dawood. He said: "O people! We have been taught the tongue of birds and given all sort of things. This is indeed a great blessing from Allah." Sulaiman gathered an army comprised of Jinns, men and birds; they all were kept under strict discipline. Once in an expedition he was marching with his army when they came across a valley of ants, one of the ants said: "O ants, get into your habitations lest Sulaiman and his army crush you under their feet without even noticing it." So Sulaiman smiled, laughing at its statement, and said: "O Rabb! Inspire me to render thanks for Your favors, which You have bestowed on me and on my parents, to do such good deeds that will please You; and admit me, by Your mercy, among Your righteous servants." " (An-Naml: 27.15-19)

12) Story of Ayub (Job,A.S.), his sickness and relief:

"Mention Our devotee Ayub (Job), when he called upon his Rabb saying: "Shaitan has afflicted me with distress and suffering," and We asked him: "Strike your foot on the ground. A cool spring will gush forth. Wash and drink to refresh yourself." And We restored to him his family and many more with them as a grace from Ourselves and a reminder for the people of understanding. Then, to fulfill his oath of giving his wife one hundred strikes which he made during his sickness, We said: "Take a bunch of twigs and strike with it and do not break your oath." Certainly We found him full of patience. He was an excellent devotee, who turned to Us over and over again. And mention Our devotees Ibrahim (Abraham), Ishaq (Isaac) and Ya'qoob (Jacob): men of power and vision. Surely We chose them for their special quality of keeping in mind the abode of hereafter. Certainly they are with Us; among the best chosen. Also mention Isma'il, Al-Yas'a (Elisha) and Zul-Kifl; all of them were among the best." (Sad: 38.41-48)

13) Story of Prophet Yusuf (Joseph,A.S.):

a. "This is the narrative of that time, when Yusuf (Joseph) said to his father: "O my father! In a dream I saw eleven stars, the sun and the moon - I saw them prostrate themselves before me!" He replied: "My dear little son! Do not say anything about this dream to your brothers, lest they plot an evil scheme against you; for Shaitan is an open enemy to human beings. It will happen, as you have seen in your dream, that you will be chosen by your Rabb for His work. He will teach you how to interpret visions, and will perfect His favor upon you and the children of Ya'qoob (Jacob), as He perfected it upon your forefathers Ibrahim (Abraham) and Ishaq (Isaac) before you. Surely your Rabb is Knowledgeable, Wise. Indeed in the story of Yusuf and his brothers, there are signs for inquirers." (Yusuf: 12.4-7)

b. Yusuf's (A.S.) prayer to live and die as a Muslim:

"When they came to Yusuf, he asked his parents to lodge with himself, and said: "Now enter the city. Allah willing, you will live here in peace." After entering the city he helped his parents to seats on the throne, and they all fell down in prostration before him. "This," said Yusuf to his father, "is the interpretation of my dream which I dreamt long before. My Rabb has really made it come true. It was His grace that He took me out of prison and brought you all here from the desert even though Shaitan had stirred up strife between me and my brothers. For sure my Rabb fulfills His plan in mysterious ways. Surely He is the One Who is the Knowledgeable, the Wise. O Rabb! You have indeed given me a kingdom and taught me the interpretation of dreams. O, the Creator of the heavens and the earth, You are my Protector in this world and in the hereafter, make me die as a Muslim and admit me among the righteous"." (Yusuf: 12.99-101)

14) Rasools were sent to the descendants of Prophet Nuh (A.S.) - similarly Prophet Musa (A.S.) and Haroon (A.S.) were sent to Pharaoh:

"Then after him We sent Rasools to their descendants. They came to them with clear signs but they would not believe what they had rejected before. Thus, do We set seals upon the hearts of those who (intentionally) exceed the limits. Then later on We sent Musa (Moses) and Haroon (Aaron) to Fir'on (Pharaoh) and his chiefs with Our signs. But they showed arrogance, for they were a guilty nation. When the truth did come to them from Us they said: "This is indeed sheer magic!" Musa replied: "Is this what you say of the Truth when it has come to you? Is this a magic? Magicians do not prosper." They said: "Have you come to turn us away from the faith of our forefathers in order that you two (Musa and Haroon) may become the leaders in the land? We will never believe in you!" Fir'on said: "Bring me every skillful magician." When the magicians came, Musa said to them: "Throw what you wish to throw!" So when they had thrown, Musa said: "The magic that you have brought, Allah will surely prove it wrong: for Allah does not promote the work of mischief-makers. By His Words Allah vindicates the truth, much as the criminals may dislike it!." " (Yunus: 10.74-82)

15) Allah bestowed His favors on Prophets Musa (A.S.) and Haroon (A.S.):

a. "We bestowed Our favor on Musa and Haroon. We delivered them with all their people from the mighty distress. We helped them so they became victorious. We gave them the Glorious Book (Torah), and guided them both to the Right Way. We left their good names among the later generations. Salutation to Musa and Haroon! Thus do We reward the righteous. Surely they were two of Our believing devotees." (As-Saffat: 37.114-122)

b. Musa (A.S.) was given nine signs; people still did not believe him:

   i. "To Musa (Moses) We gave nine clear signs. Ask the Children of Israel how, when he came to them and Fir'on told him: "O Musa! I think that you are bewitched."" (Al-Israa: 17.101)

   ii. "Then later on We sent Musa (Moses) and Haroon (Aaron) to Fir'on (Pharaoh) and his chiefs with Our signs. But they showed arrogance, for they were a guilty nation." (Yunus: 10.75)

   iii. "We afflicted Fir'on's people with several years of famine and shortages of fruit so that they might come to their senses. But whenever they had good times they said "It is our due," and whenever evil befell them they ascribed that bad luck to Musa and those with him. Behold! In fact their misfortune was in the hands of Allah; yet most of them do not know. They said to Musa: "No matter what sign you may bring us to put your magic spell, we are not going to believe you." So We plagued them with storms, locusts, lice, frogs and blood: clear cut signs, yet they persisted in their arrogance, for they were a criminal nation. Every time the plague befell them, they said: "O Musa! Pray for us to your Rabb as He has made the promise with you, if you help remove the plague from us, we shall truly believe in you and send the Children of Israel with you." But every time We removed the plague from them and the appointed time for the release of the Children of Israel came, lo! they broke their promise. Therefore, We inflicted retribution on them and drowned them in the sea, for they denied Our signs and became heedless of them." (Al-A'raf: 7.130-136)

c. Prophet Musa (A.S.) prayed to Allah:

"Musa prayed: "O Rabb! Open my heart, ease my task and remove the impediment from my speech so that people may understand what I say and grant me a minister from my family, Haroon my brother. Grant me strength through him and let him share my task, so that we may glorify You frequently and mention You often; for You are the One Who has always been watching over us." Allah responded: "Your request is granted, O Musa!"" (Ta-ha: 20.25-36)

16) Prophethood of Musa (A.S.), Isma`il (A.S.) and Idris (A.S.):

"So when he left them and the deities whom they worshipped besides Allah, We granted him descendants like Ishaq and Ya'qoob, and We made each of them a Prophet. We bestowed on them Our Mercy and We granted them honor of being mentioned with true high respect. Relate to them the story of Musa in the Book; surely he was a chosen man and was a Rasool, a Prophet.

We called him from the right side of Mount Tur and honored him to come closer for exclusive conversation. We made his brother Haroon a Prophet with Our blessing and assigned him as his assistant. Also relate to them the story of Isma`il in the Book; he was a man of his word and was a Rasool, a Prophet. He commanded his people to establish Salah and give Zakah, and was the one with whom his Rabb was well pleased. Also relate to them the story of Idris in the Book; he was a Truthful man, a Prophet whom We raised to a lofty place. These are some of the Prophets on whom Allah bestowed His favors from among the descendants of Adam and of those whom We carried in the Ark with Nuh, and of the descendants of Ibrahim and Israel, and of those whom We guided and chose. Whenever the Revelations of the Compassionate (Allah) were recited to them, they fell to prostrate and weep." (Maryam: 19. 49-58)

17) Allah accepted the prayers and blessed Prophets Isma`il (A.S.), Zulkifl (A.S.), Yunus (A.S.), Zakariya (A.S.) and also blessed Maryam (Peace be upon her):

"Likewise, We blessed Isma`il (Ishmael), Idris and Zulkifl, for all of them practised patience. We admitted them to Our Mercy, for they were of the righteous people. We blessed Zun-nun (Yunus / Jonah), when he departed in anger, thinking We would not take him to task for this, but later he prayed to Us from the depths of darkness, "There is no god but You, glory be to You! Indeed I was the one who committed wrong." We accepted his prayer and delivered him from distress; thus do We deliver the believers. We also blessed Zakariya, when he prayed to his Rabb, "O my Rabb! Do not let me remain childless even though You are the best of inheritors. We accepted his prayer and gave him Yahya (John), curing his wife for him to bear a child. They were ever quick in emulating good deeds and called on Us with hope, fear, and submission. And We blessed the woman (Maryam), who guarded her chastity, We breathed into her of Our Spirit and We made her and her son a sign for the whole world." (Al-Anbiyaa: 21.85-91)

18) Story of Prophet Yunus (Jonah, A.S.):

"Yunus (Jonah) was surely one of Our Rasools. When he ran to the laden ship, took part in casting of lots, and was condemned, a whale swallowed him for he had become blameworthy. Had he not repented and became of those who glorify Allah, he would certainly have remained inside the belly of whale till the Day of Resurrection. Then We cast him upon a desolate shore in a state of serious illness and caused a gourd plant to grow over him. Then We sent him to a nation of one hundred thousand people or more. They believed in him, so We permitted them to enjoy their life for a while." (As-Saffat: 37.139-148)

19) Ilyas (Elias, A.S.) was one of the Rasools of Allah:

"Ilyas (Elias) was surely one of Our Rasools. Behold he said to his people: "Have you no fear of Allah? Would you invoke Bal (their invented god) and forsake the best of the Creators - Allah - Who is your Rabb and the Rabb of your forefathers?" But they denied him, so they will certainly be called to account, with the exception of sincere devotees of Allah. We left his good name among the later generations. Salutation to Ilyas!" " (As-Saffat: 37.123-130)

20) Descendants of Prophet Ibrahim (A.S.) including Musa (A.S.), Isa (A.S.) and Muhammad (S.A.W.), none of them were Mushrikin:

"This was the argument which We furnished Ibrahim (Abraham) against his people. We exalt in ranks whom

We please; surely your Rabb is Wise, Aware. We gave him Ishaq (Isaac) and Ya'qoob (Jacob) and guided them all as We guided Nuh (Noah) before them, and among his descendants were Dawood (David), Sulaiman (Solomon), Ayub (Job), Yusuf (Joseph), Musa (Moses) and Haroon (Aaron); thus do We reward those who do good to others. Other descendants include Zakariya, Yahya (John), Isa (Jesus), and Ilyas (Elias); all of them were righteous; and Isma`il (Ishmael), Al-Yas'a (Elisha), Yunus (Jonah) and Lut (Lot). We exalted every one of them over the worlds as We exalted some of their forefathers, their children and their brothers. We chose them for Our service and guided them to the Right Way. This is the guidance from Allah; He bestows it upon whom He pleases of His devotees. If they had committed Shirk (worshiped anyone else besides Allah) all their deeds would have become void. Such were the people to whom We gave the Book, wisdom and Prophethood. Now if these people deny this guidance, it does not matter; We would bestow this guidance upon other people who would not disbelieve. O Muhammad, those were the people who were rightly guided by Allah, therefore, follow their guidance and tell these people: "I am not asking you any compensation for this work of delivering the Message to you, this message is nothing but a reminder to all the worlds."" (Al-An'am: 6.83-90)

21) Supplication of Zakariya (A.S.) for his son Yahya (John, A.S.):

"Thereupon Zakariya prayed to his Rabb saying: "O my Rabb! Grant me a righteous child as Your special favor; surely You hear all prayers." As he stood praying in the Mahrab (a prayer place in the sanctuary) the angels called out to him saying: "Allah gives you good news of a son to be named Yahya (John), he will confirm the word of Allah, he will be a great leader and chaste, a Prophet and a righteous man."" (Al-i'Imran: 3.38-39)

22) "To Yahya, when he became old enough, We said: "Hold firmly to the Book." We granted him wisdom, while he was yet a boy." (Maryam: 19.12)

23) The Jews and Christians who call Azra (A.S.) and Jesus (A.S.) the sons of God are Mushrikeen:

"The Jews say: "Uzair (Azra) is the son of Allah," and the Christians say: "Messiah (Christ) is the son of Allah." That is what they say with their mouths, imitating the sayings of the former unbelievers. May Allah destroy them! How perverted they are! They (Jews and Christians) have taken their rabbis and priests to be their Lords beside Allah and so they did with Messiah (Jesus) the son of Maryam (Mary), although they were commanded in the Torah and the Gospel to worship none but One Ilah (Allah); besides Whom there is none worthy of worship. Exalted be He above those whom they associate with Him. They desire to extinguish the light of Allah with their mouths but Allah will not allow it to happen, for He seeks to perfect His light even though the disbelievers may dislike it. It is He Who has sent His Rasool with guidance and true Deen (faith) to make it prevail over all other Deens (faiths) even though the Mushrikin may hate it." (At-Tauba: 9.30-33)

24) The story of Maryam (P.B.U.H.) and the miraculous birth of Isa (Jesus, A.S.):

a. O Muhammad, relate to them the story of Maryam in the Book (The Qur'an) when she withdrew from her family to a place in the East. She chose to be secluded from them. We sent to her Our angel and he appeared before her as a grown up man. She said: "I seek Rahman's (Allah's) protection against you, leave me alone if you are Godfearing." He said: "Don't be afraid, I am merely a messenger from your Rabb to tell you about the gift of a holy son." She said: "How shall I bear a son, no man has ever touched me nor am I unchaste?" The angel replied: "So shall it be - your Rabb says: `It is easy for Me. We wish to make him a Sign for mankind and a blessing from Us' - and this matter has already been decreed." So she conceived the child and she retired with him to a remote place. The pains of childbirth drove her to the trunk of a palm-tree. She cried in her anguish: "Ah! Would that I had died before this, and been long forgotten!" An angel from beneath the palm-tree consoled her, saying: "Do not grieve! Your Rabb has provided a brook at your feet. If you shake the trunk of this palm-tree, it will drop fresh ripe dates in your lap. So eat, drink and refresh yourself. If you see anyone, tell him: `I have vowed a fast to Rahman (Allah), so I will not speak to anyone today'." Carrying the baby, she came back to her people. They said: "O Maryam! You have brought something hard to believe! O sister (a woman from the noble family) of Haroon! Your father was not a bad man nor your mother an unchaste woman." In response she merely pointed towards the baby. They said: "How can we talk to a babe in the cradle?" Whereupon the baby spoke out: "I am indeed a servant of Allah. He has given me the Book and made me a Prophet. His blessing is with me wherever I go. He has commanded me to establish Salah and give Zakah as long as I shall live. He has exhorted me to honor my mother and has not made me domineering, hard to deal with. Peace be upon me the day I was born, the day I shall die and the Day I shall be raised to life again." Such was Isa (Jesus) the son of Maryam, and this is the true statement about him concerning which they are in doubt." (Maryam: 19.16-34)

b. Prophet Isa's (A.S.) Prayers:

"It is not befitting to the majesty of Allah that He Himself should beget a son! He is far above this (weakness to get a son for name, fame, help or continuity of race); for when He decrees a matter He need only say: "Be" and it is. Isa declared, "Verily Allah is my Rabb and your Rabb: therefore serve Him. This is a Right Way." Inspite of this, the sects from among them are divided concerning Jesus. So woe to the disbelievers who shall be punished after witnessing this Truth on the Great Day of Judgement. They will be able to see and hear very clearly on that Day when they will appear before Us! But today these wrongdoers, neither want to hear nor see the Truth and, are in manifest error. O Muhammad, forewarn them about the Day of intense regret when this matter will be decided, even though at present they are paying no heed and do not believe. Ultimately, all things will perish and it is We, Who will inherit the earth and all that is on it, and to Us shall they return." (Maryam: 19.35-40)

25) Advent of Prophet Muhammad (S.A.W.) was described in Torah and Gospel:

a. " "or lest you say: "If the Book had been revealed to us, we could have followed its guidance better than them," a veritable sign has now come to you from your Rabb as a guidance and mercy. Who then is more unjust than the one who denies the revelations of Allah and turns away from them? Very soon those who turn away from Our revelations will face dreadful punishment for their aversion."" (Al-An'am: 6.157)

b. Prophet Isa (Jesus, A.S.) gave good news of a Rasool coming after him whose name is Ahmed (Muhammad, S.A.W.):

"And remember when Isa (Jesus) the son of Maryam said: "O children of Israel! I am the Rasool of Allah towards you, confirming the Torah which came before me, and to give you good news of a Rasool that will come after me whose name shall be Ahmed (another name of Muhammad, meaning 'The praised one')." But when he (Muhammad) came to them with clear signs, they said "This is plain magic." Who could be more wrong than the one who invents falsehoods against Allah while he is being called towards Islam? Allah does not guide those who are wrongdoers. They seek to extinguish the Light of Allah with their mouths, but Allah will perfect His Light, much as the unbelievers may dislike it. It is He Who has sent His Rasool with the guidance and the religion of truth so that he may proclaim it over all religions, much as the Mushrikin may dislike it." (As-Saff: 61.6-9.)

c. Allah appointed Muhammad (S.A.W.) as a Rasool:

"All that is in the heavens and earth declares the glory of Allah, the King, the Holy, the Mighty, the Wise. It is He Who has raised among the unlettered people a Rasool of their own, who recites to them His revelations, purifies them, and teaches them the Book and Wisdom, though prior to this they were in gross error, he is also sent for others of them who have not yet joined them (become Muslims). He is the Mighty, the Wise. That is the grace of Allah, which He bestows on whom He pleases. Allah is the Lord of mighty grace." (Al-Jamu'a: 62.1-4)

d. Reaffirming the Prophethood of Muhammad (P.B.U.H.) Ranks of Rasools:

   "These are the revelations of Allah; We recite them to you in truth. Surely you, O Muhammad, are one of Our Rasools. These are the Rasools (which We have sent for the guidance of mankind). We have exalted some above others. To some Allah spoke directly; others He raised high in ranks; to Isa (Jesus) the son of Maryam (Mary) We gave clear Signs and supported him with the Holy Spirit. If Allah wished the people who received the clear signs would not have fought against each other; but they disputed as a result, there were some who believed while others rejected. Yet if Allah wanted, they would not have fought each other; but Allah does what He intends." (Al-Baqara: 2.252-253)

e. The Life of Rasoolallah (Muhammad- S.A.W.) is the best Model:

   "You have indeed, in the life of Rasool-Allah, the 'Best Model' for him whose hope is in Allah and the Day of the Hereafter, and who engages himself much in the remembrance of Allah. When the true believers saw the confederate forces they said: "This is what Allah and His Rasool had promised us: Allah and his Rasool were absolutely true." This increased them all the more in their faith and their zeal in obedience. Among the believers there are men who have been true to their covenant with Allah: of them some have completed their vow through sacrificing their lives, and some others are waiting for it, and have not changed their determination in the least. All this happens so that Allah may reward the truthful for their truth and punish the hypocrites or accept their repentance if He wills: for Allah is Forgiving, Merciful." (Al-Ahzab: 33.21-24)

f. Allah has sent Muhammad (P.B.U.H.) as a blessing for all the worlds (Humans, Jinns and others):

   "O Muhammad, We have not sent you but as a blessing for all the worlds. Tell them: "It has been revealed to me that your God is One God - will you then become Muslims?" If they give no heed, tell them: "I have warned you all alike in complete fairness; now I do not know whether what you are threatened with is near or far. It is He Who knows your spoken words and hidden thoughts. I do not know whether this delay is a trial for you or you are being given respite for an appointed time."Finally the Prophet said: "O Rabb! Pass Your Judgment with fairness. And O People! Our Rabb is most Compassionate, Whose help we seek against the blasphemies you utter."" (Al-Anbiyaa: 21.107-112)

g. Scene of the 1st Revelation, brought by angel Gabriel to Prophet Muhammad (S.A.W.) and Allah gave him a tour of heavens, paradise and other great signs:

   "By the star when it set, your companion (Muhammad) is neither astray, nor misguided, nor does he speak out of his own desire. This Qur'an is but an inspired revelation. He is being taught by one who is mighty, powerful (angel Gabriel); the one free from defects who became stable in the view. He stood poised at the uppermost horizon, then he drew near, coming closer within the length of two bows or even closer, and revealed to Allah's servant that what he was supposed to reveal. His (Muhammad's) own heart did not deny that which he saw. How can you, O unbelievers, then question what he saw? And he (Muhammad) saw him once again near Sidra-tul-Muntaha (the Lot-tree at the farthest end of the seven heavens, beyond which none can pass). Near it is Janna-tul-M'awa (the rest-house of paradise). When that Lot-tree was covered with what covered it, his eyes did not turn aside nor did it exceed the limit: and he did indeed see some of his Rabb's greatest signs." (An-Najm: 53.1-18)

h. Prophet (S.A.W) is sent as a bearer of good news, a Warner and a lamp spreading light:

"Muhammad is not the father of any of your men (he is not going to leave any male heirs). He is the Rasool of Allah and the Seal of the Prophets. Allah has the knowledge of all things. O believers! Remember Allah as a frequent remembrance, and glorify Him morning and evening. It is He Who sends His blessings on you (believers) and so do His angels, that He may bring you out of darkness into light, for He is Merciful to the believers. On the Day of their meeting with Him, their greeting shall be: "Salaam (peace)!" and He has prepared for them a generous reward. O Prophet! Surely We have sent you as a witness, as a bearer of good news and as a Warner, and to call the people towards Allah by His leave and a lamp spreading light (guidance). Give good news to the believers that they shall have great blessings from Allah. Do not obey the unbelievers and the hypocrites, disregard their annoyances and put your trust in Allah; for Allah is sufficient as a disposer of affairs." (Al-Ahzab: 33.40-48)

i. Characteristics of Muhammad (pbuh) and his followers:

"It is He who has sent His Rasool with Guidance and the religion of truth, so that He may exalt this religion over all other religions: and sufficient is Allah as a witness. Muhammad, the Rasool of Allah, and those with him are strong against the unbelievers and compassionate to each other among themselves. When you see them, you will find them making Rakuh (bowing down) and Sajud (prostrate in prayers), and craving for the blessings from Allah and His good pleasure. They have mark of Sajud (prostration) on their foreheads, the traces of their prostration. This is their similitude in the Taurat (Torah); and their similitude in the Injeel (Gospel): they are like the seed which puts forth its sprout, then strengthens it, then becomes thick and stands firmly on its stem, delighting the sowers of the seed, so that through them He may enrage the unbelievers. Yet to those of them who will believe and do good deeds, Allah has promised forgiveness and a great reward." (Al-Fath: 48.28-29)

j. Muhammad (P.B.U.H.) is no more than a Rasool of Allah:

"Muhammad is no more than a Rasool of Allah, like the Rasools that passed away before him. If he dies or is killed will you turn back on your heels (become unbelievers)? He that turns back on his heels will do no harm to Allah; but Allah will reward the thankful." (Al-i'Imran: 3.144)

k. "Indeed Allah and His angels send blessings on the Prophet. O believers, call for Allah's blessings on him and salute him with all respect." (Al-Ahzab: 33.56)

## 5) To believe in the day of Doom, Resurrection and Judgement.

"As for the dooms day, it shall come, when the Trumpet will be blown with a single blast and the earth with all its mountains will be lifted up and crushed into pieces with a single stroke. On that day the Great Event will come to pass, heaven shall split asunder, and the day shall seem flimsy. The angels will stand all around and eight of them will be carrying the Throne of your Rabb above them. That shall be the day when you will be brought before your Rabb, and none of your secrets shall remain hidden." (Al-Haqqa: 69.13-18)

1) Everyone has to die:

   "Every soul shall taste death. You shall receive your full reward for everything which you have striven for, on the Day of Resurrection. Whoever is spared from the fire and is admitted into paradise will have attained the objective of this worldly life; for the life of this world is nothing but an illusory enjoyment." (Al-i'Imran: 3.185)

2) There is no escape from death:

   "Have you reflected on the case of thousands of people (Israelites) who fled their homes for fear of death? Allah said to them: "Die" (gave them death). Then He gave them life again. Surely Allah is bountiful to mankind, but most of the people are ungrateful." (Al-Baqara: 2.243)

3) Life and death is from Allah:

   "O believers! Do not be like the unbelievers who speak of those brethren of theirs who die during their travels on the earth or while engaged in fighting: "Had they but stayed with us they would not have died or been killed." Allah makes such thinking a cause of regret and anguish in their hearts. It is Allah who gives life and death. Allah is observant of all your actions. If you should die or get killed in the cause of Allah, His forgiveness and mercy will be far better than all the riches you could gather. Whether you die or get killed, all of you will be brought before Allah." (Al-i'Imran: 3.156-158)

4) Similitude of worldly life and its relationship with the life of hereafter:

"O Prophet! Give them the similitude of the life of this world. It is like the vegetation of the earth that flourishes with the rain from the sky, but afterwards the same vegetation turns into dry stubble which is blown away by the winds. Allah is the One Who has power over everything. Likewise, wealth and children are an attraction of this worldly life; yet honorable deeds that last forever are better rewarded by your Rabb and hold for you a better hope of salvation. You should prepare for that Day when We will set the mountains in motion and you will see the earth as a barren waste; when We shall assemble mankind all together, leaving not even a single soul behind. They all will be brought before your Rabb standing in rows and Allah will say: "Well! You see that you have returned to Us as We created you at first: even though you claimed that We had not fixed any time for the fulfillment of this promise of meeting with Us!" Then the book of their deeds will be placed before them. At that time you will see the sinners in great terror because of what is recorded therein. They will say: "Woe to us! What kind of a book is this? It leaves out nothing small or large: all is noted down!" They will find all that they did recorded therein. Your Rabb will not be unjust to anyone in the least." (Al-Kahf: 18.45-49)

5) Believer's and unbeliever's life in this world and their life hereafter:

"Man says: "What! Once I am dead, shall I be raised to life again?" Does not the man remember that We created him before out of nothing? By your Rabb, We will call them to account in the company of all their Shaitans and set them on their knees around the Fire of Hell; then from every set We will certainly drag out its stoutest rebels against the Compassionate (Allah). Certainly We know best who deserves most to be burned therein. There is not a single one of you, who shall not pass over it, this absolute decree of your Rabb is unavoidable; then We will deliver those who were pious during their life on earth and leave the wrongdoers therein humbled on their knees." (Maryam: 19.66-72)

6) There is a life after death:

"If you could witness the scene, when they will be made to stand before the hellfire! They will say: "We wish we could return to earthly life again; then we would not deny the revelations of our Rabb, and we would join the believers!" In fact, they will say this because they had come to know the reality which they were concealing before. As a matter of fact even if they be sent back, they would certainly repeat the same things which they had been forbidden to do. Indeed they are liars. Today they say: "There is no other life except the life on this earth and we shall never be raised to life again." If you could witness the scene when they will be brought before their Rabb; He will ask, "Is this not a reality?" They will say: "Yes, our Rabb, this is the reality." He will order: "Well, then taste the punishment for denying this reality." " (Al-An'am: 6.27-30)

7) On the Day of Judgement the Book of Deeds will be laid open and justice will be done with all fairness:

"Therefore, worship Allah and be among His thankful servants. They have not recognized the worth of Allah as his worth should be recognized. On the Day of

Resurrection the whole earth shall be in His grasp and all the heavens shall be rolled up in His right hand. Glory be to Him! Exalted be He above what they associate with Him. The Trumpet shall be blown, and all that is in the heavens and the earth shall swoon except those whom Allah will please to exempt. Then the Trumpet will be blown for the second time and behold! They shall all stand up, looking around. The earth will be shining with the light of her Rabb, the Book of record will be laid open, the Prophets and other witnesses will be brought in, and justice shall be done between people with all fairness: none shall be wronged. Every soul will be paid in full according to its deeds, for He knows fully well as to what they did." (Az-Zumar: 39.66 -70)

8) The day of judgement will be equal to fifty thousand years:

"A questioner asked you about the punishment which is bound to happen. It is for the disbelievers and there is none to avert it. It will come from Allah, the Owner of the Ways of Ascent. The angels and the Spirit ascend to Him in a Day the measure of which is fifty thousand years. Therefore, endure with graceful patience. They see it (Day of Judgement) to be far-off: but We see it quite near. On that Day, the sky shall become like molten brass and the mountains like tufts of wool; even a close friend will not ask of his friend, though they will see each other. To save himself from the punishment of that Day, the culprit (disbeliever) will wish to give his children, his wife, his brother, his relatives - who gave him shelter - and all that is in the earth, in ransom to save himself. By no means! It will be the fire of hell, eager to pluck out his skull, it will be calling all those who try to escape and turn their back, who collected wealth and withheld it. Indeed, man has been created impatient, when evil befalls him, he becomes despondent; but when blessed with good fortune, he becomes stingy; with the exception of those who offer the Salah (prayer), remain steadfast in their Salah, set aside a due share in their wealth for the beggars and the deprived, accept the truth of the Day of Judgement, dread the punishment of their Rabb - for none is secure from the punishment of their Rabb - and guard their private parts, except from their wives and those whom their right hands possess, for in their case they are not blameworthy. As for those who seek to go beyond this, they are transgressors. Those who keep their trusts and honor their promises, who stand firm in their testimonies and strictly guard their Salah. It is they who shall live with honor in paradise." (Al-Ma'arij: 70.1-35)

9) Man's accountability in the court of Allah:

"About what are they asking? About the mighty event - the theme of their disputes. Very soon they shall come to know; We repeat, very soon they shall come to know. Is it not true that We have spread the earth like a bed, and the mountains as pegs, created you in pairs, provided you rest in sleep, made the night a mantle, made the day to work for earning your livelihood, built above you seven firmaments, placed therein a shining lamp, sent down abundant water from the clouds, bringing forth grain, vegetation and gardens of luxurious growth? The Day of decision is already fixed. On that Day, the Trumpet shall be sounded and you shall come forth in multitude. The sky shall be opened as if there were doors. The mountains shall vanish as if they were a mirage. For sure, the hell shall lie in ambush, to become a home for the transgressors. There they shall live for ages, in it they shall taste neither refreshment nor drink, except scalding water and decaying filth: a fitting recompense for their deeds. For they never expected to be accountable, and wittingly rejected Our revelations. But We had recorded everything in a Book. It will be said: "Taste the fruits of your deeds! You shall have nothing but increase in punishment." On that Day, the righteous will certainly achieve their heart's desires: beautiful gardens, vineyards; and young women of their own age, and overflowing cups; they shall hear no vanity, nor any falsehood; - a recompense from your Rabb and a gift beyond their account from the Compassionate, Who is the Rabb of the heavens, the earth and all that lies between them; before Whom no one shall be able to speak. On that Day, the Spirit (Gabriel) and the angels shall stand in their ranks; none shall speak except the one to whom the Compassionate (Allah) shall grant permission to speak, and he will speak straight to the point. That Day is a sure reality. Let him who desires, seek a way back to his Rabb. Indeed We have forewarned you of an imminent punishment which lies close-at-hand, on the Day when man shall see what his hands have sent forth and the unbeliever will cry: "I wish I could remain merely dust."" (Al-Nabaa: 78.1-40)

10) All that exist will perish except Allah, Who is busy in heavy tasks all the time:

"All that exists on the earth will perish, but the Face of your Rabb will remain full of Majesty and Glory. Then, O jinn and men, which of your Rabb's glories will both of you deny? All who dwell in the heavens and the earth, implore Him for their needs, every moment He is busy in some mighty task. Then, O jinn and men, which of your Rabb's honors will both of you deny? O you, the two burdens (jinns and mankind)! Soon We shall find the time to call you to account. Then, O jinn and men, which of your Rabb's favors will both of you deny?" (Ar-Rahman: 55.26-32)

11) They will be called to account:

"Do they not think that they will be raised to life again on a Mighty Day, a Day when all mankind will stand before the Rabb of the worlds? Indeed not! The record of the wicked is in Sijjeen (prison register), what will explain to you, what the Sijjeen is? This is a written book of hell. Woe on that Day to the disbelievers, who deny the Day of Judgment! None denies it except the sinful transgressor!" (Al-Mutaffifin: 83.4-12)

12) Rasools as well as the people to whom they were sent shall be questioned on the Day of Judgment and a Scale of Justice shall be established:

"This Book is revealed to you; let there be no hesitation in your heart about it so that you may thereby warn the unbelievers and remind the believers. Say: "O people, follow what has been brought down to you from your Rabb and do not follow other patrons besides Him." Yet little do they take admonition. How many towns have We destroyed for their sins? Our scourge took them all of a sudden at night or while they were taking their afternoon rest, and when our scourge fell upon them, their only cry was: "We have indeed been wrongdoers." On the Day of Judgement We shall question those to whom Rasools were sent and We shall also question the Rasools about Our message and its response. Then We shall tell their whole story as an eye witness for We were never absent at any time or from any place. On that Day, the Scale of Justice shall be established. Those whose scale of good deeds will be heavy, they are the ones who will attain felicity, and those whose scale is light, they shall find themselves in loss for they had done injustice to Our revelations!" (Al-A'raf: 7.2-9)

13) There is no escape from the day of resurrection and judgement:

"I swear by the Day of Resurrection, and I swear by the self reproaching soul! Does man think that We shall not be able to put his bones together? Why not? We are able to put together, in perfect order, the very tips of his fingers. But man wishes to keep on doing evil in the future as well. He questions: "When will this Day of Resurrection be?" Well, it will come when the sight shall be dazed, the moon will be eclipsed, and the sun and the moon will be brought together on that Day man will ask: "Is there any way to escape?" Nay! There will be no refuge. On that Day, the refuge will only be towards your Rabb. On that Day man shall be told about all his deeds, from the first to the last. Indeed, man shall bear witness against himself, even though he shall plead with excuses." (Al-Qiyamat: 75.1-15)

14) Surely the day of judgement shall come to pass:

"They ask: "When will the Day of Judgment be?" It will be the Day when they will be punished in the fire, and it will be said: "Taste your chastisement! This is what you were seeking to haste."" (Al-Zariat: 51.12-14)

15) Scale of Justice shall be set up on the Day of Judgement:

"On the Day of Judgement We shall set up Scales of Justice so that no one will be dealt with unjustly in any way; even if someone has an act as small as a grain of a mustard seed, We will bring it to account, and sufficient are We to settle the accounts." (Al-Anbiyaa: 21.47)

16) After Judgement unbelievers will be driven to Hell and the righteous will be led to Paradise:

"After the Judgement, the Unbelievers will be driven to hell in groups. When they reach there, its gates will be opened and its keepers will say: "Did there not come to you Rasools from among yourselves, who recited to you the revelations of your Rabb and forewarned you about the meeting of this Day?" "Yes," they will answer. But at that time the sentence of punishment would have been already announced against the unbelievers. They will be told: "Enter the gates of hell to live therein forever. Evil shall be the abode of the arrogant." As for those who fear their Rabb, they shall be led towards paradise in groups. When they reach there, its gates will be opened, and its keepers will say: "Peace be upon you! You have done well, now enter to live therein forever." They will say: "Praise be to Allah Who has truly fulfilled His promise and gave us this land to inherit, now we can live in paradise wherever we like." How excellent will be the reward for the righteous? You will see the angels surrounding the Divine Throne, glorifying their Rabb with His praises. The judgement between the people will be made with perfect justice, and it will be proclaimed: "Praise be to Allah the Rabb of the worlds!"." (Az-Zumar: 39.71-75)

17) The day of judgement will be very difficult especially for those who deny Allah's revelations and oppose His cause:

"When the Trumpet will be sounded, that Day will be a very difficult Day, not easy for the disbelievers. Leave Me and the one (Walid bin Mughirah, a staunch opponent of the Prophet) whom I created, alone. I gave him abundant resources, thriving sons, and made his life smooth and comfortable. Yet he hopes that I shall give him more. By no means! Because he has stubbornly denied Our revelations. Soon I shall make him suffer mounting calamities, surely he pondered and devised a plot. May he perish, how he plotted! Again, may he perish, how he plotted! He looked around, frowned and scowled, then he turned his back in scornful pride and said: "This is nothing but counterfeited magic, this is nothing but the word of a human being." Soon I shall cast him into Saqar. What will make you understand, what Saqar is? It is burning fire which leaves nothing and spares none. It shrivels human flesh. It is guarded by nineteen guards. We have appointed none but angels as wardens of the fire; and We have made their number a trial for the unbelievers, so that the People of the Book may be convinced and the faith of the true believers may be increased, and that no doubts will be left for the People of the Book and the believers, and that those in whose hearts there is a disease and the disbelievers may say: "What could Allah mean by this parable?" Thus, Allah leaves to stray whom He wills and guides whom He pleases. No one knows the forces of your Rabb except Himself, and this (Qur'an) is nothing but a reminder to mankind." (Al-Muddaththir: 74.8-31)

18) A scene from the Day of judgement:

" They ask you as to what will happen to the mountains. Tell them: "My Rabb will crush and scatter them like a fine dust. He will turn earth into a plain leveled ground, wherein you will not see neither any curve nor crease." - On that Day the people will follow the call of the Caller, no one will dare show any crookedness; their voices hushed before the Beneficent (Allah), and you shall hear nothing but the sound of the marching feet. On that Day, no intercession will avail except the one to whom the Beneficent (Allah) shall grant permission and would like to give him a hearing. He knows what is before them and what is behind them while they do not encompass any knowledge about Him. Their faces shall be humbled before the Ever-living, the Ever-existent

(Allah). The one who is carrying the burden of iniquity will be doomed: but the one who is a believer and does good deeds shall fear no tyranny or injustice." (Ta-ha: 20.105-112)

19) Fortunate people and their reward and Unfortunate people and their punishment:

"Then he, who will be given his Book of Deeds in his right hand, will say: "Here it is, read my Book of Deeds! I knew that I would certainly face my reckoning." So he will have a life of pleasure, in a lofty garden, with clusters of fruit within his reach. We shall say to him: "Eat and drink to your heart's content; this is a reward for what you did in the days gone by." While he, who will be given his Book of Deeds in his left hand, will say: "Woe to me, would that I had not been given my Book of Deeds nor known what my account was! Would that my death had ended all! My wealth had availed me nothing, and my authority has gone away from me." We shall say: "Seize him and put a chain around his neck, then cast him in the blazing fire, then fasten him with a chain seventy cubits long." (Al-Haqqa: 69.19-32)

20) If Allah were to punish for wrong-doings, He would not leave even an animal around the wrongdoers:

"If Allah were to punish mankind for its wrongdoing, He would not leave even an animal around the wrongdoers, but He gives them respite for an appointed time. But when their appointed time comes, they can neither stay behind for a moment nor can they go before it." (An-Nahl: 16.61)

Scene of the day of judgement when mankind will be divided into three groups:

"When the inevitable event will come to pass, - no one will be able to deny its coming to pass - then some shall be abased and some exalted. The earth shall be shaken with severe shaking and the mountains shall be made to crumble with awful crumbling and become like scattered dust. Then you shall be divided into three groups: those on the right hand - how blessed shall be the people of the right hand; those on the left hand - how damned shall be the people of the left hand; and foremost shall be the foremost." (Al-Waqi'a: 56.1-10)

(a) Reward for the right-hand group:

i. "Those of the right hand - happy shall be those on the right hand! They shall be among the thornless lot trees, clusters of bananas, extended thick shades, constantly flowing water, abundant fruits of unforbidden never ending supply, and will be reclining on high raised couches. We shall create their wives of special creation and make them virgins beloved by nature, equal in age, for those of the right hand." (Al-Waqi'a: 56.27-38)

ii. Food and entertainment for the righteous in paradise:

"As for the righteous, they will be in a secure place; among gardens and springs, dressed in fine silk and rich brocade, sitting face to face. Such shall be their place! And We shall wed them to Hourin-Ayn (damsels with beautiful big and lustrous eyes). There, in full peace, they shall call for every kind of fruit; and after having prior death in the world, they shall taste death no more; and He (Allah) will protect them from the torment of hell as a grace from your Rabb, and that will be the supreme achievement. Surely We have made this Qur'an easy by revealing in your own language so that they may take heed. If they do not accept the admonition then wait; surely they too are waiting." (Al-Dukhan: 44.51-59)

(b) Punishment for the left-hand group:

i. "Many of them will be from the former and many from the later generations. As for those of the left hand - how unfortunate will be the people of the left hand! They will be in the midst of scorching winds and in boiling water: in the shade of a pitch-black smoke, neither cool nor refreshing. For they lived in comfort before meeting this fate. They persisted in heinous sins and used to say: "When we are dead and turned to dust and bones, shall we then be raised to life again? And our forefathers, too?" Tell them: "Surely those of old and those of present age shall certainly be brought together on an appointed time of a known Day. Then, "O the mistaken rejecters, you shall eat of the Zaqqum tree, and fill your bellies with it; and drink on top of it scalding water; yet you shall drink it like a thirsty camel." Such will be their entertainment on the Day of Reckoning." (Al-Waqi'a: 56.39-56)

ii. Food and drink for the sinners in hell:

"Surely the Zaqqum tree shall be the food of the sinners; it will be like the drags of oil which shall boil in the belly like the boiling of scalding water. A voice will be heard: "Seize him and drag him into the depth of the hell, then pour scalding water over his head, then the voice will say: Taste it; you were such a powerful noble! This is the punishment which you use to doubt." " (Al-Dukhan: 44.43-50)

(c) Reward for the foremost group:

"When the inevitable event will come to pass - no one will be able to deny its coming to pass - then some shall be abased and some exalted. The earth shall be shaken with severe shaking and the mountains shall be made to crumble with awful crumbling and become like scattered dust. Then you shall be divided into three groups: those on the right hand - how blessed shall be the people of the right hand; those on the left hand - how damned shall be the people of the left hand; and foremost shall be the foremost. They will be nearest to Allah, in the gardens of bliss. Most of them will be from the former and a few from the later generations. They shall have the jeweled couches, reclining on them facing each other, and there shall wait on them the eternal youths with goblets, shining beakers and cups of pure wine, - which will neither pain their heads nor take away their senses. They shall have fruits of their own choice and flesh of fowls that they may desire, and dark-eyed hurs (damsels), as lovely as well guarded pearls as a reward for their good deeds that they had done. There they shall not hear any vain talk nor sinful words, but only the greetings of "Peace be upon you! Peace be upon you!"" (Al-Waqi'a: 56.1-26)

## 6) Individual's fate - good or bad:

Good or bad events are due to individual's fate; planned by the Allah to judge the action of the individual in particular circumstances.

a. Prosperity in this world is not a reward but a respite:

"We did send Rasools before you to other nations and afflicted them with suffering and adversities so that they might learn humility. Why did they not humble themselves when the sufferings overtook them? On the contrary, their hearts became hardened and Shaitan made their sinful acts seem fair to them. When they neglected the warning they had received, then, instead of punishment, We opened the gates of every kind of prosperity for them; but just as they were rejoicing in what they were given, We suddenly seized them; lo! They were plunged into despair! Thus We cut off the roots of the wrongdoers. All praises are due to Allah the Rabb of the worlds." (Al-An'am: 6.42-45)

b. Allah is the One Who delivers you from the calamities:

"Ask them: "Who delivers you from calamities in the darkness of the land and of the sea, when you call upon Him in open humility and silent terror: If You deliver us from this affliction, we shall become truly grateful." Say: "Allah delivers you from these and all other calamities, yet you commit shirk (worship false gods)!" Say: "He has the power to send calamities on you from above and from below or to split you into discordant factions to make you taste the violence of one another. See how We present Our revelations over and over again so that they may understand the reality. But your people are rejecting this (The Qur'an), although it is the very truth." Tell them: "I am not appointed as your caretaker. For every prophecy there is an appointed time, and soon you will come to know." " (Al-An'am: 6.63-67)

c. It is Allah Who gives daughters and sons as He pleases:

"To Allah belongs the kingdom of the heavens and the earth. He creates whatever He pleases. He gives daughters to whom He pleases and gives sons to whom He pleases. To some He gives both sons and daughters, and makes barren whom He will; surely He is All-knowledgeable, All-Powerful." (Ash-Shura: 42.49-50)

d. Whatever afflictions befall upon people are the result of their own misdeeds:

"Whatever affliction befalls you is the result of what your own hands have done even though for many of your misdeeds He grants forgiveness." (Ash-Shura: 42.30)

e. "He is the One Who has made you the inheritors of the earth and raised some of you in ranks over others so that He may test you in what He has given you. Surely your Rabb is swift in retribution; yet He is also very Forgiving, Merciful." (Al-An'am: 6.165)

f. "It is Allah Who has created you in a state of helplessness as a baby, then gave you strength to come out of helplessness in youth, then after strength again helplessness and grey hair in old age. He creates whatever He wills and it is He Who is the All-knowing, the Almighty." (Ar-Rum: 30.54)

g. "Allah has made some of you excel in sustenance over the others; those who are so favored, do not give away their sustenance to their slaves so as to make them their equals. How can you think that Allah will allow other deities to be His equals? Would they refuse to acknowledge the favors of Allah? It is Allah Who has made for you mates from your own species and He is the One Who gives you sons and grandsons through those wives, and provides for you good things to eat: will they then, after knowing all that, believe that falsehood and disbelieve Allah's favors? They worship those deities other than Allah, who neither provide them anything for sustenance from the heavens or the earth, nor have any power to do so?" (An-Nahl: 16.71-73)

●●●

# 4.
# The Fundamental Principles of Islam

The fundamental principles of Islam are five in number:

1. **Imaan -** The declaration of 'La ilaha illallah Muhammad-ur-rasoolullah', which means that there is no God but Allah and Muhammad (S.A.W.) is His prophet.
2. **Salaat -** The observance of obligatory prayers five times a day.
3. **Saum -** The observation of fast during the day time in the month of ramazaan.
4. **Zakaat -** Distribution of zakaat (Islamic alms-fee) by rich people among the deserving, amounting to 1/40th in one's possession for a complete year.
5. **Hajj -** The performance of Hajj (pilgrimage) to Mecca at least once in a life time, if circumstances permit.

## 1) Imaan (Faith in Allah):

a. Affirmation by heart in Kalemah. To believe that 'none is worthy of worship but Allah; Mohammad (S.A.W.) is the messenger of Allah'.

"In the name of Allah, the Compassionate, the Merciful. All praise is for Allah, the 'Rabb' of the Worlds. The Compassionate, the Merciful. Master of the Day of Judgement." (Al-Fathiha: 1.1-4)

b. "Allah has the most excellent names (over ninety-nine attributes); call on Him by them; and shun those people who use profanity in His names, such people shall be requited for their misdeeds." (Al-A'raf:7.180)

c. "Praise be to Allah, the One Who has begotten no son and Who has no partner in His Kingdom; nor He is helpless to need a protector, and glorify His greatness in the best possible way." O Prophet, say to them: "Whether you call Him Allah or call Him Rahman; it is all the same by whichever name you call Him because for Him are all the Finest names." (Al-Israa: 17.111, 110)

d. Fifteen exclusive attributes of Allah:

"Allah is He, besides Whom there is no god, the Knower of the unseen and the seen. He is the Compassionate, the Merciful. Allah is He, besides Whom there is no god, the King, the Holy, the Giver of peace, the Granter of security, the Guardian, the Almighty, the Irresistible, the Supreme: Glory be to Allah! He is far above the shirk they commit (by associating other gods with Him). He is Allah, the Creator, the Evolver, the Modeler. His are the most beautiful names. All that is in the heavens and the earth declares His glory, and He is the All-Mighty, the All-Wise." (Al-Hashr: 59.22-24)

e. "The fact is that to every Rasool whom We sent before you, We revealed the same Message: "there is no god but Me, so worship Me Alone." (Al-Anbiyaa: 21.25)

f. Live Islam, die as a Muslim, and be not divided among yourselves:

"O believers! Fear Allah as He should be feared and die not but as true Muslims. All together hold fast the rope of Allah (Faith of Islam) and be not divided among yourselves. Remember Allah's favors upon you when you were enemies; He united your hearts, so by His favor you became brethren; you were at the brink of the fiery pit and He saved you from it. Thus Allah makes His revelations clear to you, so that you may be rightly guided." (Al-i'Imran: 3.102-103)

g. "O believers! Obey Allah, obey the Rasool and those charged with authority among you. Should you have a dispute in anything, refer it to Allah and His Rasool, if you truly believe in Allah and the Last Day. This course of action will be better and more suitable." (An-Nisaa: 4.59)

h. Muhammad (P.B.U.H.) is the Prophet for the whole of mankind:

   "O Muhammad, say: "O mankind! I am the Rasool of Allah towards all of you from He to whom belongs the kingdom of the heavens and the earth. There is no deity but Him. He brings to life and causes to die. Therefore, believe in Allah and His Rasool, the unlettered Prophet (Muhammad) who believes in Allah and His Word. Follow him so that you may be rightly guided". " (Al-A'raf: 7.158)

## 2) Salaat (Namaaz):

a. Order for Wuzu (ablution) and Permission of Tayammum:

   "O believers! When you rise up for Salaah (prayer), wash your faces and your hands as far as the elbows, wipe your heads with wet hands and wash your feet to the ankles. If you had an emission of semen, then take a full bath. However, if you are sick or on a journey or you have used the toilet or you had intercourse with your women (your wife) and you do not find any water then resort to Tayammum - find clean soil and rub your faces and hands with it. Allah does not wish to burden you; He only wishes to purify you and to perfect His favor upon you, so that you may be thankful." (Al-Maida: 5.6)

b. Order to face towards Kaa'ba as Qiblah during Salaah (prayers):

"Everyone has a direction towards which he turns; therefore, emulate one another in good deeds. Wherever you are, Allah will bring all of you together; Allah has power over all things. From whatever place you come forth, turn your face during Salaah towards the Sacred Mosque; this is in fact a commandment from your Rabb. Allah is not unaware of what you do. Again, whatever place you come forth, turn your face during Salaah towards the Sacred Mosque; and wherever you are, face towards it, so that people will not have any argument against you, except those among them who are wrongdoers. Do not fear them; fear Me, so that I may perfect My favors to you and that you may be rightly guided." (Al-Baqara: 2.148-150)

c. Declare, 'My Salaah, my devotion, my life and my death are all for Allah':

"Also declare: "Surely my Salaah, my devotion, my life, and my death are all for Allah the Rabb of the Worlds." (Al-An'am: 6.162)

d. Five times daily Salaah (prayers) and extra prayer called Tahajjud for the Holy Prophet (S.A.W.) and Al-Quran is a healing and mercy for the believers:

i.. " "Establish Salah from the decline of the sun till the darkness of the night (Zuhr, Asr, Maghrib and Isha) and read at Fajr (dawn); for the reading at Fajr is witnessed (by the angels). During a part of the night, pray Tahajjud, an additional prayer for you (O Muhammad), very soon your Rabb may exalt you to 'Maqam-e-Mahmood' (a station of great glory)." " (Al-Israa: 17.78-79)

ii. "Therefore be patient with what they say. Glorify your Rabb with His praise before sunrise and before sunset, glorify Him during the hours of the night as well as at the ends of the day, so that you may find satisfaction." (Ta-ha: 20.130)

iii. "Therefore, glorify Allah in the evening and in the morning - all praise is due to Him in the heavens and the earth - so glorify Him in the late afternoon and when the day begins to decline." (Ar-Rum: 30.17-18)

iv. "Therefore, O Prophet, bear with them in patience whatever they say, and keep on glorifying your Rabb before sunrise and before sunset. And glorify Him during a part of the night and after the prostration (prayers)." (Qaf: 50.39-40)

v. "Stand in prayers at night, but not the whole night, half of it or a little less, or a little more; and recite the Qur'an with measured tone." (Al-Muzzammil: 73.2-4)

e. Guarding the Salaah (Prayers):

"Guard your Salaah (obligatory regular prayers) especially the middle Salaah and stand up with true devotion to Allah. If you are in danger, pray on foot or while riding; and when you are safe, remember Allah in the manner that He has taught you which you did not know before." (Al-Baqara: 2.238-239)

f. Commandment relating to the obligation of Friday Prayers:

"O believers! When the call for Salaah (prayer) is made on Friday (the day of congregational prayers), hasten to the remembrance of Allah and cease your business. That is better for you if you but knew. When you finish the Salaah, then disperse through the land and seek the bounty of Allah (go back to your normal business). Remember Allah frequently, so that you may prosper. Those who are still weak in Imaan (faith), when they see some bargain or some sport they rush to it and leave you standing. O Prophet, declare to them that what Allah has in store for them is far better than any sport and bargain, and Allah is the best provider." (Al-Jumu'a: 62.9-11)

g. Prohibition of drinking liquor and Tayammum - a substitute for wuzu (ablution):

"O believers! Do not offer your Salaah when you are drunk until you know what you are saying; nor after seminal emission, except when you are traveling, unless you wash your whole body. If you are sick, or on a journey, or one of you has used the toilet, or has had contact with women (sexual relation with wives) and can find no water, then make Tayammum: take some clean earth and rub your faces and hands with it. Allah is Lenient, Forgiving." (An-Nisaa: 4.43)

h. Salaat-al-Qasr, (Shortening of Salaat) during travel and in the state of war at its prescribed times:

"When you travel on the earth, there is no blame on you if you shorten your prayers, especially when you fear that the unbelievers may attack you, since the unbelievers are your open enemies. When you, O Muhammad, are with them, leading their Salaah (prayer in the state of war), let one party of them stand up to pray with you, armed with their weapons. After they finish their prostrations, let them withdraw to the rear and let the other party who have not yet prayed come forward to pray with you; and let them also be on their guard, armed with their weapons. The unbelievers wish to see you neglect your arms and your baggage, so that they could suddenly attack to overpower you all in one stroke. However, there is no blame on you if you lay aside your arms because of heavy rain or because you are sick, but you should still be on your guard. Allah has prepared a humiliating punishment for the unbelievers. When you finish your Salaah (prayers) remember Allah whether you are standing, sitting or reclining; then as soon as you are safe (out of danger) establish regular Salaah in full. Surely Salaah are made obligatory for the believers at their prescribed times. Do not show weakness in following up the enemy; if you are suffering hardships they too are suffering similar hardships; moreover, you have hope to receive reward from Allah while they have none. Allah is the Knowledgeable, Wise." (Al-Nisaa: 4.101-104)

i. "Therefore establish Salaah, pay Zakah and obey the Rasool, so that you may be shown mercy." (An-Nur: 24.56)

ii. "The one who will take admonition and purify himself shall be successful, who remembers the name of his Rabb and prays." (Al-A'la: 87.14-15)

iii. Salaat keeps one away from the shameful deeds:

   "Recite from this Book (Al-Qur'an) which has been revealed to you and establish Salaah (prayers). Surely Salaah keeps one away from shameful and evil deeds; and surely the remembrance of Allah (during your prayers and Allah's mention of your name in response to your prayers) is the greatest of all deeds, Allah knows what you do." (Al-Ankabut: 29.45)

iv. "The reasons which prevent their contributions from being accepted are: that they disbelieve in Allah and His Rasool, that they come to offer Salaah but reluctantly, and that they offer contributions but unwillingly." (At-Tauba: 9.54)

i. Allah's Light is found in the places of worship which are built for his remembrance by His devotees:

   "His Light is found in those houses which Allah has sanctioned to be built for the remembrance of His name; where His praise is sung, in the mornings and in the evenings again and again, by such people whom neither business nor business profit can divert from the remembrance of Allah, nor from establishing Salaah and nor from paying Zakah, for they fear the Day of Judgement when hearts will be overturned and eyes will be petrified." (An-Nur: 24.36-37)

j. Mushrikins are forbidden to be the caretakers of Masjids:

   i. It is not for the Mushrikin to maintain the mosques of Allah while they bear witness against themselves about their unbelief. It is they whose deeds are in vain and in the hellfire shall they live forever. The mosques of Allah should be maintained by those who believe in Allah and the Last Day, establish Salaah (prayers), and pay Zakah (poor-due) and fear none except Allah. It is they who are expected to follow the true guidance." (At-Tauba: 9.17-18)

   ii. Do not order or prevent people from coming to the Masjid (mosque):

      "Who is more unjust than he who prevents people from the Masjid (place of worship) of Allah, forbids the mention of His name therein, and strives to ruin them? It is not proper for such people to enter in them except with His fear. For them there is disgrace in this world and grievous punishment hereafter." (Al-Baqara: 2.114)

iii. "Enjoin Salaah on your people and be diligent in its observance. We demand nothing of you; instead We provide you sustenance. Blessed shall be the end of the Righteous." (Ta-ha: 20.132)

## 3) Saum (Roza / Fasting):

Observance of one month's compulsory fasting during day by adults.

a. Obligation of fasting:

"O believers! Fasting is prescribed for you as it was prescribed for those before you so that you may learn self-restraint. Fast the prescribed number of days; except if any of you is ill or on a journey, let him fast a similar number of days later. For those who cannot endure it for medical reasons, there is a ransom: the feeding of one poor person for each missed day. But if he feeds more of his own free will, it is better for him. However, if you truly understand the rationale of fasting, it is better for you to fast." (Al-Baqara: 2.183-184)

b. Revelation of the Quran and fasting in the month of Ramazaan:

"It is the month of Ramadhan in which the Qur'an was revealed, a guidance for mankind with clear teachings showing the right way and a criterion of truth and falsehood. Therefore, anyone of you who witnesses that month should fast therein, and whoever is ill or upon a journey shall fast a similar number of days later on. Allah intends your well-being and does not want to put you to hardship. He wants you to complete the prescribed period so that you should glorify His Greatness and render thanks to Him for giving you guidance." (Al-Baqara: 2.185)

c. Allah is very close to His devotees:

"When my servants question you about Me, tell them that I am very close to them. I answer the prayer of every suppliant when he calls Me; therefore, they should respond to Me and put their trust in Me, so that they may be rightly guided." (Al-Baqara: 2.186)

d. Nights of the Fasting month and Timings of fasting:

"It is made lawful for you to approach your wives during the night of the fast; they are an apparel for you and you for them. Allah knows that you were committing dishonesty to your souls. So He has relented towards you and pardoned you. Now, you may approach your wives and seek what Allah has written for you. Eat and drink until the white thread of dawn appears to you distinct from the black thread of night, then complete your fast till nightfall. Do not approach your wives during I'htikaf (retreat in the mosques in last ten days of Ramadhan). These are the limits set by Allah: do not ever violate them. Thus Allah makes His revelations clear to mankind so that they may guard themselves against evil." (Al-Baqara: 2.187)

e. "The night of Qadr is better than one thousand months." (Qadr: 97.3)

## 4) Zakaat:

The word Zakaat covers two meanings. The first relates to purification - that is, purification by means of Zakaat from sins and bad qualities such as greed. The second meaning relates to growth and increase - that is, the giving of Zakaat results in growth and increase in our wealth. Both meanings are referred to in the following verse of the Qur'an:

"Take Sadaqat (this commanded Sadaqat means - Zakat-ul-Mall) from their wealth, so that they may thereby be cleansed and purified, and pray for them; for your prayer will give them comfort. Allah hears all and knows all." (At-Tauba: 9.103)

In other words, it's said to be distribution of compulsory charity among the deserving poor by wealthy people amounting to 1/40th in once possession for a complete year. Assets that have potential of growth are subject to Zakaat which may be broadly classified as follows;

a. Gold, silver and money.

b. Stock-in-trade.

c. Livestock (goats, sheeps, cows and camels, etc).

d. Agricultural produce.

The agreed amount of Zakaat payable is two and a half percent of;

a. The value of gold and silver if equal to Nisaab (minimum wealth) in weight.

b. Trading stock or its value at the time of obligation of payment of Zakaat, if the stock is equal to Nisaab.

c. Cash on hand if equal to Nisaab.

1) Qur'anic verses referring to pay Zakaat:

   a. "Yet they were commanded nothing but to worship Allah, with their sincere devotion to Him, being True in their faith; to establish Salaah (prayers); and to pay Zakah (poor-due); and that is the infallible true Religion." (Al-Baiyina: 98.5)

   b. "Who will loan to Allah a beautiful loan which Allah will increase manifold? Allah alone can decrease and increase wealth, and to Him you all shall return." (Al-Baqara: 2.245)

   c. "O believers! Spend out of the sustenance which We have provided for you before the arrival of that

Day when there will be no bargaining, friendship or intercession. It is the unbelievers who are wrongdoers." (Al-Baqara: 2.254)

d. Rasools were commanded to pay Zakaat and also preach for it:

   i. "We made them (Ibrahim, his son Ishaq and grandson Ya'qoob) leaders who guided other people by Our command and We sent them revelations to do good deeds, establish Salaah and pay Zakah." (Al-Anbiyaa: 21.73)

   ii. "He (Ismaeel) commanded his people to establish Salaah and give Zakah, and was the one with whom his Rabb was well pleased." (Maryam: 19.55)

   iii. "His blessing is with me wherever I go. He has commanded me (Isa - Jesus) to establish Salaah and give Zakah as long as I shall live." (Maryam: 19.31)

e. Spend the best portion of your wealth:

   "O believers, spend in Allah's Way the best portion of the wealth you have lawfully earned and that which We have produced for you from the earth, and do not pick out for charity those worthless things that you yourselves would not accept but with closed eyes. Bear in mind that Allah is Self-Sufficient, Praiseworthy." (Al-Baqara: 2.267)

f. Zakaat purifies our wealth:

   "Do they not know that Allah accepts repentance from His servants and takes their Sadaqat (charity), and surely Allah is the One Who is the Accepter of Repentance, the Merciful?" (At-Tauba: 9.104)

g. Parable of spending in Zakaat:

"The parable of those who spend their wealth in the way of Allah is that of a grain that sprouts into seven ears, each bearing one hundred grains. Allah gives manifold increase to whom He wishes. Allah has boundless knowledge. Those who spend their wealth in the cause of Allah and do not follow their charity with reminders of their generosity or injure the feeling of the recipient, shall get their reward from their Rabb; they shall have nothing to fear or to regret. Kind words and forgiveness are better than charity followed by injury. Allah is Self-sufficient, Forbearing." (Al-Baqara: 2.261-263)

2) Who is eligible for Zakaat?

a) "They ask you what they should spend in charity. Say: "Whatever you spend with a good heart, give it to parents, relatives, orphans, the helpless, and travelers in need. Whatever good you do, Allah is aware of it." (Al-Baqara: 2.215)

b) "O believers, give what is due to your relatives, the needy and the traveler in need. That is best for those who seek the pleasure of Allah and it is they who will attain felicity." (Ar-Rum: 30.38)

c) "Whatever you spend in charity or whatever vow you make, surely Allah knows it. The wrongdoers shall have no helpers. To give charity in public is good, but to gives the poor in private is better and will remove from you some of your sins. Allah is aware of your actions. Charity is for those needy people who are engaged so much in the cause of Allah that they cannot move about in the land to earn their livelihood: the ignorant think that they are wealthy on account of their modest behavior. You can recognize them by their look because they do not make insistent demands on people. Whatever you spend on them, surely Allah knows it. Those who spend their wealth in charity by night and day, secretly and openly, they will have their reward from their Rabb. They shall have nothing to fear or to regret." (Al-Baqara: 2.270-271, 273-274)

d) "When they spend, are neither extravagant nor stingy, but keep the balance between those two extremes." (Al-Furqan: 25.67)

e) "In fact the Sadaqat (Zakaah) collection is for the poor, the helpless, those employed to administer the funds, those whose hearts need to be won over to the truth, ransoming the captives, helping the destitute, in the Way of Allah and for the wayfarer. That is a duty enjoined by Allah; and Allah is All-Knowledgeable, Wise." (At-Tauba: 9.60)

3) Give Zakaat of agriculture on the harvest day:

"It is He who has created all kinds of plants, trellised and untrellised, the palm trees, the field crops with produce of different kinds, the olives and pomegranates, similar in kind yet different in taste. Eat of their fruit in their season and give away their Zakaah on the harvest day. Do not be spendthrift, surely He does not love the spendthrifts." (Al-An'am: 6.141)

4) Penalty for not giving Zakaat:

a) "O believers! Indeed most of the (Jewish) rabbis and (Christian) priests misappropriate the wealth of people and hinder them from the way of Allah. To those who hoard gold and silver and do not spend it in the way of Allah, proclaim a painful punishment." (At-Tauba: 9.34)

b) Qarun; the rich man, who failed to give Zakaat was punished by Allah:

"Rather seek, by means of what Allah has given you, to attain the abode of the hereafter, while not neglecting your share in this world. Be good to others as Allah has been good to you, and do not seek mischief in the land, for Allah does not love the mischief-makers." One day he came out before his people in his worldly glitter. Those who sought the life of this world said: "Would that we had the like of Qarun's fortune! He is indeed a very lucky man." Then We caused the earth to swallow him, together with his dwelling, and he had no host to help him against Allah; nor was he able to defend himself." (Al-Qasas: 28.77, 79, 81)

## 5) Hajj (Pilgrimage to Mecca):

Hajj is a devotional act of pilgrimage performed from the 8th to 12th of the month 'zil-hijja' (12th month of Islamic calendar). All the pilgrims gather in Mecca. They perform the Tawaaf-e-Kaa'ba (seven rounds of Kaa'ba), perform special prayers at Muqam-e-Ibrahim (A.S.). Then they go to perform 'Saee' which is walking between two hills, Safa and Marwah, seven times. Thereafter they go to drink Zam-Zam (holy water). They then go to Mina (which is few kilometers away from the Kaa'ba) on the 8th of zil-hijja, and then on the 9th, they assemble in the field of Arafaat and pray there. Pilgrims pass the 9th zil-hijja's night at Muzdalfa (another place nearby); they collect pebbles and return back to Mina on 10th morning. They hurl (throw) the pebbles on 1st Shaitaan (1st pillar – the symbol of devil), thereafter they perform the Qur'baani (sacrificing goat or sheep or camel, etc) and celebrate Eid-uz-Zuha festival. Then again on 11th zil-hijja, the pilgrims hurl stones on the 2nd and 3rd Shaitaans (2nd & 3rd pillar). Then on 12th they go for the Tawaaf-e- Ziarat to Mecca. Thus all the five days are for prayers. Thereafter the pilgrims go to Madina, stay there for eight days and perform 40 (8 X 5) farz Salaats at Masjid-e-Nabvi and pay respects to Prophet Muhammad's (S.A.W.) grave. Some pilgrims go to Madina first and thereafter to Mecca to perform Hajj so as to accommodate the flow of lakhs of pilgrims visiting for Hajj.

Performance of Hajj once in a life-time is compulsory, if circumstances permit to the wealthy people; that is – if they are in a position both physically and materially to undertake the journey to Mecca and make sufficient provisions for their dependents in their absence.

## Importance of the Kaa'ba:

a. "Undoubtedly the first House for the worship of Allah ever built for mankind is the one at Bakka (Makkah), a blessed site and a guidance for all the worlds. In it are clear signs and the Station of Ibrahim (Abraham) where he used to worship. Whoever enters it is safe. Performance of Hajj (pilgrimage) to this House is a duty to Allah for all who can afford the journey to it; and the one who disobeys this commandment should know that Allah is Self-sufficient, beyond the need of anyone from the worlds." (Al-i'Imran: 3.96-97)

b. "Remember when We made the House (the Ka'bah) a center and sanctuary for mankind saying, "Take the station of Ibrahim as a place of prayer;" We entrusted Ibrahim and Isma`il to cleanse Our House for those who walk around it, who meditate in it, and who kneel and prostrate in prayers." (Al-Baqara: 2.125)

c. Prayer of Ibrahim(A.S.) for the city of Makkah:

   i. "Ibrahim said: "My Rabb make this (Makkah) a secure town and provide its people with plenty of food from fruits, those of them who believe in

Allah and the Last Day." He answered, "As for those who do not, I shall also provide for them in this life, though in the Hereafter I shall drag them to the torture of Hellfire and it is an evil destination indeed!" Ibrahim (Abraham) and Isma`il (Ishmael) raised the foundations of the House and dedicated it by saying: "Accept this from us, O Rabb, You are the one who hears all and knows all. O Rabb, make us both Muslims (submissive to You); and make our descendants a nation that will be Muslims (submissive to You). Teach us our rites of worship and forbear our shortcomings; surely, You are the Acceptor of repentance, the Merciful." (Al-Baqara: 2.126-128)

ii. "Our Rabb! Give us the good life, both in this world and in the Hereafter and save us from the torment of the fire." (Al-Baqara: 2.201)

d. Hajj and Umrah (pilgrimage to Makkah):

"Complete the Hajj (obligatory pilgrimage to Makkah) and the Umrah (optional visit to Makkah) for the sake of Allah. If you are prevented from proceeding then send such offering for sacrifice as you can afford and do not shave your head until the offerings have reached their destination. But if any of you is ill or has an ailment in his scalp which necessitates shaving, he must pay ransom either by fasting or feeding the poor or offering a sacrifice. If in peacetime anyone wants to take the advantage of performing Umrah and Hajj together, he should make an offering which he can afford; but if he lacks the means, let him fast three days during the Hajj and seven days on his return making ten days in all. This order is for the one whose household is not in the precincts of the Sacred Mosque. Fear Allah and know that Allah is strict in retribution. Hajj is in the well known months. He who undertakes to perform it must abstain from husband-wife relationship, obscene language, and wrangling during Hajj. Whatever good you do, Allah knows it. Take necessary provisions with you for the journey, and piety is the best provision of all. Fear Me, O people endowed with understanding. There is no blame on you if you seek the bounty of your Rabb during this journey. When you return from Arafaat (stop at Muzdalifah and) praise Allah near Mash'ar-il-Haram. Praise Him as He has guided you, for before this you were from the people who had lost the Right Way. Then return from where the others return and ask Allah's forgiveness; surely Allah is Forgiving, Merciful. When you have fulfilled your sacred duties, praise Allah as you used to praise your forefathers or with deeper reverence. There are some who say: "Our Rabb! Give us abundance in this world." Such people will not have any share in the hereafter. Celebrate the praises of Allah during these appointed days. If anyone hastens to leave Mina after two days or stays there a day longer there is no blame on him provided he spends these days in piety. Fear Allah and remember that you will surely be gathered before Him." (Al-Baqara: 2.196-203)

e. "Behold! Safa and Marwah (two hills in the Sacred Mosque) are among the symbols of Allah. So anyone who performs Hajj or Umrah (pilgrimage) to the House, there is no blame if one goes around both of them; and anyone who does good voluntarily should know that surely Allah knows the grateful." (Al-Baqara: 2.158)

f. Sacred elements of Hajj:

"Allah has made the Ka'bah of the Sacred House an eternal value for mankind, and so are the Sacred Months, the animal offerings, and the animals which are collared as a mark of dedication; so you must know that Allah has knowledge of what is in the heavens and in the earth and that Allah is well aware of everything." (Al-Maida: 5.97)

g, Fulfill your obligations, promises and agreements:

"O believers! Fulfill your contract obligations. All four-legged animals from livestock are lawful to you other than those which are hereby announced. However do not violate the prohibition of hunting while you are in Ihram (Hajj dress). Indeed Allah orders whatever He pleases. O believers! Do not violate the sanctity of the Symbols of Allah: the Sacred Month , the animals brought for sacrifice, the garlands that mark such animals, and those people visiting the Sacred House (Ka'bah) to seek the grace and good pleasure of their Rabb. When you put off your Ihram (pilgrimage is over) then you are allowed to hunt. Let not the hatred of some people - who once hindered you from the Sacred Mosque - incite you to commit transgression. Cooperate with one another in righteousness and piety, and do not cooperate in sin and transgression. Have fear of Allah. Allah is stern in punishment." (Al-Maida: 5.1-2)

h. Prohibition of hunting during Hajj Ihram (wearing pilgrim garb) and Kaffarah (penalty) for hunting during Hajj Ihram:

"O believers! Do not kill game while you are in Ihram (pilgrim garb). If anyone kills game intentionally, he will have to pay a penalty through an offering brought to the Ka'bah of a domestic animal equivalent to the one which was killed as determined by two just men among you; or as an expiation, either feed a few indigent or fast their equivalent days, so that he may taste the evil consequences of what he did. Allah has forgiven what happened in the past; but if anyone repeats it now, Allah will inflict retribution on him. Allah is Mighty, Capable of Retribution. Game of the sea and its use as food is lawful for you and the seafarers, but the game of the land is forbidden as long as you are in Ihram (pilgrim garb). Have fear of Allah to whom you shall all be assembled." (Al-Maida: 5.95-96)

. It is not the meat or the blood of the sacrificed animals that reaches Allah:

"For every nation We prescribed a way of sacrifice so that they may pronounce the name of Allah over the cattle which He has given them for food, but the object is one and the same: to remember that your God is one God; so submit yourselves to Him as a Muslim, and O Prophet, give good news to the humble, whose hearts tremble at the mention of Allah; who endure adversity with patience, who establish Salaah and spend in charity out of what we have given them. We have included the sacrificial camels among the Symbols of Allah, for there is much good for you in them. Therefore, pronounce the name of Allah over them while standing, and when they fall down on their sides after slaughter, when their movement completely stops, then eat of their meat, feed the contented (poor who do not ask) and the beggars (poor who ask). Thus We have subjected these animals to you so that you may be grateful. It is neither their meat nor their blood that reaches Allah; it is your piety that reaches Him. Thus, He has subjected these animals to you so that you may glorify Allah for giving you guidance, and O Prophet, give good news to those who do good to others." (Al-Hajj: 22.34-37)

j. The number of months in the book of Allah is 12, of which 4 are sacred:

"The number of months ordained by Allah is twelve in the Book of Allah since the day He created the heavens and the earth. Of these, four are sacred; that is the established principle of Deen. Therefore, do not wrong yourselves by violating them. But you may fight against the Mushrikin in all these months if they fight against you in all of them. Know that Allah is with the righteous." (At-Tauba: 9.36)

k. Prohibition of Mushrikin from entering Masjid-al-Haram:

   "O believers! Know that Mushrikin are unclean; therefore, do not let them come near the Masjid-al-Haram after this year's pilgrimage. If you fear poverty, soon Allah - if He so wills - enrich you out of His bounty. Allah is All-Knowledgeable, All-Wise." (At-Tauba-9.28)

l. Order to fight for a just cause:

   "Fight in the cause of Allah with those who fight against you, but do not exceed the limits. Allah does not like transgressors. Kill them wherever they confront you in combat and drive them out of the places from which they have driven you. Though killing is bad, creating mischief is worse than killing. Do not fight them within the precincts of the Sacred Mosque unless they attack you there; but if they attack you put them to the sword; that is the punishment for such unbelievers." (Al-Baqara: 2.190-191)

# 5. The Rights and Duties

There are three types of rights:

## (a) Rights of Allah (Haquooqul Allah):

1) Believe in Imaan and obey the orders contained in Qur'an in the way demonstrated by the prophet Hazrat Muhammad (S.A.W.).

   i. Believers are required to believe wholeheartedly:

   "O believers! Believe in Allah, His Rasool, the Book which He has revealed to His Rasool, and every Book which He previously revealed. He who denies Allah, His angels, His Books, His Rasools and the Last Day has gone far astray." (An-Nisaa: 4.136)

   ii. Order to obey and follow the Prophet (S.A.W.):

   "Tell the people O Muhammad: "If you sincerely love Allah, then follow me; Allah will also love you and forgive you your sins. Allah is Forgiving, Merciful." Also tell them, "Obey Allah and His Rasool." Inspite of this, if they turn back then warn them, that Allah does not love the disobedient. Indeed Allah exalted Adam, Nuh (Noah), the family of Ibrahim (Abraham) and the family of Imran above all the worlds. They were the offsprings of one another. Allah hears all and knows all." (Al-Imran: 3:31-34)

iii. "It is not fitting for a believing man or a believing woman to have an option in their affairs when a matter has been decided by Allah and His Rasool; and whoever disobeys Allah and His Rasool has indeed strayed into a clearly wrong path." (Al-Ahzab: 33.36)

2) Consult before making a decision, once the decision is made then be firm:

"O Muhammad, it is a great Mercy of Allah that you are very gentle with them; had you been rough or hard-hearted, they would have deserted you. Therefore pardon them and ask Allah's forgiveness for them. Consult them in the conduct of affairs; and when you make a decision to do something, then put your trust in Allah (hold fast to your decision). Allah loves those who put their trust in Him." (Al-i'Imran: 3.159)

3) Do not utter evil words and do not draw a line between Allah and His Rasools in obedience:

"Allah does not like evil words to be uttered except by someone who is truly wronged. Allah hears all and knows all. If you do good deeds openly or in private or forgive an evil, then surely Allah is Pardoning, Powerful. Those who deny Allah and his Rasool and those who intend to draw a line between Allah and His Rasools saying: "We believe in some, and reject the rest" - desiring to take a middle way between belief and unbelief - these are the real unbelievers and We have prepared for such unbelievers a humiliating punishment. As for those who believe in Allah and His Rasools and do not discriminate between any of them, We shall soon give them their due rewards. Allah is Forgiving, Merciful." (An-Nisaa: 4.148-152)

**(b) Rights of self (Haquooqun Nafs):**

1) Acquiring knowledge is the birth-right of all mankind as Allah gave wisdom to Adam (A.S.) also and made humans the superior-most status amongst all His creatures:

   "when your Rabb said to the angels: I am going to place a vicegerent on earth." (Al-Baqara: 2.30)

   "and taught him how to convey his feelings and thoughts." (Ar-Rahman: 55.4)

2) Command of Allah to wear decent and proper dress, and to eat good and healthy food:

   a. "O Children of Adam! We have sent down to you clothing to cover your nakedness and as an adornment, however, the best clothing is the clothing of piety. This is one of Allah's revelations so that the people may learn a lesson." (Al-A'raf: 7.26)

   b. "O Children of Adam! Put on your adornment (decent proper dress) when you attend your Masjid at the time of every prayer. Eat and drink, but do not be extravagant; surely He does not love the extravagant." (Al-A'raf: 7.31)

   c. "O Muhammad, ask them: "Who has forbidden you to wear decent clothes or to eat the good food which Allah has provided for His devotees?" Say: "All these things are for the enjoyment of the believers in the life of this world though shared by others; but these shall be exclusively theirs on the Day of Resurrection. Thus do We make Our revelations clear for those who understand." " (Al-A'raf: 7.32)

3) Respond to greetings with even better greetings:

   "When anyone greets you in a courteous manner, let your greetings be better than his - or at least return the same. Allah keeps account of everything." (An-Nisaa: 4.86)

4) Command not to compromise in the matters of religion:

"Say: O unbelievers! I worship not that you worship, nor will you worship that which I worship. I shall never worship those gods whom you worship, nor it appears will you ever worship Allah, whom I worship. To you be your religion, and to me mine." (Al-Kafirun: 109.1-6)

5) Restrictions on number of wives:

"If you fear that you shall not be able to treat the orphans with fairness, then you should not marry the women with orphan children; marry other women of your choice: two, three or four. But if you fear that you will not be able to maintain justice between your wives, then marry only one or any slave girl you may own. That will be more suitable, so that you may not deviate from the right way." (An-Nisaa: 4.3)

6) Obligation of 'Nihlah' (Mehr):

'Nihlah' signifies the giving of something willingly, of one's own accord, without expecting a return for it, by the groom to his bride. Prophet Muhammad (S.A.W.) clarified that 'even an iron ring' may be enough if the bride is willing to accept it or short of that. It is to be noted that the amount of Nihlah has not been circumscribed by the law; it depends entirely on the agreement of the two parties, and may consist of anything, even a mere token. Qur'anic verses referring to imparting the bride is given below.

a. "And give the women (on marriage) their dower as a free gift; but if they of their own good pleasure remit any part of it to you take it and enjoy it with right good cheer." (An-Nisaa: 4.4-A.Yusuf Ali's translation)

b. Do not take 'mehr' and essential utility items back from women:

   "If you wish to marry another wife in place of the one you already have, do not take back anything of what you have given her even if it be a heap of gold. Would you take it back through slander and open sin (accusing her unjustly)? And how could you take it back when you have enjoyed conjugal happiness and she had taken from you a firm pledge of marriage?." (An-Nisaa: 4.20 -21)

7) Commandment of Hijaab (dress code) for women:

   a. "O Prophet! Enjoin your wives, daughters and the believing women that they should draw their outer garments over their persons. That is more proper, so that they may be recognized and not bothered." (Al-Ahzab: 33.59)

   b. "There is no blame on the ladies if they appear before their fathers, their sons, their brothers, their brothers' sons, their sisters' sons, their familiar women and those whom their right hands possess (slaves). O Ladies! Have fear of Allah: for Allah is a witness to all things." (Al-Ahzab: 33.55)

8) Women that are prohibited for marriage – 'Mahram' relations:

   "Forbidden to you for marriage are: your mothers, your daughters, your sisters, your paternal aunts, your maternal aunts, daughters of your brothers, daughters of your sisters, your foster-mothers, your foster-sisters, the mothers of your wives, your stepdaughters under your guardianship from those wives with whom you have consummated your marriage, but there is no blame on you in marrying your step daughters if you have not consummated your marriage with their mothers, whom you have divorced, and the wives of your own real sons; and you are also forbidden to take in marriage two sisters at one and the same time except what happened prior to this commandment; surely Allah is Forgiving, Merciful." (An-Nisaa: 4.23)

9) Establishment of justice for women:

   a. "They ask your decision concerning the women. Tell them: Allah makes His decision concerning them and along with it reminds you about those commandments, recited to you in the Book (The Qur'an), relating to orphan girls to whom you do not give their lawful rights and to whom you do not wish to marry. He also reminds you regarding the helpless children, and to stand firm for justice to orphans. Whatever good you do, Allah surely knows it. If a women fears cruelty or desertion from her husband, there is no blame if both of them agree to reconcile by means of a compromise, after all compromise is better. Human souls are prone to narrow-mindedness, but if you show generosity and fear Allah in your dealings, surely Allah is well aware of your actions. It is not possible for you to do justice between your wives even if you wish to do so; therefore, in order to comply with Divine Law, do not lean towards one wife to the extent that you leave the other hanging in air. If you work out a friendly understanding and fear Allah, Allah is Forgiving, Merciful. If the spouses do separate, Allah will make each one independent of the other out of His own limitless resources, Allah is Ample-giving, Wise." (An-Nisaa: 4.127-130)

b. Women should not be mistreated:

"O believers! It is not lawful for you to consider women as a part of your inheritance and retain them against their will in order that you may force them to give up a part of the dowry (mehr) you have given them, unless they are guilty of proven fornication. Treat them with kindness even if you dislike them; it is quite possible that you dislike something in which Allah has placed much good." (An-Nisaa: 4.19)

10) Advise of Luqman about moral behavior and interaction:

"Luqman further said: "O my son! Allah will bring all things to light, be they as small as a grain of a mustard seed, be they hidden inside a rock or high above in the heavens or deep down in the earth. Allah is well aware of all things to their finest details. O my son! Establish Salaah, enjoin good and forbid the evil. Endure with patience whatever befalls you, surely this shows your determination in conducting the affairs. Do not speak to the people with your face turned away, nor walk proudly on earth; for Allah does not love any self-conceited boaster. Be moderate in your pace and lower your voice; for the harshest of voices is the braying of a donkey." " (Luqman: 31.16-19)

## (c) Rights of people (Haquooqul Ibaad):

Every individual has to attend to the rights of parents, relatives, neighbours, friends and all other creatures. They are also supposed to pass on the same to fellow Muslims in particular and others in general.

1) "Serve Allah and do not commit shirk (associate any partner) with Him, and be good to your parents, kinfolk, orphans, the helpless, near and far neighbors who keep company with you, the travelers in need, and the slaves you own. Allah does not love those who are arrogant and boastful." (An-Nisaa: 4.36)

2) Your Rabb has decreed to you that: You shall worship none but Him, and you shall be kind to your parents; if one or both of them live to their old age in your lifetime, you shall not say to them any word of contempt nor repel them and you shall address them in kind words. You shall lower to them your wings of humility and pray: "O Rabb! Bestow on them Your blessings just as they cherished me when I was a little child." " (Al-Israa: 17.23-24)

3) Those who treat their parents with kindness shall be rewarded and those who rebuke their parents shall be punished:

   "We have enjoined man concerning his parents - his mother carries him in her womb while suffering weakness upon weakness and then weans him for two years - That's why We commanded him: "Give thanks to Me and to your parents, and keep in mind that, to Me is your final goal.. If they argue with you to commit shirk, of which you have no knowledge, then do not obey them; however you should still treat them kindly in this world, but follow the way of that individual who has turned to Me. After all, to Me is your return; then I will inform you about the reality of all that you have done". " (Luqman: 31.14-15)

4) Stand firm for justice:

   a) "We said: "O Dawood! We have made you a vicegerent on the earth, so rule among the people with justice and do not follow your own desires lest they mislead you from the Way of Allah. As for those who go astray from the Way of Allah, they shall surely have a severe punishment because of forgetting the Day of Reckoning." (Sad: 38.26)

b) "O believers! Stand firm for justice and bear true witness for the sake of Allah, even though it be against yourselves, your parents or your relatives. It does not matter whether the party is rich or poor - Allah is well-wisher of both. So let not your selfish desires swerve you from justice. If you distort your testimony or decline to give it, then you should remember that Allah is fully aware of your actions." (An-Nisaa: 4.135)

5) Muslims are the best nation ever evolved to enjoin good and forbid evil and some righteous people of the Book:

"You are the best nation which has ever been raised for the guidance of mankind. You enjoin good, forbid evil, and believe in Allah. Had the People of the Book (Jews and Christians) believed, it would surely have been better for them; among them some are believers but most of them are transgressors. Anyhow, they can do no harm to you except a trifling annoyance; if they do fight against you, they will turn their backs and run, getting no help from anywhere. Disgrace will be branded on them wherever they are found except when they get refuge under the favor of Allah or the patronage of other people; they have incurred the wrath of Allah and have been branded with misery because they disbelieved Allah's revelations and slew His prophets unjustly and because they disobeyed and transgressed the limits. Yet they are not all alike: there are some among the People of the Book who are upright, who recite the revelations of Allah all night long and then prostrate before Him; they believe in Allah and the Last Day they enjoin good and forbid evil and rush in emulating each other in good deeds. These are the righteous people. Whatever good they do, its reward will not be denied to them; Allah knows the righteous." (Al-i'Imran: 3.110-115)

6) Command of Allah to wear decent proper dress and eat good food:

"O believers! Eat the clean things which We have provided you and give thanks to Allah, if you worship only Him." (Al-Baqara: 2.172)

●●●

# 6.
# Social Customs

Islam believes that the root of all is one, i.e., Adam (A.S.).

Allah-the Almighty commands establishment of peace, justice, human brotherhood, dignity, amity, equality, love for all and hatred for none. Hence all are our brothers and sisters and deserve supportive and sympathetic treatment.

1) Behavior with parents, relatives, and the community at large:

   a. "Your Rabb has decreed to you that: You shall worship none but Him, and you shall be kind to your parents; if one or both of them live to their old age in your lifetime, you shall not say to them any word of contempt nor repel them and you shall address them in kind words. You shall lower to them your wings of humility and pray: "O Rabb! Bestow on them Your blessings just as they cherished me when I was a little child." Your Rabb knows best what is in your hearts. If you do good deeds, certainly He is most forgiving to those who turn to Him in repentance. You shall give to your relatives their due and to the needy and to the wayfarers. You shall not be a spendthrift - as spendthrifts are the brethren of Shaitan and Shaitan is ever ungrateful to His Rabb. You shall speak courteously to needy persons if you are waiting for your Rabb's bounty and you lack the means to assist them. You shall neither tie your hands to your neck (be miserly) nor stretch them forth to their utmost reach (be prodigal), lest you sit back, blameworthy, destituteYou shall not kill your children for fear of want, for it is We Who provide sustenance for them as well as for you; surely killing them is a great blunder. You shall not commit adultery; surely it is a shameful deed and an evil way (opening the door to other evils). You shall not kill anyone whom Allah has forbidden, except for a just cause under the law. If anyone is killed unjustly, We have granted the right of retribution to his heir, but let him not carry his vengeance too far in killing the culprit through taking the law in his own hands, as he is supported by the law. You shall not go near the property of an orphan, except with the good intention of improving it, until he attains his maturity. You shall fulfill your pledges; surely you shall be held accountable for your pledges. You shall give full measure, when you measure, and weigh with even scale; this is the best way and will prove to be the best in the end. You shall not follow anyone blindly in those matters of which you have no knowledge, surely the use of your ears and the eyes and the heart - all of these, shall be questioned on the Day of Judgement. You shall not walk arrogantly on the earth, for you can neither rend the earth asunder nor attain the height of the mountains. All these and their evil aspects are hateful in the sight of your Rabb. This is but a part of the wisdom which your Rabb has revealed to you. Do not associate other deities as object of worship, lest you should be cast into hell, blameworthy rejected.

What! Has your Rabb preferred to give you sons and adopted angels as daughters for Himself? Certainly you are uttering a monstrous statement." (Al-Israa: 17.23-40)

b. Allah commands to do justice, do well to others, and give to near relatives; and He forbids indecency, wickedness, and rebellion:

"Allah commands doing justice, doing good to others, and giving to near relatives, and He forbids indecency, wickedness, and rebellion: He admonishes you so that you may take heed." (An-Nahl: 16.90)

c. "O believers! Stand firm for justice and bear true witness for the sake of Allah, even though it be against yourselves, your parents or your relatives. It does not matter whether the party is rich or poor - Allah is well- wisher of both. So let not your selfish desires swerve you from justice. If you distort your testimony or decline to give it, then you should remember that Allah is fully aware of your actions." (An-Nisaa: 4.135)

d. "Say: "My Rabb has forbidden all indecencies whether open or secret, sin and rebellion against justice, committing shirk with Allah for which He has granted no sanction, and saying things about Allah of which you have no knowledge."" (Al-A'raf: 7.33)

e. "Therefore, do not treat the orphan with harshness and do not chide away the beggar." (Adh-Dhuha: 93.9-10)

f. Avoid heinous sins and do not be jealous:

"If you avoid the heinous sins which you have been forbidden, We will do away with your small sins and cause you to enter a place of great honor (paradise).

Do not envy that Allah has given some of you more than the others. Men will be rewarded according to their deeds and women will be rewarded according to theirs. Ask Allah for His grace. Surely Allah has perfect knowledge of everything." (An-Nisaa: 4.31-32)

g. "Fulfill the covenant of Allah when you have pledged to do so, and do not break your oaths after you have sworn them; for swearing in His name you have made Allah your surety; surely Allah has knowledge of all your actions." (An-Nahl: 16.91)

h. "O believers! Do not take oaths to deceive each other, lest your foot slip after being firmly fixed upon guidance; and taste the evil consequences for debarring others from the Way of Allah and incur a mighty punishment." (An-Nahl: 16.94)

2) Etiquettes for:

   a. Consulting the Rasool (S.A.W.) in private:

      "O believers! When you want to consult the Rasool in private, offer something in charity before your consultation, that is best and purest for you. But if you lack the means, know that Allah is Oft-Forgiving, Most Merciful." (Al-Mujadila: 58.12)

   b. Entering the houses other than your own:

      "O believers! Do not enter houses other than your own until you have sought permission and said greetings of peace to the occupants; this is better for you, so that you may be mindful. If you do not find the person you wanted to see, then do not enter until permission is given to you; and if you are asked to go back, then go back; this is more fitting for you; and Allah is cognizant of what you do." (An-Nur: 24.27-28)

c. Moral behaviour:

"O believers! Let no men laugh at other men who may perhaps be better than themselves; and let no woman laugh at another woman, who may perhaps be better than herself. Do not defame through sarcastic remarks about one another, nor call one another by offensive nicknames. It is an evil thing to be called by a bad name after being a believer, and those who do not repent are the ones who are the wrongdoers. O believers! Avoid immoderate suspicion, for in some cases suspicion is a sin. Do not spy on one another, nor backbite one another (to say something about another behind one's back that if one hears it, dislikes it). Would any of you like to eat the flesh of his dead brother? Surely you would abhor it. Fear Allah; for Allah is the Accepter of repentance, Merciful." (Al-Hujurat: 49.11-12)

d. In gatherings of males and females:

"Say to the believing men that they should lower their gaze and guard their modesty: that will make for greater purity for them: and Allah is well acquainted with all that they do. And say to the believing women that they should lower their gaze and guard their modesty; that they should not display their beauty and ornaments except what (must ordinarily) appear thereof; that they should draw their veils over their bosoms and not display their beauty except to their husbands their fathers their husbands' fathers their sons their husbands' sons their brothers or their brothers' sons or their sisters' sons or their women or the slaves whom their right hands possess or male servants free of physical needs or small children who have no sense of the shame of sex; and that they should not strike their feet in order to draw attention to their hidden ornaments. And O ye Believers! turn ye all together towards Allah that ye may attain Bliss." (An-Nur: 24.30-31–A Yusuf's Qur'an translation)

3) Duties of righteous person;

   a. "Have We not given him two eyes to observe? One tongue and two lips to control it? Then shown him the two high ways (good leading towards paradise and evil leading towards hell)? Yet he does not attempt to tackle the Aqabah (steep path)! And what will explain to you what the Aqabah is? It is the freeing of a neck (slave) from bondage; or the giving of food in a day of famine to an orphan relative, or to a needy in distress; besides this, he should be of those who believe, enjoin fortitude, encourage kindness and compassion. Such are the people of the right hand (going towards paradise)." (Al-Balad: 90.8 -18)

   b. "You shall not falsely declare with your tongues: "This is lawful, and that is forbidden," in order to ascribe false things to Allah, for those who forge lies against Allah will never prosper. Brief is their enjoyment of this life, and they shall have a painful punishment." (An-Nahl: 16.116-117)

4) Men are given authority over women and corrective measures for disobedient women and arbitration in family disputes:

   "Men are overseers over women because Allah has given the one more strength than other, and because men are required to spend their wealth for the maintenance of women. Honorable women are, therefore, devoutly obedient and guard in the husband's absence what Allah require them to guard their husband's property and their own honor. As to those women from whom you fear disobedience, first admonish them, then refuse to share your bed with them, and then, if necessary, beat them. Then if they obey you, take no further actions against them and do not make excuses to punish them. Allah is Supremely Great and is aware of your actions." (An-Nisaa: 4.34)

5) Investigate properly before jumping to conclusion:

"O believers! When you struggle in the way of Allah, investigate carefully, and do not say to anyone who offers you a salutation: "You are not a believer" in order to seek worldly gain by this. Allah has abundant spoils for you. Remember that you yourselves were in the same condition before, Allah has conferred His favors on you. Therefore, make a thorough investigation before considering someone an unbeliever. Allah is well aware of all your actions." (An-Nisaa: 4.94)

6) Stand for true witness:

"Remember Allah's favor to you and the covenant which He ratified with you when you said: "We hear and we obey." Have fear of Allah; surely Allah knows the secrets of your hearts." (Al-Maida: 5.7)

7) All good and clean things are made lawful:

   a. "They ask you what food is lawful for them, say: All good clean things are lawful for you, as well as what you have taught your hunting birds and beasts to catch, trained by you with the knowledge given to you by Allah. Eat what they catch and hold for you, however, pronounce the name of Allah over it. Have fear of Allah. Allah is swift in settling the accounts." (Al-Maida: 5.4)

b. Prohibited (Haraam) food:

   i. "He has forbidden you to eat dead meat, blood, the flesh of swine, and that on which any name other than Allah has been invoked; but if someone is compelled by absolute necessity, intending neither to sin nor to transgress, he shall incur no sin. Surely Allah is Forgiving, Merciful." (Al-Baqara: 2.173)

   ii. "You are forbidden to eat the meat of any animal that dies by itself (dead body), blood, the flesh of swine (pork) and that on which any name other than Allah has been invoked; also that which is strangled to death, killed by a violent blow, killed by a headlong fall and of those beaten or gored to death; and that which has been partly eaten by a wild animal unless you are able to slaughter it before its death; also that which is sacrificed on altars or is divided by raffling of arrows. All these are sinful acts." (Al-Maida: 5.3)

8) Prohibition of intoxicants (liquor and drugs):

   a. "O believers! Intoxicants and gambling (games of chance), dedication to stones (paying tribute to idols) and division by arrows (lottery) are the filthy works of Shaitan. Get away from them, so that you may prosper. Shaitan desires to stir up enmity and hatred between you with intoxicants and gambling and to prevent you from the remembrance of Allah and from Salaah (prayers). Will you not abstain?" (Al-Maida: 5.90-91)

   b. Drinking and gambling is prohibited :

   "They ask you about drinking and gambling. Tell them: "There is great sin in both, although they may have some benefit for men; but the sin is greater than the benefit." They ask you what they should spend; tell them: "Whatever you can." Thus Allah makes His revelations clear to you, so that you may reflect upon." (Al-Baqara: 2.219)

9) Duties and obligations of the Islamic State towards Muslims living in a non-Muslim country:

"Those who believed (embraced Islam), migrated and made Jihad (exerted their utmost struggle) with their wealth and their persons in the cause of Allah; as well as those who gave them asylum and help, are indeed the protecting friends of one another. As to those who believed (embraced Islam) but did not emigrate (to Dar-ul-Islam, the Islamic State), you are under no obligation to protect them until they emigrate; yet it is your obligation to help them in the matters of faith if they ask for your help, except against a people with whom you have a treaty. Allah is observant of all your actions." (Al-Anfal: 8.72)

10) Defend themselves when oppressed :

"and when they are oppressed, help and defend themselves. The recompense for an injury is an injury proportionate to it; but if a person forgives and makes reconciliation he shall be rewarded by Allah; He does not like the wrongdoers. Those who avenge themselves when wronged cannot be blamed. The blameworthy are those who oppress their fellow men and conduct themselves with wickedness and injustice in the land. It is they who will have painful punishment. Those who endure with fortitude and forgive others, surely exhibit great courage in conducting their affairs." (Ash-Shura: 42.39-43)

# 7.
# Financial Matters

Islam has streamlined the principles for the professionals engaged in households, business communities, cultivators, factories, science and technology as stated in the Qur'anic verses below:

1) Islamic society is, thus based upon righteousness and mutual help:

   "Cooperate with one another in righteousness and piety, and do not cooperate in sin and transgression" (Al-Maida: 5.2)

2) Islamic society has enunciated many rules like payment by installment allowed to the debtor, if he is in strained circumstances based on the Qur'anic command:

   "If the debtor is in a difficulty, grant him time till it is easy for him to repay; but if you waive the sum by way of charity it will be better for you, if you understand it." (Al-Baqara: 2.280)

3) Prohibition of usury (includes interest also):

   a. "Those who devour usury will not stand except as stands one whom the Evil One by his touch hath driven to madness. That is because they say: "Those who live on usury will not rise up before Allah except like those who are driven to madness by the touch of Shaitan. That is because they claim: "Trading is no different than usury, but Allah has made trading lawful and usury unlawful. He who has received the admonition from his Rabb and has mended his way may keep his previous gains; Allah will be his judge. Those who turn back (repeat this crime), they shall be the inmates of hellfire wherein they will live for ever. Allah has laid His curse on usury and blessed charity to prosper. Allah does not love any ungrateful sinner." (Al-Baqara: 2.275-276)

b. "O You who believe! Fear Allah and waive what is still due to you from usury if you are indeed believers." (Al-Baqara: 2.278)

c. "That usury which you give to increase the wealth of people, does not increase with Allah: but the Zakah that you give to seek the pleasure of Allah, shall be repaid to you many times over." (Ar-Rum: 30.39)

4) If writing is not possible, take a security deposit:

"If you are on a journey and cannot find a scribe to write down the transaction, then transact your business by taking possession of a pledge. If one of you entrust another with a pledge, let the trustee deliver the pledged property to its owner, and let him fear Allah, his Rabb. Do not conceal testimony, and whoever conceals it, his heart is surely sinful. Allah is aware of all your actions." (Al-Baqara: 2.283)

5) "He has raised the heaven on high and created the balance: don't ever tamper with this balance. Therefore, you also establish weight with justice and do not give less measure." (Ar-Rahman: 55.7-9)

6) Bribe is a sin:

"Do not misappropriate one another's property unjustly, nor bribe the judges, in order to misappropriate a part of other people's property, sinfully and knowingly." (Al-Baqara: 2.188)

7) "People whom neither business nor business profit can divert from the remembrance of Allah, nor from establishing Salaah and nor from paying Zakaah, for they fear the Day of Judgement when hearts will be overturned and eyes will be petrified." (An-Nur: 24.37)

8) "When you finish the Salaah (jumu'a), then disperse through the land and seek the bounty of Allah (go back to your normal business). Remember Allah frequently, so that you may prosper." (Al-Jumu'a: 62.10)

## Concepts of Banking in Islam:

A developed system of banking can be had, under Islamic law, in consonance with the spirit of Islam. The interest-free economy practiced in the early days of Islam is neither capitalistic nor communistic, yet it has good features of both. It can create a healthy society which blossomed in the past and in which there was no accumulation of wealth in a few hands, no hoarding and no profiteering. Based on the principle of 'neither do harm, nor be harmed', it worked well and guaranteed to the poor their sustenance. Every citizen was provided with means of livelihood, peace and prosperity. This was due to the fact that interest was eliminated from the society for all.

According to the Islamic law, partnerships are of various kinds but the one best suited to the purpose of banking is 'shirkat-ul-inan' or partnership where by two or more persons join in business each of them being an agent of and for the other. The capital is not necessarily to be shared equally but the profit has to be distributed according to the terms agreed between them, under the principle or 'what is forbidden is permissible'. An Islamic bank may be a company, an association or a concern owned by an individual. Partnership then must be distinguished from a company. The main practical difference between a company and a partnership is this that the formation and existence of a partnership depends upon the mutual trust in and personal relationship of, the members to each others, whereas the formation and existence of a company does not depend to any extent on this; further, whilst in partnership every member is entitled to take part in the management of a business unless he bargains away his rights, in a company the management is left to specified officers. To avoid 'riba' (interest or usury) it may be lawful to adopt investment based on sharing in of the profit and loss according to the specified terms.

## Central Bank of a Muslim State:

Bait-al-mal, the 'fiscal' or treasury of a Muslim state is often spoken of as the central bank of the Muslim state but it is entirely concerned with the public finance, its collection and expenditure on the poor and needy.Revenues of the state were collected under the following heads.

1) Zakaat revenue and Sadaqat (obligatory to Muslims),
2) The revenues under Jizia and Kharaj (poll and land tax),
3) The booty revenue (leftover arms and materials in a battle),
4) General materials lost and found.

## Loans and Securities:

Loans are of two kinds;

a. Loan for a fixed time (Salaf which may include short, immediate and long term loans),
b. Loan recoverable on demand (Qarz).

The Qur'anic verse which deals with transactions involving future obligations is given below:-

All business dealings must be reduced to writing and Witnesses are required in all major business transactions:

"O believers! When you deal with each other in lending for a fixed period of time, put it in writing. Let a scribe write it down with justice between the parties. The scribe, who is given the gift of literacy by Allah, should not refuse to write; he is under obligation to write. Let him who incurs the liability (debtor) dictate, fearing Allah his Rabb and not diminishing anything from the settlement. If the borrower is mentally unsound or weak or is unable to dictate himself, let the guardian of his interests dictate for him with justice. Let two witnesses from among you bear witness to all such documents, if two men cannot be found, then one man and two women of your choice should bear witness, so that if one of the women forgets anything the other may remind her. The witnesses must not refuse when they are called upon to do so. You must not be averse to writing (your contract) for a future period, whether it is a small matter or big. This action is more just for you in the sight of Allah, because it facilitates the establishment of evidence and is the best way to remove all doubts; but if it is a common commercial transaction concluded on the spot among yourselves, there is no blame on you if you do not put it in writing. You should have witnesses when you make commercial transactions. Let no harm be done to the scribe or witnesses; and if you do so, you shall be guilty of transgression. Fear Allah; it is Allah that teaches you and Allah has knowledge of everything." (Al-Baqara: 2.282)

The first part of the text deals with transactions involving future payments and the second part deals with transactions in which the payments and delivery are made on the spot. As to the transactions of the first part written documents are recommended while the transactions performed on the spot require no evidence in writing except oral witnesses and even these oral witnesses are dispensed with if the parties trust each other.

## Islamic Laws:

A careful study of the Islamic law and its application to modern requirements is of vital importance. The Islamic laws are universal and can be followed for all times to come; as its laws are based upon broad principles that admit of interpretation to cover all the aspects of life. If there be anything essentials uncovered then recourse may had to be 'Rule of Necessity and Need' which has to be consulted with Islamic authorities of the time.

### 1) Laws of Inheritance:

"Men will have a share in what their parents and their near relatives leave; and women will have a share in what their parents and their near relatives leave: whether it be a little or much, they shall be legally entitled to their shares. If the relatives, orphans or needy are present at the time of the division of an inheritance, give them something out of it, and speak to them kind words. Let those (disposing of an estate) have the same fear in their minds as they would have for their own if they were to leave a helpless family behind: they should, therefore, fear Allah and speak for justice. In fact, those who misappropriate the property of orphans unjustly, swallow but fire into their bellies; they will soon be cast into the blazing fire!" (An-Nisaa: 4.7-10)

a. Prescribed shares in inheritance:

"In regard to inheritance Allah commands you concerning your children: that the share of a boy shall be twice that of a girl. In the case where there are more than two girls, their share will be two thirds of the estate; but if there is only one girl, her share will be one half of the estate. If the deceased left children behind, each of the parents shall get one sixth of the estate, but if the deceased left no children and the parents are the only heirs, the mother shall get one third of the estate, but if the deceased left brothers and sisters, then the mother will get one sixth of it. The distribution in all cases shall be after fulfilling the terms of the last will and the payment of debts. With regards to your parents and your children, you do not know who is more beneficial to you, therefore, Allah issued this ordinance. Surely Allah is Knowledgeable, Wise." (An-Nisaa: 4.11)

b. Commandment of Allah to make a 'Will':

- Last will and testament, and testimony of witnesses:

  "O believers! When death approaches any one of you, let two just men from among yourselves act as witnesses at the time of making your last will; or from the non-Muslims if you are traveling through the land and the calamity of death overtakes you. If you doubt their honesty, detain them after prayer and let them both swear by Allah: "We will not sell our testimony for any price, even to a relative, and we will not hide the testimony which we will be giving for the sake of Allah; for we shall be sinners if we do so!"." (Al-Maida: 5.106)

- Obligation of executing the 'Last Will and Testament':

  "Those of you who die and leave widows should bequeath for them a year's maintenance without causing them to leave their homes; but if they leave the residence on their own there is no blame on you for what they chose for themselves in a fair way. Allah is Mighty, Wise. Reasonable provisions must also be made for divorced women. That is an obligation upon those who fear Allah. That's how Allah makes His Revelations clear to you so that you may understand." (Al-Baqara: 2.240-242)

c. Inheritance of spouse's property:

"You shall inherit one half of your wives' estate if they leave no child, but if they leave behind a child then you will get one fourth of their estate, after fulfilling the terms of their last will and the payment of debts. Your wives shall inherit one fourth if you leave no child behind you; but if you leave a child, then they shall get one-eighth of your estate; after fulfilling the terms of your last will and the payment of debts. If a man or a woman leaves neither ascendant nor descendants but has left a brother or a sister, they shall each inherit one sixth, but if they are more than two, they shall share one third of the estate; after fulfilling the terms of the last will and the payment of debts; without prejudice to the rights of the heirs. Thus is the commandment of Allah. Allah is Knowledgeable, Forbearing." (An-Nisaa: 4.12)

d. Legal decision relating to the inheritance of childless persons:

"They ask you for a legal decision relating to inheritance in the case of a childless person. Say: Allah gives you His decision about those who leave no descendants or ascendants as heirs. If a man dies childless and leaves behind a sister, she shall inherit one-half of his estate. If a woman dies childless, her brother will inherit all of her estate. If the childless person leaves behind two sisters, they both shall inherit two-third of his estate; but if he leaves more than two brothers and sisters, the share of each male shall be equal to that of two females. Thus Allah makes His commandments clear to you lest you go astray. Allah has perfect knowledge of everything." (An-Nisaa: 4.176)

## 2) Property of the Orphans:

"Give orphans the property which belongs to them when they are able to handle it themselves and do not substitute your worthless things for their valuable ones; and do not cheat them of their possession through mixing it up with your own. For this would indeed be a great sin." (An-Nisaa: 4.2)

## 3) Laws Relating to Divorce:

a. "Pronouncement of revocable divorce is only allowed twice: then she should be allowed to stay with honor or let go with kindness after the third pronouncement. It is not lawful for husbands to take anything back which they have given them except when both parties fear that they may not be able to follow the limits set by Allah; then if you fear that they both will not be able to keep the limits of Allah, there is no blame if, by mutual agreement the wife compensates the husband to obtain divorce. These are the limits set by Allah; do not transgress them, and those who transgress the limits of Allah are the wrongdoers. So if a husband divorces his wife three times, it is not lawful for him to remarry her until after she has married another man and gotten divorced. In that case there is no blame on either of them if they reunite in marriage, provided they think that they can keep the limits of Allah. Such are the limits of Allah which He makes clear to the people of understanding." (Al-Baqara: 2.229-230)

b. Dowry and divorce:

   "There is no blame on you if you divorce women before the marriage is consummated or the dowry is settled. Pay them something anyhow, the rich man according to his means and poor according to his, a reasonable amount in all fairness. This is an obligation on the righteous people. And if you divorce them before the marriage is consummated but after the fixation of a dowry, give them half of their dowry unless the woman wants to waive it or the man in whose hand is the marriage tie is generous enough (to pay the dowry in full). It is more appropriate that the man should act generously. Do not forget to show kindness to each other. Surely Allah observes your actions." (Al-Baqara: 2.236-237)

c. Laws of divorce and Iddat (waiting period):

"O Prophet! If you and the believers divorce your wives, divorce them at the end of their prescribed periods, and count their prescribed periods accurately. Fear Allah, your Rabb. Do not expel them from their homes during their waiting period, nor they themselves should leave, unless they have committed an open lewdness. These are limits set by Allah; he that transgresses the limits of Allah will wrong his own soul. You never know, Allah may, thereafter, bring about some new situation of reconciliation. Then when their waiting period ends, either keep them honorably or part with them in an honorable way. Call to witness two honest persons among you, and O witnesses, bear witness equitably for the sake of Allah. This advice is being given to all who believe in Allah and the last Day. He that fears Allah may be provided a way out by Him, and given sustenance from the sources he could never imagine: for Allah is all sufficient for the person who puts his trust in Him. Surely Allah brings about what He pleases, and Allah has set a measure for all things. If you have any doubt concerning those of your wives who have ceased menstruating, then you should know that their waiting period will be three months, and the same will apply to those who have no menstruation due to young age or a disease. As for those who are pregnant, their waiting period will end with delivery. Allah will ease the hardship of those who fear Him. This is the command of Allah which He has sent down to you. He that fears Allah, will have his sins removed and his reward enlarged. Let those women, during their waiting period ('Iddat), live where you yourselves live according to your means. You shall not harass them so as to make life intolerable for them. If they are pregnant, maintain them until their delivery: and if, after that, they suckle your offspring, compensate them and settle the matter of compensation with mutual consultation and in all fairness. But if you cannot bear with each other then let another woman suckle the baby for you.Let the rich man give according to his means, and the poor man give according to what Allah has given him. Allah does not charge a man with more than He has given him; soon Allah may bring ease after hardship." (At-Talaq: 65.1-7)

- Waiting period after divorce:

  "Divorced women must keep themselves waiting for three menstrual periods, it is not lawful for them to hide what Allah has created in their wombs if they believe in Allah and the Last Day. In such cases their husbands have a right to take them back in that period if they desire reconciliation. Women have rights similar to those exercised against them in an equitable manner, although men have a status (degree of responsibility) above them. Allah is Mighty, Wise." (Al-Baqara: 2.228)

- Divorce when no Iddat (waiting period for remarriage) is required:

  "O believers! If you marry believing women and divorce them before the marriage is consummated, you are not required to observe the Iddat (waiting period) which you should count for them, so give them some present and relieve them gracefully." (Al-Ahzab: 33.49)

- Treatment to the divorced women:

  "When you divorce women and they have reached the end of their waiting period (Iddat) either allow them to stay with honor or let them go with kindness; but you should not retain them to harm them or to take undue advantage; if anyone does that he wrongs his own soul. Do not take Allah's revelations as a joke. Remember the favors of Allah upon you and the fact that He sent down the Book and Wisdom for your guidance. Fear Allah and know that Allah has knowledge of everything." (Al-Baqara: 2.231)

d. There is no restriction on divorcees to remarry:

   - "When you have divorced women and they have reached the end of their waiting period do not prevent them from marrying their prospective husbands if they have come to an honorable agreement. This is enjoined on everyone amongst you who believes in Allah and the Last Day. This is more virtuous and chaste for you; Allah knows what you do not know." (Al-Baqara: 2.232)
   - "As for those of you who die and leave widows behind, let them abstain from marriage for four months and ten days: when they have reached the end of this period, there is no blame on you for what they do for themselves in a decent manner. Allah is aware of what you do." (Al-Baqara: 2.234)
   - There is no restriction on the remarriage of widows:

     "There is no blame on you if you make a proposal of marriage during their waiting period openly or keep it in your hearts. Allah knows that you will naturally cherish them in your hearts; however, be careful not to make any secret agreement, and if you wish to marry, speak to them in an honorable manner. Do not confirm the marriage tie until the prescribed waiting period expires. You should know that Allah is aware of what is in your hearts, so fear Him. Bear in mind that Allah is Forgiving, Forbearing." (Al-Baqara: 2.235)

## 4) The punishment for guilty of lewdness:

"If any of your women are guilty of fornication, ask for four reliable witnesses from among yourselves against them; and if they testify and their guilt is proved, confine them to their houses until they die or Allah opens some other way out for them. And the two, whether married or unmarried, who are guilty of this offense, punish them both. If they repent and mend their ways, leave them alone. Surely Allah is the Acceptor of Repentance, Merciful." (An-Nisaa: 4.15-16)

## 5) Prohibition of adoption of a child:

"Allah has not put two hearts in a person's body: nor does He regard your wives whom you divorce through Zihar (divorcing a wife saying; from now on you are as my mother, depriving her conjugal rights yet keeping her like a slave nor letting her marry anyone else) as your mothers: nor does He regard your adopted sons as your sons. These are mere words which you utter with your mouths; but Allah declares the Truth and guides you to the Right Way. Name your adopted sons after their fathers; that is more just in the sight of Allah, and if you don't know who their fathers are, then call them as your brothers in faith and your friends. There is no blame on you for an unintentional mistake, but you will be held responsible for what you do with the intention of your hearts; Allah is Forgiving, Merciful." (Al-Ahzab: 33.4-5)

## 6) Pagans' practice of divorce through 'Zihar' (calling his wife as his mother) is prohibited and Penalty for practicing 'Zihar':

"Those of you who divorce their wives by Zihar (calling them to be like their mothers) should know that they are not their mothers. Their mothers are only those who gave birth to them. Surely the words they utter are absurd and false. Allah could punish them for this but He forgave them, surely Allah is All-Pardoning, All-Forgiving. Those who divorce their wives by Zihar, then wish to retract the words they uttered, shall have to free a slave before they touch each other. This is enjoined as a penalty for doing so. Allah is well aware of all your actions. He that has no slave, shall fast two consecutive months before they touch each other. He that cannot fast, shall feed sixty poor people. This is enjoined so that you may have faith in Allah and His Rasool. These are the limits set by Allah, and the violators shall have a painful punishment. Those who resist Allah and His Rasool, shall be humiliated as were those before them. We have sent down clear revelations; the disbelievers shall have a humiliating punishment. On the Day of Judgement Allah will raise them all back to life, then inform them about what they have done. Allah has kept full record of their deeds even though they may have forgotten, for Allah is a witness over all things." (Al-Mujadila: 58.2-6)

## 7) Respect the ownership of one another's properties:

"O believers! Do not consume one another's wealth through unlawful means; instead, do business with mutual consent; do not kill yourselves by adopting unlawful means. Indeed Allah is Merciful to you. Anyone who commits such acts of aggression and injustice will soon be thrown into hellfire, and this is very easy for Allah to do." (An-Nisaa: 4.29-30)

## 8) Do not entrust property to feeble-minded people:

"Do not entrust your property which Allah has made a means of support for your family, to feeble-minded people for investment in business, however, provide such people with food and clothing and speak to them nicely and give them good advice." (An-Nisaa: 4.5)

## 9) Train the orphans to manage their properties:

"Observe the orphans through testing their abilities until they reach the age of marriage, then if you find them capable of sound judgment, hand over to them their property; and do not consume it wastefully in haste lest they grow up to demand it. If the guardian is well-off, he should not take compensation from the orphan's property, but if he is poor let him take a just and reasonable remuneration. When you hand over their property to them, call in some witnesses; even though Allah is sufficient in taking the accountability." (An-Nisaa: 4.6)

## 10) Rules about the distribution of the spoils of war:

"Know that one-fifth of the booty (spoils of war) is for Allah, His Rasool, close relatives of the Rasool, orphans, the needy and the wayfarer, if you do believe in Allah and in what We revealed to Our servant on the day of distinction (between right and wrong), the day when two armies met in combat. Allah has power over everything. Remember when you were on this side of the valley and they on the farther side, and the caravan was on lower ground than you both. If you had made a mutual appointment to fight, you would have certainly failed; but Allah sought to accomplish what He has ordained, that those who were destined to perish might die by clear proof and those who were destined to live might survive by clear proof. Surely,

Allah is He Who hears all and knows all. Also remember that Allah made them appear in your dream as few in number; if He had shown them to you as many in number, you would surely have been discouraged and you would have disputed in your decision. But Allah saved you; surely He knows the very secrets of the hearts. And remember when you met them in the encounter, He showed them to you as few in number in your eyes and He made you appear as a few in number in their eyes so that Allah might accomplish what He had ordained: for ultimately all affairs return to Allah for decision." (Al-Anfal: 8.41-44)

## 11) The Islamic laws of retribution:

"O believers! Retaliation is prescribed for you in the cases of murder: a free man for a free man, a slave for a slave, and a female for a female. But if anyone is pardoned by his aggrieved brother, then blood wit (a ransom for manslaughter) should be decided according to the common law and payment should be made with gratitude. This is a concession and a mercy from your Rabb. Now, whoever exceeds the limits after this, shall have a painful punishment. O men of understanding! There is security of life for you in the law of retaliation, so that you may learn self-restraint." (Al-Baqara: 2.178-179)

## 12) Punishment for theft:

"Male or female, whoever is guilty of theft, cut off the hand (that was used in theft) of either of them as a punishment for their crime. This is exemplary punishment ordained by Allah. Allah is Mighty, Wise. But whoever repents after committing the crime and reforms his conduct, Allah will surely turn to him with forgiveness. Allah is Forgiving, Merciful. Don't you know that Allah has sovereignty over the heavens and the earth? He may punish whom He pleases and forgive whom He pleases. Allah has power over everything." (Al-Maida: 5.38-40)

**13)** "The worst of animals in the sight of Allah are those who reject the truth and do not become believers. Those who make treaties with you and time after time violate their treaties, and have no fear of Allah. If you encounter them in combat, make them a fearsome example for others who would follow them so that they all may learn a lesson. If you fear treachery from any of your allies, you may fairly retaliate by breaking off the treaty with them (through properly notifying them to that effect), for Allah does not love the treacherous." (Al-Anfal: 8.55-58)

# 8.
# Islam and Science

Numerous translations and commentaries on the Qur'an have been written by Islamic scholars. It is now required that scientific hidden meanings of various Qur'anic verses are to be correlated with the latest scientific developments. As interpretations of the holy Qur'an holds true even in the terms of modern science. A number of facts that had been already explained in the Qur'an are now proven by the development of scientific technologies. Qur'an clarifies various theories on various principles related to astrology, geology, medical sciences, plant and animal kingdom etc. There are many verses, whose obvious meanings are easily understood but some which conceal scientific meanings are yet as starling; it is only Allah who will reveal those at appropriate time to the scientists of His choice.

## (1) Astrology –

### a. Skies / Heavens:

(i) The skies and earth were once one mass, Allah split them asunder, and He created all living things from water:

"Have not the unbelievers ever considered that the skies and the earth were once one mass, then We split them asunder? And We have created every living thing from water. Will they still not believe?" (Al-Anbiyaa: 21.30)

(ii) Allah has created seven skies with heavenly bodies; one above another without any flaw:

"Allah is the One Who raised the heavens without any pillars that you can see, then firmly established Himself on the throne of authority and subjected the sun and the moon to His law - each one pursuing its course for an appointed time. He regulates all affairs. He has spelled out His revelations so that you may believe in meeting your Rabb." (Ar-R'ad: 13.2)

(iii) "He has raised the heaven on high and created the balance." (Ar-Rahman: 55.7)

(iv) "And We have made the sky a safe canopy: yet they are heedless to these signs." (Al-Anbiyaa: 21.32)

(v) "And We have (from of old) adorned the lowest heaven with Lamps and We have made such (Lamps) (as) missiles to drive away the Evil Ones and have prepared for them the Penalty of the Blazing Fire." (Al-Mulk: 67.5–A.Yusuf Ali's Qur'an translation)

(vi) "It is He Who created the heavens and the earth in six periods, then firmly established Himself on the throne of authority. He knows all that enters the earth and all that emerges from it, all that comes down from Heaven and all that ascends to it; and He is with you wherever you are. Allah is aware of all your actions." (Al-Hadid: 57.4)

(vii) "He is the One to Whom belongs the kingdom of the heavens and the earth, has begotten no son and has no partner in His kingdom; He has created everything and ordained them in due proportions." (Al-Furqan: 25.2)

## b. Expansion of the Firmament:

Qur'an also seems to allude to one of the most imposing discoveries of the modern science, the expansion of the Firmament.

(i) "With the power and skill did We construct the Firmament: for it is We Who create the vastness of Space." (Az-Zariyat: 51.47 – A. Yusuf's Qur'an translation)

(ii) "And it is we who have built the universe with (our creative) power; and, verily, it is we who are steadily expanding it." (Az-Zariyat: 51.47 – M. Asad's Qur'an translation)

## c. The Sun and Moon: The Day and Night:

The Qur'an distinguishes between the sun and the moon by use of different terms: Mantle (noor / light ) for the moon, and lamp (Siraj) for the sun. The moon is an inert body which reflects light whereas the sun is a celestial body in a state of combustion producing both light and heat.

"...provided you rest in sleep, made the night a mantle, made the day to work for earning your livelihood, built above you seven firmaments, placed therein a shining lamp." (An-Nabaa: 78.9-13)

Now that the man has landed on the moon and observed that the earth was spinning on its own axis and that the dark half of the globe appears to wind itself around the light half and the light half appears to wind itself around the dark. The following Qur'anic verses seems to be totally valid at the time when Qur'an was revealed.

(i) "The sun and the moon are also assigned for your benefit, which steadfastly pursue their courses, to cause the night and the day for your benefit." (Ibrahim: 14.33)

(ii) "He causes the night to pass into the day and the day into the night, and He has made the sun and the moon to serve you; each one follows its course for an appointed term. Such is Allah, your Rabb; His is the kingdom; and those to whom you pray besides Him do not even own a thread of a date-stone." (Fatir: 35.13)

(iii) The moon is to determine Time periods:

"They question you about the new moon. Tell them: it is to determine the periods of time for the benefit of mankind and for the Hajj (pilgrimage)." (Al-Baqara: 2.189)

(iv) "The sun and the moon move along their computed courses." (Ar-Rahman: 55.5)

(v) "He has subjected to your service the night and the day, the sun and the moon: and likewise the stars also serve you by His command: surely there are signs in this for people who use their common sense." (An-Nahl: 16.12)

(vi) "He created the heavens and the earth to manifest the Truth. He causes the night to succeed the day and the day to overtake the night. He has subjected the sun and the moon to His law, each one following a course for an appointed term. Is not He the All-Mighty, the All-Forgiving?" (Az-Zumar: 39.5)

(vii) "Allah alternates the night and the day; there is indeed a lesson in it for those who possess insight." (An-Nur: 24.44)

(viii) "He causes the daybreak from the dark. He makes the night for rest and makes the rising and setting of the sun and the moon for you to determine times (days, weeks, months and years), these are the arrangements of the Almighty, the All-Knowing." (Al-A'nam: 6.96)

## d. The Solar Apex:

Modern astronomy confirms that the solar system is indeed moving in its space at the rate of 12 miles per second towards a point situated in the constellation of Hercules (alpha lyrae) whose exact location has been precisely calculated. Astronomers have even given it a name, the Solar Apex. Qur'an indicates an exact appointed place and time 'settled places' given in the following quote:

"Another sign for them is the night; when We withdraw the daylight from it, and behold they are in darkness. The sun runs its course, this course is pre-estimated for it by the Almighty, the All-Knowing. As for the moon, We have designed phases for it till it again becomes like an old dry palm branch. Neither it is possible for the sun to overtake the moon, nor for the night to outstrip the day: each floats along in its own orbit." (Yasin: 36.37-40)

## e. Orbits:

Galaxy is balanced by the position of stars and planets in well defined orbits, as well as the interplay of gravitational forces produced by their masses and the speed of their moments. This is what the Qur'an describes which has become comprehensible in modern times.

"He is the One Who has created the night and the day and the sun and the moon: all (the celestial bodies) move swiftly in an orbit of their own." (Al-Anbiyaa: 21.33)

## f. Stars and Planets:

Stars are heavenly bodies producing their own light like the sun.

(i) "He is the One Who has made the stars for you, so that you might find your way thereby in the darkness whether you are on the land or the sea. We have spelled out Our revelations very clearly for people of common sense." (Al-A'nam: 6.97)

(ii) Star burns and consumes itself as it pierces the shadow of the night.

"It is the star of piercing brightness." (At-Tariq: 86.3)

Planets (Kawkab in Qur'an) which are celestial bodies that reflect light and do not produce their own light like the sun.

"Lo! We have adorned the lowest heaven with an ornament, the planets." (As-Saffat: 37.6 – M. Pickthall's Qur'an translation)

### g. Conquest of space:

One of the modern science's achievements is the 'conquest of space' which has resulted in man's journey to the moon. The prediction of this event surely springs to mind when we read the chapter 'Ar-Rahman' in the Qur'an. The authorities to travel in the space can only come from the creator of the laws which govern movement and space. The whole of the above chapter invites humankind to recognize Allah's beneficence.

"O you, the assembly of jinns and men! If you have the power to get away from the boundaries of the heavens and the earth (to escape from His punishment), then get away! You cannot get away except with Our Own authority." (Ar-Rahman: 55.33)

## (2) Geology –

The Qur'anic reflections deal not only with the physical phenomena observed on earth but also with details concerning the living organisms that inhabit it.

### a. The Earth:

(i) "On the Earth He has created things of different colors: surely there is a sign in this for those who want to learn a lesson." (An-Nahl: 16.13)

(ii) "He is the One Who spread out the earth and placed thereon mountains and rivers, created fruits of every kind in pairs, two and two and makes the night cover the day. Certainly in these things there are signs for those who use their common-sense." (Ar-R'ad: 13.3)

### b. Reduction of the land:

Similarly, the most imposing discovery of modern science is the reduction of land.

"Do they not see that We are gradually reducing the land in their control through curtailing its borders? When Allah commands, there is none to reverse His command and He is swift in taking accountability." (Ar-Ra'd: 13.41)

### c. Mountains:

(i) He set mountains to stabilize earth:

"He has set mountains on the earth - lest it should move away with you. He also made rivers and roads so that you may find your way; and likewise made landmarks and the stars for your guidance." (An-Nahl: 16.15-16)

(ii) Pegs, which are driven into the ground like those used to anchor a tent, are the deep foundations of geological folds:

"Is it not true that We have spread the earth like a bed, and the mountains as pegs?" (An-Nabaa: 78.6-7)

### d. Oceans:

(i) Allah is the Rabb of the east and west and put the laws to regulate oceans, its products and ships:

"He has made the two oceans apparently meeting together, yet between them is a barrier which they cannot cross. He produces pearls and coral from both of them. His are the ships looming up like mountains on the sea. So, O jinn and men, which of your Rabb's favors will both of you deny?" (Ar-Rahman: 55.19-20, 22, 24-25)

(ii) "He is the One Who has made the two seas rolling, the one sweet and fresh, the other salty and bitter, and set a rampart between them, an insurmountable barrier." (Al-Furqan: 25.53)

(iii) Subjected the sea to your service:

"It is He Who has subjected the sea to your service, that you may eat fresh meat there from and that you may bring out of it ornaments to wear; and you see that ships plough their course through it. He has done all this so that you may seek His bounty and so that you may pay thanks to Him." (An-Nahl: 16.14)

(iv) "The two bodies of water, of which one is sweet and pleasant to drink and the other is salty and bitter, are not alike. Yet from each kind of water you eat fresh meat and extract ornaments which you wear; and you see the ships plough their course through them to seek the bounty of Allah, that you may be grateful." (Fatir: 35.12)

## e. Water cycle in nature:

If one compares the facts of modern hydrology with the data found in numerous verses of the Qur'an on this subject, one cannot fail to notice the remarkable degree of agreement between the two.

(i) "Do you not see that Allah makes the clouds move gently, then joins them together, then piles them up in masses, then you see the rain coming from inside them? He also sends down hail from the clouds that look like mountains in the sky, afflicting therewith whom He wills and turning it away from whom He pleases; the flash of His lightning almost takes away sight." (An-Nur: 24.43)

(ii) "Do you not see how Allah sends down water from the sky which penetrates the earth and comes out through springs? With it He brings forth a variety of crops with different colors, then they wither and you see them turning yellow, and then finally He crumbles them to dust. Surely, in this example, there is a lesson for the people of understanding." (Az-Zumar: 39.21)

Now we know that it is the infiltration of rain water into the ground that comes forth as springs.

## (3) Plant and Animal Kingdom –

The holy Qur'an has dealt with living things, both in the plant and animal kingdom, especially with regard to reproduction.

The Qur'anic verses referring to plants:

a. It is He Who sends down water from the sky for drinking and agriculture:

- "It is He Who sends down rainwater from the sky and therewith produces vegetation of all kinds: He brings forth green crops producing grain piled up in the ear (seed-bearing part), palm-trees laden with clusters of dates hanging within reach, gardens of grapes, olives, and pomegranates; though their fruit resembles in kind yet is different in variety. Look at their fruits as they yield and ripen. Behold! In these things there are signs for true believers." (Al-A'nam: 6.99)
- "It is He Who sends down water from the sky, which provides drinking water for you and brings forth fodder to pasture your cattle. With it He grows for you crops, olives, date-palms, grapes, and every kind of fruit: surely there is a great sign in this for those who think." (An-Nahl: 16.10-11)

b. Trees, fruits, vegetables and their tastes are the signs of Allah:

"In the earth there are tracts side by side: gardens of grapes, cornfields and palm trees with single and double trunks - they are all watered with the same water, yet We make some of them excel others in taste. Surely in this, there are signs for people who use their common sense." (Ar-Ra'd: 13.4)

c. "Surely it is Allah Who causes the seed and the fruit-stone to split and sprout. He brings forth the living from the dead and the dead from the living. It is Allah, Who does all this; then why are you being misled?" (Al-A'nam: 6.95)

d. "Likewise in the fruits of the date-palm and the grapes, from which you derive intoxicants and wholesome food, certainly there is a sign for those people who use their common sense." (An-Nahl: 16.67)

e. "He laid out the earth for His creatures, with all its fruits and palms having sheathed cluster, and grain with husk and scented herbs. So, O jinn and men, which of your Rabb's favors will both of you deny?" (Ar-Rahman: 55.10-13)

f. Created two sexes of every plant:

- "And sends down water from the sky with which We produce pairs of various kinds of vegetation." (Ta-ha: 20.53)
- "Created fruits of every kind in pairs." (Ar-Ra'd: 13.3)
- Allah has created all things in pair:

  "The dead land may serve as a sign for them; We give it life and produce from it grain for them, which they eat. We also produce from it gardens with date-palms and vines, and We cause springs to gush forth from it. So that they may enjoy the fruits thereof. It was not their hands that made all this; should they not then give thanks? Glory be to Allah Who created all things in pairs: the plants of the earth, mankind themselves and other living things which they do not know." (Yasin: 36.33-36)

The Qur'anic verses referring to animal kingdom:

a. "Allah has created from water every living creature: of them there are some that creep upon their bellies, some that walk on two legs, and yet some that walk on four; Allah creates what He pleases; surely Allah has power over everything." (An-Nur: 24.45)

b. He has created cattle for the benefit of human beings:

   - "He also created for you eight heads of cattle in pairs." (Az-Zumar: 39.6)
   - "He created cattle, which provide you clothing, food, and other benefits. How pleasant they look to you when you bring them home in the evening and drive them to pasture in the morning. They carry your heavy loads to far-off towns that you could not otherwise reach without painful toil; indeed your Rabb is Kind and Merciful. He has also created horses, mules, and donkeys for you to ride and put on show, and He has created other things which are beyond your knowledge." (An-Nahl: 16.5-8)

c. There is a lesson for mankind in the lives of animals, i.e., milk-producing animals and the honeybee:

   "Surely there is a lesson for you in cattle. We give you to drink of what is in their bellies, between bowels and blood - pure milk - pleasant for those who drink it. Behold! Your Rabb inspired the bees to build their hives in the mountains, in the trees, and in anything which men may build for beekeeping, and feed on every kind of fruit and follow the smooth ways of your Rabb. From its belly comes forth a syrup of different colours, which contains healing for mankind. Certainly in this there is a sign for those who think." (An-Nahl: 16.66, 68-69)

d. There are also signs of Allah in the lives of the birds and the animals:

"Do they not see the birds, that wing their flight in the air towards the sky? Who holds them up but Allah? Surely in this there are signs for the true believers. Allah has made your homes the place for your rest, and animal skins for tent-like houses so that you may find them light when you travel and easy to pitch when you stop; while from their wool, fur, and hair He provides you household items and articles of convenience for your prescribed term of life." (An-Nahl: 16.79-80)

## (4) Medical Science –

There are multitudes of statements in the Qur'an on the subject of human reproduction which constitute a challenge to the embryologist seeking a human explanation for them. It was only after the birth of the basic sciences which contributed to our knowledge of biology and the invention of the microscope, that humans were able to understand the depth of those Qur'anic statements. It was impossible for human beings living in the early seventh century to have accurately expressed such ideas. Today there are many Muslim scientists possessing a thorough knowledge of Qur'an and natural sciences that have recognized the amazing similarity between the verses of the Qur'an dealing with reproduction and modern scientific knowledge.

### Creation of human being:

a. "He created man from sounding clay similar to pottery, and created jinns from smokeless fire." (Ar-Rahman: 55.14-15)

b. "O mankind! Have fear of your Rabb, the One who created you from a single soul, from that soul He created its mate, and through them He spread countless men and women. Fear Allah, the One in whose name you demand your rights from one another and the ties of relationship; surely Allah is watching you very closely." (An-Nisaa: 4.1)

c. "He is the One Who has created you from a single soul and granted you dwelling on Earth and a resting place in the hereafter. We have spelled out Our revelation very clearly for people of understanding." (Al-An'am: 6.98)

d. "He is the one who created you from a single being and from that being He created his mate, so that he might find comfort with her. When he covers her, she conceives a light burden and walks around with it. When it grows heavy they both pray to Allah their Rabb saying: "If You will grant us a healthy child, we will be truly thankful." " (Al-A'raf: 7.189)

## Fertilization:

The complexity of the semen and the fact that an infinitely small quantity is required to ensure fertilization is given in Qur'an.

"Indeed, We have created man from the sperm drop containing both sexes." (Ad-Dahr: 76.2)

The Arabic word 'Nutfah' has been translated as small quantity. It comes from the verb meaning 'to dribble, to trickle'. The verse correctly implies that the fertilization is performed by only a small volume of the liquid. On the other hand, mingled fluids (Amshaaj) have been understood by early competitors to refer to mixture of male and female discharges. Modern authors have corrected this view and noted that sperm is made of various components. When the Qur'an talks of a fertilizing fluid composed of different components it also informs us that human progeny will be formed from something extracted from this fluid. This is the meaning of the following verse: "And made his progeny from a quintessence of the nature of a fluid despised." (As-Sajda: 32.8 – A. Yusuf Ali's Qur'an translation)

## Implantation:

Once the egg has been fertilized in the fallopian tube, it descends to lodge itself inside the uterus. This process is called the 'implantation of the egg'. It's a result of development of villosities, which, like roots in the soil, draw nourishment from the wall of the uterus and make the egg literally cling to the womb. The process of implantation is appropriately described in several verses by the word 'alaq' as given in the following verse of the Qur'an:

"- created man from a leechlike mass." (Al-Alaq: 96.2)

## Embryo:

The evolution of the embryo inside the maternal uterus is only briefly described but the description is accurate because the simple word referring to it corresponds exactly to the fundamental stages in its growth. This is what we read in a verse from the Qur'an.

The term 'chewed flesh' (muzghah) corresponds exactly to the appearance of the embryo at a certain stage in its development. It is known that the bones develop inside this mass and that they are then with muscle. This is the meaning of the term intact flesh (lahm).

"And then we create out of the drop of the sperm a germ-cell, and then We create out of the germ-cell an embryonic lump, and then We create within the embryonic lump bones, and then We clothe the bones with flesh – and then We bring [all] this into being as a new creation: hallowed, therefore, is God, the best artisans!" (Al-Muminun: 23.14 – M. Asad's Qur'an translation)

The embryo passes through a stage where some parts are partly formed and some are partly unformed with what is later to become the individual. This is the obvious meaning of a verse in the holy Qur'an:

"...then from a morsel of flesh, partly formed and partly unformed." (Al-Hajj: 22.5)

Next, we have references to the appearance of the senses and internal organs in the following verses of the holy Qur'an:

"...then He fashioned him in due proportion and breathed into him His spirit. He gave you ears, eyes and heart; yet you are seldom thankful." (As-Sajda: 32.9)

"Created man and taught him how to convey his feelings and thoughts." (Ar-Rahman: 55.3-4)

## Exact age in womb and future of the embryo:

a. "He creates you in the wombs of your mothers in stages, one after another, in three layers of darkness. This is Allah, your Rabb. To Him belongs the sovereignty. There is no god but Him. How can you then turn away from Him?" (Az-Zumar: 39.6)

b. "It is He Who shapes your bodies in the wombs of your mothers as He pleases. There is no god but Him; the Mighty, the Wise." (Al-i'Imran: 3.6)

c. "Allah knows what every female bears in her womb. He is fully aware of what decrease or increase (miscarriage or a long wait) takes place in the womb. Everything has a due measure with Him." (Ar-R'ad: 13.8)

d. "No female conceives or delivers without His knowledge. No long-lived man grows old or has his life cut short but is written in a Book; surely all this is easy for Allah." (Fatir: 35.11)

## Physiology:

a. "Indeed We have created man from an essence of clay, then placed him as a drop of semen in a firm resting place." (Al-Muminun: 23.12-13)

b. "He is created from an emitted fluid that is produced from between the loins and the ribs." (At-Tariq: 86.6-7)

c. "We have created you: will you not then testify about Our power of creation? Have you ever considered the semen you discharge: Is it you who create the child from it, or are We the Creator?" (Al-Waqi'a: 56.57-59)

d. "We have indeed created man in the best stature;" (At-Tin: 95.4)

e. "Who created you, fashioned you, proportioned you, and moulded you in whatever form He pleased?" (Al-Infitar: 82.7-8)

f. "Allah brought you forth from the wombs of your mothers when you knew nothing, and He gave you hearing, sight and intelligence so that you may give thanks to Him." (An-Nahl: 16.78)

g. "Out of what Allah has created him? Out of a semen-drop! Allah created him and then fashioned him in due proportion, then makes his way of life smooth for him, then causes him to die and stows him in a grave. Then He will surely bring him back to life when He pleases." (Abasa: 80.18-22)

## Question about Menstruation:

"They ask you about menstruation. "Tell them: This is a discomfort; therefore, keep away from women (do not have sexual intercourse) during their menstrual periods and do not approach them until they are clean again. When they have cleansed themselves then you may approach them in the manner

Allah has enjoined for you. Surely Allah loves those who turn to Him in repentance and keep themselves clean. Your wives are your tilth; so go to your tilth when you like. Take care of your future and refrain from the displeasure of Allah. Bear in mind that you shall meet Him in the Hereafter, and give good news to the believers". " (Al-Baqara: 2.222-223)

## Birth Control:

Requirement of breast-feeding babies and Waiting period of at least 39 months or more between two children:

a. "The mothers shall breast-feed their offspring for two whole years if the father wishes the breast-feeding to be completed." (Al-Baqara: 2.233)

b. "With much trouble his mother bore him, and much pain did she give him birth. His bearing and his weaning took thirty months". (Al-Ahqaf: 46.15)

c. Abortion is prohibited:

   - "O Muhammad, say: "Come, I will recite what your Rabb has forbidden to you: not to commit shirk with Him, to be kind to your parents, not to kill your children making the excuse of inability to support them - We provide sustenance for you and for them - not to commit shameful deeds whether open or secret, not to kill any soul forbidden by Allah except for the requirements of justice. These are the things which He enjoined you so that you may learn wisdom." (Al-An'am: 6.151)
   - "Whenever the news of a female child is announced to any one of them, his face darkens and he chokes with inward gloom. He hides himself from his people because of the bad news he has heard, asking himself whether he should retain her with disgrace or bury

her in the dust. Beware! Evil is the judgement they make about Allah." (An-Nahal: 16.58-59)

**Birth of child to barren lady is possible:**

The story of Zakariya (A.S.), his wife and their son Yahya (John) (A.S.):

"This is a reminder of blessings that your Rabb bestowed on His servant Zakariya, when he invoked his Rabb in secret, saying: "O Rabb! Surely my bones have weakened and the hair of my head glistens with grey, while I have never been disappointed in my prayer to You, O Rabb! Yet I fear about my relatives after me, for my wife is barren, grant me a heir by Your grace who should inherit me and inherit the posterity of Ya'qoob, and make him, O my Rabb, a desirable person!" We answered his prayer saying: "O Zakariya! Surely We give you the good news of a son, his name shall be Yahya (John): a name that no one has had before him." He asked: "O Rabb! How shall I have a son when my wife is barren and I have become impotent from old age?" The answer came: "So shall it be. Your Rabb says: 'It shall not be a difficult task for Me, just as I created you before, when you were nothing at all!" Zakariya said "O my Rabb! Give me a sign." He said: "Your sign is that for three nights you shall not be able to speak to the people even being sound in health." After this Zakariya came out of the shrine and asked his people, through sign language, to glorify Allah in the morning and in the evening. To Yahya, when he became old enough, We said: " Hold firmly to the Book." We granted him wisdom, while he was yet a boy, and also granted him kindness and purity by Our grace, and he grew up a pious man; dutiful to his parents - he was neither arrogant nor disobedient. Peace be on him the day he was born, the day of his death and the Day he will be raised to life again!" (Maryam: 19.2-15)

**Birth of child is also possible without conception of male:**

The story of Maryam (P.B.U.H.) and the miraculous birth of Isa (Jesus -A.S.):

a. "O Muhammad, relate to them the story of Maryam in the Book (The Qur'an) when she withdrew from her family to a place in the East. She chose to be secluded from them. We sent to her Our angel and he appeared before her as a grown up man. She said: "I seek Rahman's (Allah's) protection against you, leave me alone if you are God-fearing". He said: "Don't be afraid, I am merely a messenger from your Rabb to tell you about the gift of a holy son." She said: "How shall I bear a son, no man has ever touched me nor am I unchaste?" The angel replied: "So shall it be - Your Rabb says: "It is easy for Me. We wish to make him a Sign for mankind and a blessing from Us - and this matter has already been decreed." So she conceived the child and she retired with him to a remote place. The pains of childbirth drove her to the trunk of a palm-tree. She cried in her anguish: "Ah! Would that I had died before this, and been long forgotten!" An angel from beneath the palm-tree consoled her, saying: "Do not grieve! Your Rabb has provided a brook at your feet. If you shake the trunk of this palm-tree, it will drop fresh ripe dates in your lap. So eat, drink and refresh yourself. If you see anyone, tell him: 'I have vowed a fast to Rahmaan (Allah), so I will not speak to anyone today!!'"" (Maryam: 19.16-26)

b. Maryam brought her baby (Jesus) to her people, and the baby spoke to his people in the cradle to defend his mother and proclaim his assignment to be their Prophet:

"Carrying the baby, she came back to her people. They said: "O Maryam! You have brought something hard to believe! O sister (a woman from the noble family) of Haroon! Your father was not a bad man nor your mother an unchaste woman." In response she merely pointed towards the baby. They said: "How can we talk to a baby in the cradle?" Whereupon the baby spoke out: "I am indeed a servant of Allah. He has given me the Book and made me a Prophet. His blessing is with me wherever I go. He has commanded me to establish Salaah and give Zakah as long as I shall live. He has exhorted me to honor my mother and has not made me domineering, hard to deal with. Peace be upon me the day I was born, the day I shall die and the Day I shall be raised to life again." Such was Isa (Jesus) the son of Maryam, and this is the True statement about him concerning which they are in doubt." (Maryam: 19. 27-34)

## Coma Patients:

Some were awakened up by Allah after 309 years:

"Now We tell you their real story. They were young men who believed in their Rabb, and on them We had bestowed Our guidance. If you could see them, you might have thought them awake, though they were asleep. We turned them about to their right and left sides, while their dog lay stretched out with his forepaws at the entrance. Had you looked at them you would have certainly turned your back and their sight would have made you flee in terror. Some say they stayed in their cave three hundred years and some add another nine." (Al-Kahf: 18.13, 18, 25)

## Example of bringing Dead to Life:

"Or take another example of the one (Prophet Ezra) who passed by a town which has fallen down upon its roofs. He exclaimed: "How can Allah bring this dead township back to life?" Thereupon Allah caused him to die, and after one hundred years brought him back to life. Allah asked: "How long did you remain here?" Ezra replied: "Perhaps a day or part of a day." Allah said: "Nay! You have remained here for one hundred years: now just have a look at your food and drink; they have not rotten; and then look at your donkey and see that his very bones have decayed. We have done this to make you a Sign for mankind. Look at the bones of your donkey how We bring them together then clothe them with flesh and bring him back to life! When this all was shown clearly to him he said: "Now I know that Allah has power over everything."" (Al-Baqara: 2.259)

●●●

# References:

All Qur'anic verses are referred from F. Malik's Qur'an translation, a few are from M. Asad and A. Yusuf Ali's Qur'an translation. As described in The Alim of ISL Software Corp, USA. Available online at

**http://www.alim.org/Alim_-_Islamic_Knowledge_Platform/index.html**

| Verse Name | Verse & Sura No. | Page No. |
|---|---|---|
| Abasa | 80.18-22 | 161 |
| Ad-Dahr | 76.1 | 18 |
| Ad-Dahr | 76.2 | 158 |
| Adh-Dhuha | 93.9-10 | 125 |
| Al-A'la | 87.14-15 | 098 |
| Al-A'raf | 7.2-9 | 83 |
| Al-A'raf | 7.11-18 | 19 |
| Al-A'raf | 7.26 | 114 |
| Al-A'raf | 7.31 | 114 |
| Al-A'raf | 7.32 | 114 |
| Al-A'raf | 7.33 | 123 |
| Al-A'raf | 7.35 -39 | 50 |
| Al-A'raf | 7.35 -36 | 27 |
| Al-A'raf | 7.54 -55 | 18 |
| Al-A'raf | 7.56 | 030 |
| Al-A'raf | 7.59-64 | 054 |
| Al-A'raf | 7.65-72 | 056 |
| Al-A'raf | 7.73-79 | 056 |
| Al-A'raf | 7.73-74 | 024 |
| Al-A'raf | 7.80-84 | 059 |
| Al-A'raf | 7.85-87 | 059 |
| Al-A'raf | 7.85 | 024 |
| Al-A'raf | 7.130-136 | 065 |
| Al-A'raf | 7.145-147 | 041 |
| Al-A'raf | 7.158 | 034 |
| Al-A'raf | 7.158 | 094 |
| Al-A'raf | 7.180 | 023 |
| Al-A'raf | 7.179 | 029 |
| Al-A'raf | 7.189 | 158 |
| Al-Ahqaf | 46.15 | 162 |
| Al-Ahzab | 33.4-5 | 142 |
| Al-Ahzab | 33.21-24 | 073 |
| Al-Ahzab | 33.36 | 113 |
| Al-Ahzab | 33.40 | 022 |
| Al-Ahzab | 33.40-48 | 075 |
| Al-Ahzab | 33.49 | 116 |
| Al-Ahzab | 33.49 | 140 |
| Al Ahzab | 33.55 | 116 |
| Al-Ahzab | 33.56 | 076 |
| Al-Ahzab | 33.59 | 116 |
| Al-Alaq | 96.2 | 159 |
| Al-An'am | 6.19-20 | 045 |
| Al-An'am | 6.27-30 | 078 |
| Al-An'am | 6.42-45 | 089 |
| Al-An'am | 6.63-67 | 090 |
| Al-An'am | 6.83-90 | 068 |
| Al-An'am | 6.91 | 040 |
| Al-An'am | 6.95 | 155 |
| Al-An'am | 6.96 | 149 |
| Al-An'am | 6.97 | 150 |

| Al-An'am | 6.98 | 158 |
|---|---|---|
| Al-An'am | 6.99 | 154 |
| Al-An'am | 6.141 | 105 |
| Al-An'am | 6.151 | 162 |
| Al-An'am | 6.154-157 | 041 |
| Al-An'am | 6.156-158 | 47 |
| Al-An'am | 6.157 | 071 |
| Al-An'am | 6.159 | 030 |
| Al-An'am | 6.162 | 095 |
| Al-An'am | 6.165 | 090 |
| Al-Anbiyaa | 21.25 | 093 |
| Al-Anbiyaa | 21.25-29 | 029 |
| Al-Anbiyaa | 21.30 | 146 |
| Al-Anbiyaa | 21.32 | 147 |
| Al-Anbiyaa | 21.33 | 150 |
| Al-Anbiyaa | 21.47 | 083 |
| Al-Anbiyaa | 21.48-50 | 041 |
| Al-Anbiyaa | 21.73 | 102 |
| Al-Anbiyaa | 21.72-75 | 060 |
| Al-Anbiyaa | 21.78-82 | 060 |
| Al-Anbiyaa | 21.85-91 | 066 |
| Al-Anbiyaa | 21.92-93 | 026 |
| Al-Anbiyaa | 21.107-112 | 073 |
| Al-Anfal | 8.41-44 | 144 |
| Al-Anfal | 8.55-58 | 145 |
| Al-Anfal | 8.72 | 129 |
| Al-Ankabut | 29.45 | 098 |
| Al-Asr | 103.1-3 | 028 |
| Al-Baiyina | 98.5 | 102 |
| Al-Balad | 90.8 -18 | 126 |
| Al-Balad | 90.17-18 | 028 |
| Al-Baqara | 2.2-5 | 045 |
| Al-Baqara | 2.11-12 | 030 |
| Al-Baqara | 2.30 | 018 |
| Al-Baqara | 2.30 | 114 |
| Al-Baqara | 2.34 | 035 |
| Al-Baqara | 2.35 | 018 |
| Al-Baqara | 2.36 | 019 |
| Al-Baqara | 2.38-39 | 019 |
| Al-Baqara | 2.49-50 | 025 |
| Al-Baqara | 2.97-98 | 036 |
| Al-Baqara | 2.114 | 099 |
| Al-Baqara | 2.125 | 107 |
| Al-Baqara | 2.126-128 | 107 |
| Al-Baqara | 2.148-150 | 095 |
| Al-Baqara | 2.158 | 108 |
| Al-Baqara | 2.172 | 120 |
| Al-Baqara | 2.173 | 127 |
| Al-Baqara | 2.178-179 | 145 |
| Al-Baqara | 2.183-184 | 100 |
| Al-Baqara | 2.185 | 100 |
| Al-Baqara | 2.186 | 100 |
| Al-Baqara | 2.187 | 101 |
| Al-Baqara | 2.188 | 132 |
| Al-Baqara | 2.189 | 149 |
| Al-Baqara | 2.190-191 | 111 |
| Al-Baqara | 2.196-203 | 107 |
| Al-Baqara | 2.201 | 107 |
| Al-Baqara | 2.213 | 020 |
| Al-Baqara | 2.215 | 104 |
| Al-Baqara | 2.219 | 128 |
| Al-Baqara | 2.222-223 | 161 |
| Al-Baqara | 2.228 | 140 |
| Al-Baqara | 2.229-230 | 138 |
| Al-Baqara | 2.231 | 141 |
| Al-Baqara | 2.232 | 141 |

| Al-Baqara | 2.233 | 161 |
|---|---|---|
| Al-Baqara | 2.234 | 141 |
| Al-Baqara | 2.235 | 141 |
| Al-Baqara | 2.236-237 | 138 |
| Al-Baqara | 2.238-239 | 096 |
| Al-Baqara | 2.240-242 | 136 |
| Al-Baqara | 2.243 | 076 |
| Al-Baqara | 2.245 | 102 |
| Al-Baqara | 2.252-253 | 072 |
| Al-Baqara | 2.254 | 102 |
| Al-Baqara | 2.255 | 033 |
| Al-Baqara | 2.256 | 028 |
| Al-Baqara | 2.259 | 165 |
| Al-Baqara | 2.261-263 | 103 |
| Al-Baqara | 2.267 | 103 |
| Al-Baqara | 2.270-271, 273-274 | 104 |
| Al-Baqara | 2.275-276 | 131 |
| Al-Baqara | 2.278 | 131 |
| Al-Baqara | 2.280 | 130 |
| Al-Baqara | 2.282 | 134 |
| Al-Baqara | 2.283 | 131 |
| Al-Baqara | 2.286 | 051 |
| Al-Dukhan | 44.43-50 | 088 |
| Al-Dukhan | 44.51-59 | 087 |
| Al-Fat-h | 48.28-29 | 075 |
| Al-Fathiha | 1.1-4 | 093 |
| Al-Fathiha | 1.1-7 | 015 |
| Al-Falaq | 113.1-5 | 271 |
| Al-Furqan | 25.2 | 147 |
| Al-Furqan | 25.25 | 037 |
| Al-Furqan | 25.53 | 152 |
| Al-Furqan | 25.67 | 104 |

| Al-Hadid | 57.4 | 147 |
|---|---|---|
| Al-Hadid | 57.25 | 040 |
| Al-Hadid | 57.26-29 | 057 |
| Al-Hajj | 22.5 | 159 |
| Al-Hajj | 22.34-37 | 111 |
| Al-Hajj | 22.39-41 | 031 |
| Al-Hajj | 22.75 | 048 |
| Al-Hajj | 22.78 | 022 |
| Al-Haqqa | 69.13-18 | 076 |
| Al-Haqqa | 69.17 | 037 |
| Al-Haqqa | 69.19-32 | 086 |
| Al-Hashr | 59.22-24 | 093 |
| Al-Hud | 11.47-48 | 023 |
| Al-Hujurat | 49.9 | 026 |
| Al-Hujurat | 49.9-10 | 028 |
| Al-Hujurat | 49.11-12 | 125 |
| Al-Hujurat | 49.13 | 020 |
| Al-i'Imran | 3.2-3 | 042 |
| Al-i'Imran | 3.6 | 160 |
| Al-i'Imran | 3.8-9 | 051 |
| Al-i'Imran | 3.18-20 | 033 |
| Al-i'Imran | 3.33-34 | 053 |
| Al-i'Imran | 3.38-39 | 068 |
| Al-i'Imran | 3.31-34 | 112 |
| Al-i'Imran | 3.47-51 | 043 |
| Al-i'Imran | 3.64 | 29 |
| Al-i'Imran | 3.83 | 021 |
| Al-i'Imran | 3.84 | 021 |
| Al-i'Imran | 3.84 | 042 |
| Al-i'Imran | 3.85 | 021 |
| Al-i'Imran | 3.96-97 | 107 |
| Al-i'Imran | 3.102-103 | 094 |
| Al-i'Imran | 3.104 | 023 |

| | | |
|---|---|---|
| Al-i'Imran | 3.110 | 022 |
| Al-i'Imran | 3.110-115 | 120 |
| Al-i'Imran | 3.144 | 076 |
| Al-i'Imran | 3.147-148 | 051 |
| Al-i'Imran | 3.156-158 | 077 |
| Al-i'Imran | 3.159 | 113 |
| Al-i'Imran | 3.164 | 034 |
| Al-i'Imran | 3.185 | 076 |
| Al-i'Imran | 3.190-194 | 052 |
| Al-i'Imran | 3.200 | 031 |
| Al-Infitar | 82.7-8 | 161 |
| Al-Infitar | 82.10-12 | 036 |
| Al-Israa | 17.23-24 | 119 |
| Al-Israa | 17.23-40 | 122 |
| Al-Israa | 17.78-79 | 095 |
| Al-Israa | 17.101 | 064 |
| Al-Israa | 17.111,110 | 093 |
| Al-Jamu'a | 62.1-4 | 072 |
| Al-Jamu'a | 62.9-11 | 097 |
| Al-Jamu'a | 62.10 | 132 |
| Al-Kafirun | 109.1-6 | 115 |
| Al-Kahf | 18.13 | 165 |
| Al-Kahf | 18.18 | 165 |
| Al-Kahf | 18.25 | 165 |
| Al-Kahf | 18.45-49 | 078 |
| Al-Ma'arij | 70.1-35 | 080 |
| Al-Maida | 5.1-2 | 109 |
| Al-Maida | 5.2 | 130 |
| Al-Maida | 5.3 | 022 |
| Al-Maida | 5.3 | 128 |
| Al-Maida | 5.4 | 127 |
| Al-Maida | 5.6 | 095 |
| Al-Maida | 5.7 | 127 |

| | | |
|---|---|---|
| Al-Maida | 5.38-40 | 145 |
| Al-Maida | 5.44-45 | 042 |
| Al-Maida | 5.46 | 043 |
| Al-Maida | 5.90-91 | 128 |
| Al-Maida | 5.95-96 | 110 |
| Al-Maida | 5.97 | 109 |
| Al-Maida | 5.106 | 136 |
| Al-Muddaththir | 74.8-31 | 085 |
| Al-Muddaththir | 74.30-31 | 038 |
| Al-Mujadila | 58.2-5 | 143 |
| Al-Mujadila | 58.12 | 124 |
| Al-Mulk | 67.5(A.Y.'s) | 147 |
| Al-Muminun | 23.12-13 | 160 |
| Al-Muminun | 23.14(MA's) | 159 |
| Al-Mutaffifin | 83.4-12 | 082 |
| Al-Muzzammil | 73.2-4 | 096 |
| Al-Qadr | 97.1-5 | 044 |
| Al-Qadr | 97.3 | 101 |
| Al-Qaf | 50.9 | 036 |
| Al-Qaf | 50.20-23 | 037 |
| Al-Qaf | 50.39-40 | 096 |
| Al-Qasas | 28.51-55 | 047 |
| Al-Qasas | 28.76-77 | 025 |
| Al-Qasas | 28.77,79,81 | 105 |
| Al-Qasas | 28.81 | 025 |
| Al-Qiyamat | 75.1-15 | 083 |
| Al-Waqi'a | 56.1-10 | 086 |
| Al-Waqi'a | 56.27-38 | 087 |
| Al-Waqi'a | 56.1-26 | 089 |
| Al-Waqi'a | 56.39-56 | 088 |
| Al-Waqi'a | 56.57-59 | 160 |
| An-Nabaa | 78.1-40 | 081 |
| An-Nabaa | 78.6-7 | 152 |

| | | |
|---|---|---|
| An-Nabaa | 78.9-13 | 148 |
| An-Nahl | 16.2 | 035 |
| An-Nahl | 16.5-8 | 156 |
| An-Nahl | 16.10-11 | 154 |
| An-Nahl | 16.12 | 149 |
| An-Nahl | 16.13 | 151 |
| An-Nahl | 16.14 | 153 |
| An-Nahl | 16.15-16 | 152 |
| An-Nahl | 16.28-29 | 038 |
| An-Nahl | 16.30-32 | 038 |
| An-Nahl | 16.58-59 | 162 |
| An-Nahl | 16.61 | 086 |
| An-Nahl | 16.66 | 156 |
| An-Nahl | 16.67 | 155 |
| An-Nahl | 16.68 | 161 |
| An-Nahl | 16.68-69 | 156 |
| An-Nahl | 16.71-73 | 091 |
| An-Nahl | 16.79-80 | 157 |
| An-Nahl | 16.90 | 123 |
| An-Nahl | 16.94 | 124 |
| An-Nahl | 16.116-117 | 126 |
| An-Nahl | 16.125-128 | 023 |
| An-Najm | 53.1-18 | 074 |
| An-Naml | 27.15-19 | 061 |
| An-Naml | 27.90 | 029 |
| An-Nas | 114.1-6 | 171 |
| An-Nazia't | 79.1-5 | 037 |
| An-Nisaa | 4.1 | 157 |
| An-Nisaa | 4.2 | 137 |
| An-Nisaa | 4.3 | 115 |
| An-Nisaa | 4.4 (A.Y.'s) | 115 |
| An-Nisaa | 4.5 | 143 |
| An-Nisaa | 4.6 | 144 |

| | | |
|---|---|---|
| An-Nisaa | 4.7-10 | 135 |
| An-Nisaa | 4.11 | 136 |
| An-Nisaa | 4.12 | 137 |
| An-Nisaa | 4.15-16 | 142 |
| An-Nisaa | 4.19 | 117 |
| An-Nisaa | 4.20 -21 | 116 |
| An-Nisaa | 4.23 | 116 |
| An-Nisaa | 4.29-30 | 143 |
| An-Nisaa | 4.31-32 | 123 |
| An-Nisaa | 4.34 | 126 |
| An-Nisaa | 4.36 | 118 |
| An-Nisaa | 4.43 | 097 |
| An-Nisaa | 4.59 | 094 |
| An-Nisaa | 4.86 | 114 |
| An-Nisaa | 4.92 | 030 |
| An-Nisaa | 4.94 | 127 |
| An-Nisaa | 4.101-104 | 098 |
| An-Nisaa | 4.127-130 | 117 |
| An-Nisaa | 4.135 | 119 |
| An-Nisaa | 4.135 | 123 |
| An-Nisaa | 4.136 | 033 |
| An-Nisaa | 4.136 | 112 |
| An-Nisaa | 4.163-166 | 040 |
| An-Nisaa | 4.148-152 | 113 |
| An-Nisaa | 4.176 | 137 |
| An-Nur | 24.27-28 | 124 |
| An-Nur | 24.30-31 | 125 |
| An-Nur | 24.36-37 | 099 |
| An-Nur | 24.37 | 132 |
| An-Nur | 24.43 | 153 |
| An-Nur | 24.44 | 149 |
| An-Nur | 24.45 | 156 |
| An-Nur | 24.56 | 098 |

| Ar-Ra'd | 13.2 | 147 |
|---|---|---|
| Ar-Ra'd | 13.3 | 151 |
| Ar-Ra'd | 13.3 | 155 |
| Ar-Ra'd | 13.4 | 154 |
| Ar-Ra'd | 13.8 | 160 |
| Ar-Ra'd | 13.11 | 036 |
| Ar-Ra'd | 13.25 | 029 |
| Ar-Ra'd | 13.38-41 | 050 |
| Ar-Ra'd | 13.41 | 152 |
| Ar-Rahman | 55.3-4 | 160 |
| Ar-Rahman | 55.4 | 114 |
| Ar-Rahman | 55.5 | 149 |
| Ar-Rahman | 55.7 | 147 |
| Ar-Rahman | 55.7-9 | 131 |
| Ar-Rahman | 55.10-13 | 155 |
| Ar-Rahman | 55.14-15 | 020 |
| Ar-Rahman | 55.14-15 | 157 |
| Ar-Rahman | 55.19-20 | 152 |
| Ar-Rahman | 55.22 | 152 |
| Ar-Rahman | 55.24-25 | 152 |
| Ar-Rahman | 55.26-32 | 082 |
| Ar-Rahman | 55.33 | 151 |
| Ar-Rum | 30.17-18 | 096 |
| Ar-Rum | 30.38 | 104 |
| Ar-Rum | 30.39 | 131 |
| Ar-Rum | 30.54 | 090 |
| Ash-Shura | 42.30 | 890 |
| Ash-Shura | 42.39-43 | 129 |
| Ash-Shura | 42.49-50 | 090 |
| Ash-Shu'araa | 26.150-152 | 024 |
| Ash-Shu'araa | 26.181-184 | 025 |
| As-Saff | 61.6-9 | 072 |
| As-Saffat | 37.6 (M.P.'s) | 151 |

| As-Saffat | 37.75-82 | 055 |
|---|---|---|
| As-Saffat | 37.83-98 | 058 |
| As-Saffat | 37.114-122 | 064 |
| As-Saffat | 37.123-130 | 067 |
| As-Saffat | 37.131-138 | 059 |
| As-Saffat | 37.139-148 | 067 |
| As-Saffat | 37.164-166 | 035 |
| As-Sajda | 32.2 | 044 |
| As-Sajda | 32.8 (A.Y.'s) | 158 |
| As-Sajda | 32.9 | 159 |
| As-Sajda | 32.11 | 037 |
| At-Takwir | 81.19-21 | 035 |
| At-Talaq | 65.1-7 | 140 |
| At-Tariq | 86.6-7 | 160 |
| At-Tariq | 86.3 | 150 |
| At-Tauba | 9.17-18 | 099 |
| At-Tauba | 9.28 | 111 |
| At-Tauba | 9.30-33 | 069 |
| At-Tauba | 9.34 | 105 |
| At-Tauba | 9.36 | 111 |
| At-Tauba | 9.54 | 098 |
| At-Tauba | 9.60 | 105 |
| At-Tauba | 9.71-72 | 207 |
| At-Tauba | 9.103 | 101 |
| At-Tauba | 9.104 | 103 |
| At-Tin | 95.4 | 160 |
| Az-Zariyat | 51.12-14 | 083 |
| Az-Zariyat | 51.47 (A.Y.'s) | 148 |
| Az-Zariyat | 51.47 (M.A.'s) | 148 |
| Az-Zariyat | 51.56 | 028 |
| Az-Zumar | 39.5 | 149 |

| | | |
|---|---|---|
| Az-Zumar | 39.6 | 160 |
| Az-Zumar | 39.6 | 156 |
| Az-Zumar | 39.21 | 153 |
| Az-Zumar | 39.66 -70 | 079 |
| Az-Zumar | 39.71-75 | 084 |
| Fatir | 35.1 | 035 |
| Fatir | 35.2-3 | 036 |
| Fatir | 35.11 | 160 |
| Fatir | 35.12 | 153 |
| Fatir | 35.13 | 148 |
| Ha-Mim | 41.9-12 | 017 |
| Ibrahim | 14.4 | 048 |
| Ibrahim | 14.33 | 148 |
| Ibrahim | 14.35-41 | 058 |
| Luqman | 31.14-15 | 119 |
| Luqman | 31.16-19 | 116 |
| Maryam | 19.2-15 | 163 |
| Maryam | 19.12 | 068 |
| Maryam | 19.16 26 | 164 |
| Maryam | 19.16-34 | 070 |
| Maryam | 19. 27-34 | 164 |
| Maryam | 19.31 | 103 |
| Maryam | 19.55 | 103 |
| Maryam | 19.35-40 | 071 |
| Maryam | 19.49-58 | 066 |
| Maryam | 19.58 | 049 |
| Maryam | 19.66-72 | 078 |

| | | |
|---|---|---|
| Sad | 38.41-48 | 062 |
| Sad | 38.26 | 119 |
| Ta-ha | 20.25-36 | 065 |
| Ta-ha | 20.42-43 | 025 |
| Ta-ha | 20.53 | 155 |
| Ta-ha | 20.55 | 020 |
| Ta-ha | 20.130 | 096 |
| Ta-ha | 20.132 | 099 |
| Ta-ha | 20.100-112 | 085 |
| Ta-ha | 20.116-124 | 053 |
| Ya-Sin | 36.13-21 | 052 |
| Ya-Sin | 36.33-36 | 155 |
| Ya-Sin | 36.37-40 | 150 |
| Yunus | 10.13 | 029 |
| Yunus | 10.25-27 | 028 |
| Yunus | 10.37 | 046 |
| Yunus | 10.37-40 | 045 |
| Yunus | 10.47-52 | 048 |
| Yunus | 10.57-60 | 046 |
| Yunus | 10.71-72 | 054 |
| Yunus | 10.74-82 | 063 |
| Yunus | 10.75 | 064 |
| Yunus | 10.99-103 | 029 |
| Yusuf | 12.2-3 | 044 |
| Yusuf | 12.4-7 | 062 |
| Yusuf | 12.99-101 | 0063 |

# 9. Selected Ahadies for a Few Verses of the Holy Qur'an

The reports of the Prophet's sayings and deeds are called Ahadith (Ahadies).

"Sahih Bukhari" is a collection of sayings and deeds of Prophet Muhammad (s.a.w.), also known as the Sunnah / Sunnat. Bukhari lived a couple of centuries after the Prophet's death and worked extremely hard to collect his Ahadith. Bukhari (full name Abu Abdullah Muhammad bin Ismail bin Ibrahim bin al-Mughira al-Ja'fai) was born in 194 A.H. and died in 256 A.H. His collection of Hadith is considered second to none. He spent sixteen years compiling it, and ended up with 2,602 Hadith (9,082 with repetition). His criteria for acceptance into the collection were amongst the most stringent of all the scholars of Ahadith. Each report in his collection was checked for compatibility with the Qur'an, and the veracity of the chain of reporters had to be painstakingly established. Bukhari's collection is recognized by the overwhelming majority of the Muslim world to be one of the most authentic collections of the Sunnah of the Prophet (s.a.w.).

It is important to realize, however, that Bukhari's collection is not complete: there are other scholars who worked as Bukhari did and collected other authentic reports.

**Six major Hadith collections**

| Name | Collector |
|---|---|
| Sahih Bukhari | Imam Bukhari (d. 870) |
| Sahih Muslim | Muslim Ibn al-Hajjaj (d. 875) |
| Sunan Abi Da'ud | Abu Da'ud (d. 888) |
| Sunan al-Tirmidhi | al-Tirmidhi (d. 892) |
| Sunan al-Sughra | al-Nasa'i (d. 915) |
| Sunan Ibn Maja | Ibn Maja (d. 886) |

"In the name of Allah, the Compassionate, the Merciful. All praise is for Allah, the 'Rabb' of the Worlds. The Compassionate, the Merciful. Master of the Day of Judgment. O'Allah! You alone we worship and You alone we call on for help. O'Allah! Guide us to the right way. The way of those whom You have favored; not of those who have earned Your wrath, or of those who have lost the way." (Al-Fathiha: 1.1-7)1

## (1) a. Narrated by Ubaida bin As-Samit (r.a.a.):

"Allah's Apostle said, "Whoever does not recite Al-Fatiha in his prayer, his prayer is invalid." (Sahih Al-Bukhari: 1.723)

## b. Narrated by Abu Huraira (r.a.a.):

Allah's Apostle said, "When the Imam says: 'Ghair-il-Maghzubi 'Alaihim Walaz-zuallin (i.e., not the path of those who earn Your Anger, nor the path of those who went astray,' (1.7)), then you must say, 'Aameen', for if one's utterance of 'Aameen' coincides with that of the angels, then his past sins will be forgiven." (Sahih Al-Bukhari: 6.2)

"If anyone is looking for a religion other than Islam, then let it be known that it will not be accepted from him; and in the Hereafter he will be among the losers." (Al-i'Imran: 3.85)2

## (2) Narrated by Abu Huraira (r.a.a.):

"Then he further asked, "What is Islam?" Allah's Apostle replied, "To worship Allah Alone and none else, to offer prayers perfectly to pay the compulsory charity (Zakat) and to observe fasts during the month of Ramadan." Then the Prophet said,

"That was Gabriel who came to teach the people their religion." Abu 'Abdullah said: "He (the Prophet) considered all that as a part of faith." (Sahih Al-Bukhari: 1.47)

"Strive in the Way of Allah as you ought to strive with sincerity and discipline; He has chosen you and has not laid upon you any hardship in the observance of your faith - the faith of your father Ibrahim (Abraham). He named you Muslims before in prior scriptures and in this (The Qur'an), so that His Rasool may testify against you and you yourselves may testify against rest of the mankind. Therefore, establish Salaah, pay Zakah and hold fast to Allah; Who is your Protector - so what an excellent Protector and what a splendid Supporter!" (Al-Haj: 22.78)3

## (3) Narrated by Ibn 'Umar (r.a.a.):

"Zaid bin 'Amr bin Naufil went to Sham, enquiring about a true religion to follow. He met a Jewish religious scholar and asked him about their religion. He said, "I intend to embrace your religion, so tell me something about it." The Jew said, "You will not embrace our religion unless you receive your share of Allah's anger." Zaid said, "'I do not run except from Allah's anger, and I will never bear a bit of it if I have the power to avoid it. Can you tell me of some other religion?" He said, "I do not know any other religion except the Hanif." Zaid enquired, "What is Hanif?" He said, "Hanif is the religion of (the prophet) Abraham who was neither a Jew nor a Christian, and he used to worship none but Allah (Alone)." When Zaid heard their statement about (the religion of) Abraham, he left that place, and when he came out, he raised both his hands and said, "O Allah! I make You my Witness that I am on the religion of Abraham." (Sahih Al-Bukhari: 5.169)

"The fact is that Qarun (Korah) was one of Musa's people, but he rebelled against them. We had given him such treasures that their very keys were a heavy burden to a band of strong men. When his people said to him: "Do not exult, for Allah does not love the exultant. Rather seek, by means of what Allah has given you, to attain the abode of the Hereafter, while not neglecting your share in this world. Be good to others as Allah has been good to you, and do not seek mischief in the land, for Allah does not love the mischief-makers." Then We caused the earth to swallow him, together with his dwelling, and he had no host to help him against Allah; nor was he able to defend himself." (Al-Qasas: 28.76-77, 81)4

## (4) Narrated by Abu Huraira (r.a.a.):

"The Prophet (or 'Abul Qasim) said, "While a man was walking, clad in a two-piece garment and proud of himself with his hair well-combed, suddenly Allah made him sink into the earth and he will go on sinking into it till the Day of Resurrection." (Sahih Al-Bukhari: 7.680)

"Permission to fight back is hereby granted to the believers against whom war is waged and because they are oppressed (before this revelation, Muslims were not allowed to fight even for self defence); certainly Allah has power to grant them victory - those who have been unjustly expelled from their homes only because they said, "Our Lord is Allah." Had not Allah repelled some people by the might of others, the monasteries, churches, synagogues, and mosques in which Allah's praise is daily celebrated, would have been utterly demolished. Allah will certainly help those who help His cause; most surely Allah is Mighty, Powerful. These are the people who, if We establish them in the land, will establish Salaah and pay Zakah, enjoin justice and forbid evil; the final decision of all affairs is in the hands of Allah." (Al-Hajj: 22.39-41)5

## (5) Narrated by Malik (r.a.a.):

"We came to the Prophet and we were young men nearly of equal ages and we stayed with him for twenty nights. Allah's Apostle was a very kind man and when he realized our longing for our families, he asked us about those whom we had left behind. When we informed him, he said, "Go back to your families and stay with them and teach them (religion) and order them (to do good deeds). The Prophet mentioned things some of which I remembered and some I did not. Then he said, "Pray as you have seen me praying, and when it is the time of prayer, one of you should pronounce the call (Adhan) for the prayer and the eldest of you should lead the prayer." (Sahih Al-Bukhari: 9.352)

– "O believers! Believe in Allah, His Rasool, the Book which He has revealed to His Rasool, and every Book which He previously revealed. He who denies Allah, His angels, His Books, His Rasools and the Last Day has gone far astray." (An-Nisaa: 4.136)6

## (6) Narrated by Abu Huraira (r.a.a.):

One day while the Prophet was sitting in the company of some people, (the angel) Gabriel came and asked, "What is faith?" Allah's Apostle replied, 'Faith is to believe in Allah, His angels, (the) meeting with Him, His Apostles, and to believe in Resurrection."(Sahih Al-Bukhari: 1.47)

"Allah! There is no god but Him: the Living, the Eternal. He neither slumbers nor sleeps. To Him belongs all that is in the Heavens and the Earth. Who can intercede with Him without His permission? He knows what is before them and what is behind them. They cannot gain access to anything out of His knowledge except what He pleases. His throne is more vast than the heavens and the earth, and guarding of these both does not fatigue Him. He is the Exalted, the Supreme." (Al-Baqara: 2.255)7

## (7) Narrated by Abu Masud (r.a.a.):

"The Prophet said, "If somebody recited the last two Verses of Surat Al-Baqara at night, that will be sufficient for him."

Narrated Abu Huraira: "Allah's Apostle ordered me to guard the Zakat revenue of Ramadan. Then somebody came to me and started stealing of the foodstuff. I caught him and said, "I will take you to Allah's Apostle!" Then Abu Huraira described the whole narration and said:" That person said (to me), "(Please don't take me to Allah's Apostle and I will tell you a few words by which Allah will benefit you.) When you go to your bed, recite Ayat-al-Kursi (2.255) for then there will be a guard from Allah who will protect you all night long, and Satan will not be able to come near you till dawn." (When the Prophet heard the story) he said (to me), "He (who came to you at night) told you the truth although he is a liar; and it was Shaitan." (Sahih Al-Bukhari: 6.530)

"Allah Himself has testified to the fact that there is no god but Him and so do the angels and those who are well grounded in knowledge standing firm on justice. There is no Ilah (God) except Him, the Mighty, the Wise. Surely the only Deen (true religion and the Right Way of life) in the sight of Allah is Al-Islam: Those to whom the Book was given did not adopt ways different than this except out of envy among themselves, and after the true knowledge had come to them. They should know that Allah is swift in calling to account those who deny His revelations. So if they argue with you (O Muhammad), tell them: "I have submitted myself entirely to Allah and so have those who follow me." Then ask those who are given the Book and those who are illiterates: "Will you also submit yourselves to Allah?" If they become Muslims they shall be rightly guided but if they turn back, you need not worry, because your sole responsibility is to convey the Message. Allah is watching all His servants very closely." (Al-i'Imran: 3.18-20)8

## (8) a. Narrated by Abu Huraira (r.a.a.):

"Then he further asked, "What is Ihsan (perfection)?" Allah's Apostle replied, "To worship Allah as if you see Him, and if you cannot achieve this state of devotion then you must consider that He is looking at you."

(Sahih Al-Bukhari: 1.47)

**b.** "Then he further asked, "When will the Hour be established?" Allah's Apostle replied, "The answerer has no better knowledge than the questioner. But I will inform you about its portents.

- When a slave (lady) gives birth to her master.
- When the shepherds of black camels start boasting and competing with others in the construction of higher buildings. And the Hour is one of five things which nobody knows except Allah.

The Prophet then recited: "Verily, with Allah (Alone) is the knowledge of the Hour--." (31. 34) Then that man (Gabriel) left and the Prophet asked his companions to call him back, but they could not see him. Then the Prophet said, "That was Gabriel who came to teach the people their religion." Abu 'Abdullah said: He (the Prophet) considered all that as a part of faith. (Sahih Al-Bukhari: 1.47)

"Allah has done a great favor to the believers that He raised among them a Rasool from among themselves, reciting to them the Revelations of Allah, sanctifying them and teaching them the Book and Wisdom, although before this they were in manifest error." (Al-i'Imram: 3.164)9

### (9) Narrated by Hudhaifa (r.a.a.):

"Allah's Apostle said to us, "Honesty descended from the Heavens and settled in the roots of the hearts of men (faithful believers), and then the Qur'an was revealed and the people read the Qur'an, (and learnt it from it) and also learnt it from the Sunnah." Both Qur'an and Sunnah strengthened their (the faithful believers') honesty." (Sahih Al-Bukhari: 9.381)

"O Muhammad, say: "O mankind! I am the Rasool of Allah towards all of you from He to whom belongs the kingdom of the heavens and the earth. There is no deity but Him. He brings to life and causes to die. Therefore, believe in Allah and His Rasool, the unlettered Prophet (Muhammad) who believes in

Allah and His Word. Follow him so that you may be rightly guided." " (Al-A'raf: 7.158)10

## (10) Narrated by Jabir bin Abdullah (r.a.a.):

"The Prophet said, "I have been given five things which were not given to anyone else before me.

a. Allah made me victorious by awe, (by His frightening my enemies) for a distance of one month's journey.

b. The earth has been made for me (and for my followers) a place for praying and a thing to perform Tayammum, therefore anyone of my followers can pray wherever the time of a prayer is due.

c. The booty has been made Halal (lawful) for me yet it was not lawful for anyone else before me.

d. I have been given the right of intercession (on the Day of Resurrection).

e. Every Prophet used to be sent to his nation only but I have been sent to all mankind. (Sahih Al-Bukhari: 1.331)

You should know that guardian angels have indeed been appointed over you, who are noble writers, they know all that you do." (Al-Infitar: 82.10-12)11

## (11) Narrated by Ibn Abbas (r.a.a.):

"The Prophet narrating about his Lord and, "Allah ordered (the appointed angels over you) that the good and the bad deeds be written, and He then showed (the way) how (to write). If somebody intends to do a good deed and he does not do it, then Allah will write for him a full good deed (in his account with Him); and if he intends to do a good deed and actually did it, then Allah will write for him (in his account) with Him (its reward equal) from ten to seven hundred times to many more times: and if somebody intended to do a bad deed and he does not do it, then Allah will write a full good deed (in his account) with Him, and if he intended to do it (a bad deed) and actually did it, then Allah will write one bad deed (in his account)." (Sahih Al-Bukhari: 8.498)

"Each person has been assigned guardian angels before him and behind him, who watch him by the command of Allah. The fact is that Allah never changes the condition of a people until they intend to change it themselves. If Allah wants to afflict a people with misfortune, none can ward it off, nor they can find any protector besides Him." (Ar-Ra'd: 13.11)12

### (12) Narrated by Abu Huraira (r.a.a.):

The Prophet said, "Angels keep on descending from and ascending to the Heaven in turn, some at night and some by daytime, and all of them assemble together at the time of the Fajr and 'Asr prayers. Then those who have stayed with you overnight ascend unto Allah Who asks them, and He knows the answer better than they, "How have you left My slaves?" They reply, "We have left them praying as we found them praying." If anyone of you says "Aameen" (during the prayer at the end of the recitation of Surat-al-Fatiha), and the angels in Heaven say the same, and the two sayings coincide, all his past sins will be forgiven." (Sahih Al-Bukhari: 4.446)

"Certainly, We granted to Musa (Moses) and Haroon (Aaron) the Criterion of right and wrong, a light and a reminder for those righteous people who fear their Rabb though they have not seen Him, and dread the Day of Judgment. And now We have revealed this blessed Reminder (The Qur'an). Will you then deny it ?. " (Al-Anbiyaa: 21.48-50)13

### (13) a. Narrated by Abu Jamra (r.a.a.):

"I used to sit with Ibn 'Abbas and he made me sit on his sitting place. He requested me to stay with him in order that he might give me a share from his property. So I stayed with him for two months. Once he told (me) that when the delegation of the tribe of 'Abdul Qais came to the Prophet, the Prophet asked them, "Who are the people (i.e., you)? (Or) who are the delegates?" They replied, "We are from the tribe of Rabi'a." Then the Prophet said to them, "Welcome! O people (or O delegation of 'Abdul Qais)! Neither will you have disgrace nor will you regret." They said, "O Allah's Apostle! We cannot come to you except in the sacred month and there is the infidel tribe of Mudar intervening between you and us. So please order us to do something good (religious deeds) so that we may inform our people whom we have left behind (at home), and that we may enter Paradise (by acting on them)." Then they asked about drinks (what is legal and what is illegal). The Prophet ordered them to do four things and forbid them from four things. He ordered them to believe in Allah Alone and asked them, "Do you know what is meant by believing in Allah Alone?" They replied, "Allah and His Apostle know better." Thereupon the Prophet said, "It means:

- To testify that none has the right to be worshipped but Allah and Muhammad is Allah's Apostle.
- To offer prayers perfectly.
- To pay the Zakat (obligatory charity).
- To observe fast during the month of Ramadan.
- And to pay Al-Khumus (one fifth of the booty to be given in Allah's Cause).

Then he forbade them four things, namely, Hantam, Dubba, Naqir Ann Muzaffat and Muqaiyar: (These were the names of pots in which alcoholic drinks were prepared). (The Prophet mentioned the container of wine and he meant the wine itself). The Prophet further said (to them): "Memorize them (these instructions) and convey them to the people whom you have left behind." (Sahih Al-Bukhari: 1.50)

**b. Narrated by Abu Huraira (r.a.a.):**

"The Prophet said, "The Israelis used to be ruled and guided by Prophets: Whenever a prophet died, another would take over his place. There will be no prophet after me, but there will be Caliphs who will increase in number." The people asked, "O Allah's Apostle! What do you order us (to do)?" He said, "Obey the one who will be given the pledge of allegiance first. Fulfil their (i.e., the Caliphs) rights, for Allah will ask them about (any shortcoming) in ruling those Allah has put under their guardianship." (Sahih Al-Bukhari:)

"Then in the footsteps of those Prophets, We sent Isa (Jesus) the son of Maryam (Mary) confirming whatever remained intact from the Taurat in his time, and gave him the Injeel (Gospel) wherein was guidance and light, corroborating what was revealed in the Taurat; a guidance and an admonition to those who fear Allah." (Al-Maida: 5.46)14

## (14) Narrated by Abu Huraira (r.a.a.):

I heard Allah's Apostle saying, "I am the nearest of all the people to the son of Mary, and all the prophets are paternal brothers, and there has been no prophet between me and him (i.e. Jesus)." (Sahih Al Bukhari: 4.651)

"Surely We have revealed this (Qur'an) in the night of Qadr. And what will make you understand, what the night of Qadr is! The night of Qadr is better than one thousand months. The angels and the Spirit (Gabriel) come down with every decree, by the leave of their Rabb, that night is the night of Peace, till the break of dawn!. " (Al-Qadr: 97.1-5)15

## (15) Narrated by Aisha (r.a.a.):

"Allah's Apostle said, "Search for the Night of Qadr in the odd nights of the last ten days of Ramadan." (Sahih Al-Bukhari: 3.234)

"This Qur'an is not such as could be produced by anyone other than Allah; in fact it is the confirmation of prior revelations (Psalms, Torah, and Gospel) and fully explains the Holy Book (prior scriptures); there is no doubt in this fact that it is (revealed) from the Rabb of the Worlds. Do they say: "He (the Prophet) has forged it?" Tell them: "If what you say be true; then produce one Surah like this, you may even call to your aid anyone you want other than Allah." Nay! They do not believe that which they cannot grasp, for they have not yet seen its prophecy fulfilled. The same way those who passed before them disbelieved. But see what was the end of the wrongdoers! Of these people there are some who will believe in it and some will not: and your Rabb best knows the troublemakers." (Yunus: 10.37-40) 16

## (16) Narrated by Abu Huraira (r.a.a.):

"The Prophet said, "There was no prophet among the prophets but was given miracles because of which people had security or had belief, but what I was given was the Divine Inspiration which Allah revealed to me. So I hope that my followers will be more than those of any other prophet on the Day of Resurrection." (Sahih Al-Bukhari: 9.379)

"This is The Book in which there is no doubt. (Since its Author, Allah, the Creator of this universe, possesses complete knowledge, there is no room for doubt about its contents.) It is a guide for those who are God-conscious, who believe in the Unseen, who establish Salaah (five regular daily prayers) and spend in charity out of what We have provided for their sustenance; who believe in this Revelation (The Qur'an) which is sent to you (O Muhammad) and the Revelations which were sent before you (Torah, Psalms, "Gospel...) and firmly believe in the Hereafter. They are on True Guidance from their Rabb and they are the ones who will attain salvation." (Al-Baqara: 2.2-5)17

## (17) Narrated by Abu Huraira (r.a.a.):

The Prophet said, "Allah does not listen to a prophet as He listens to a prophet who recites the Qur'an in a loud and pleasant tone." Sufyan said, "This saying means: a prophet who regards the Qur'an as something that makes him dispense with many worldly pleasures." (Sahih Al-Bukhari: 6.542)

"This Qur'an is not such as could be produced by anyone other than Allah; in fact it is the confirmation of prior revelations (Psalms, Torah, and Gospel) and fully explains the Holy Book (prior scriptures); there is no doubt in this fact that it is (revealed) from the Rabb of the Worlds." (Yunus: 10.37)18

## (18) Narrated by Abu Huraira (r.a.a.):

"Allah's Apostle said, "Not to wish to be the like of except two men: A man whom Allah has taught the Qur'an and he recites it during the hours of the night and during the hours of the day, and his neighbor listens to him and says, 'I wish I had been given what has been given to so-and-so, so that I might do what he does'; and a man whom Allah has given wealth and he spends it on what is just and right, whereupon an other man may say, 'I wish I had been given what so-and-so has been given, for then I would do what he does.' "(Sahih Al-Bukhari: 6.544)

"Lest you say: "The Book was revealed only to two parties before us and we were unaware of what they read," or lest you say: "If the Book had been revealed to us, we could have followed its guidance better than them," a veritable sign has now come to you from your Rabb as a guidance and mercy. Who then is more unjust than the one who denies the revelations of Allah and turns away from them? Very soon those who turn away from Our revelations will face dreadful punishment for their aversion. Are they waiting for the angels or your Rabb to come down to them or are they waiting to be given a certain sign of your Rabb! On the Day when that certain sign of your Rabb appears, the belief will not profit that soul which did not believe before, or who, while professing to believe did not do good deeds. Say to them: "Wait if you will; we too are waiting"." (Al-An'am: 6.156-158)19

## (19) a. Narrated by Abu Huraira (r.a.a.):

"Allah's Apostle said, "The Hour will not be established until the sun rises from the West: and when the people see it, then whoever will be living on the surface of the earth will have faith, and that is (the time) when no good will it do to a soul to believe then, if it believed not before." (Sahih Al-Bukhari: 6.159)

## b. Narrated by Anas (r.a.a.):

The Prophet said, "No prophet was sent but that he warned his followers against the one-eyed liar (Ad-Dajjal). Beware! He is blind in one eye, and your Lord is not so, and there will be written between his (Ad-Dajjal's) eyes (the word) Kafir (i.e., disbeliever)." (This Hadith is also quoted by Abu Huraira and Ibn 'Abbas). (Sahih Al-Bukhari: 9.245.)

"We have conveyed Our Word to them over and over again in order that they may take heed. Those to whom the scriptures were given before this (Jews and Christians), they do recognize the Truth and believe in this (Qur'an). When it is recited to them they say: "We believe in it, surely this is the Truth from our Rabb: indeed we were Muslims even before this." They are the ones who will be given their reward twice, because they have endured with fortitude, repelling evil with good and giving in charity out of what We have given them. When they hear vain talk, they withdraw from it saying: "Our deeds are for us and yours for you; peace be on to you: we do not desire the way of ignorant"." (Al-Qasas: 28.51-55)20

## (20) Narrated by Anas (r.a.a.):

When the news of the arrival of the Prophet at Medina reached 'Abdullah bin Salam, he went to him to ask him about certain things, He said, "I am going to ask you about three things which only a Prophet can answer: What is the first sign of the Hour? What is the first food which the people of Paradise will eat? Why does a child attract the similarity to his father or to his mother?" The Prophet replied, "Gabriel has just now informed me of that." Ibn Salam said, "He (i.e. Gabriel) is the enemy of the Jews amongst the angels. The Prophet said, "As for the first sign of The Hour, it will be a fire that will collect the people from the East to the West. As for the first meal which the people of Paradise will eat, it will be the caudate (extra) lobe of the fish-liver. As for the child, if the man's discharge proceeds the woman's discharge, the child attracts the similarity to the man, and if the woman's discharge proceeds the man's, then the child attracts the similarity to the woman." On this, 'Abdullah bin Salam said, "I testify that none has the right to be worshipped except Allah, and that you are the Apostle of Allah." and added, "O Allah's Apostle! Jews invent such lies as make one astonished, so please ask them about me before they know about my conversion to Islam." The Jews came, and the Prophet said, "What kind of man is 'Abdullah bin Salam among you?" They replied, "The best of us and the son of the best of us and the most superior among us, and the son of the most superior among us." The Prophet said, "What would you think if 'Abdullah bin Salam should embrace Islam?" They said, "May Allah protect him from that." The Prophet repeated his question and they gave the same answer. Then 'Abdullah came out to them and said, "I testify that none has the right to be worshipped except Allah and that Muhammad is the Apostle of Allah!" On this, the Jews said, "He is the most wicked among us and the son of the most wicked among us." So they degraded him. On this, he (i.e. 'Abdullah bin Salam) said, "It is this that I was afraid of, O Allah's Apostle." (Sahih Al-Bukhari: 5.275.)

"Allah does not burden any human being with more than he can bear. Everyone will enjoy the credit of his deeds and suffer the debits of his evil-doings. The believers say: "Our Rabb!

Do not punish us if we forget or make a mistake. Our Rabb! Do not place on us a burden as You placed on those before us. Our Rabb! Lay not on us the kind of burden that we have no strength to bear. Pardon us, Forgive us, Have mercy on us. You are our Protector, help us against the unbelievers"." (Al-Baqara: 2.286)21

## (21) a. Narrated by Abu Masud Al Badri:

"Allah's Apostle said, "It is sufficient for one to recite the last two Verses of Surat-al-Baqara at night." (Sahih Al-Bukhari: 5.345)

## b. Narrated by Abu Burda's father (r.a.a.):

"Allah's Apostle said, "Any man who has a slave girl whom he educates properly, teaches good manners, manumits and marries her, will get a double reward. And if any man of the people of the Scriptures believes in his own prophet and then believes in me too, he will (also) get a double reward. And any slave who fulfills his duty to his master and to his Lord, will (also) get a double reward." (Sahih Al-Bukhari: 7.20.)

"So when he left them and the deities whom they worshipped besides Allah, We granted him descendants like Ishaq and Ya'qoob, and We made each of them a Prophet. We bestowed on them Our Mercy and We granted them honor of being mentioned with true high respect. Relate to them the story of Musa in the Book; surely he was a chosen man and was a Rasool, a Prophet. We called him from the right side of Mount Tur and honored him to come closer for exclusive conversation. We made his brother Haroon a Prophet with Our blessing and assigned him as his assistant. Also relate to them the story of Isma`il in the Book; he was a man of his word and was a Rasool, a Prophet. He commanded his people to establish Salaah and give Zakah, and was the one with whom his Rabb was well pleased. Also relate to them the story of Idris in the Book; he was a Truthful man, a Prophet. Whom We raised to a lofty place. These are some of the

Prophets on whom Allah bestowed His favors from among the descendants of Adam and of those whom We carried in the Ark with Nuh, and of the descendants of Ibrahim and Israel, and of those whom We guided and chose. Whenever the Revelations of the Compassionate (Allah) were recited to them, they fell to prostrate and weep." (Maryam: 19. 49-58)22

## (22) Narrated by Abdullah bin Umar (r.a.a.):

"Allah's Apostle said, "Surely! Everyone of you is a guardian and is responsible for his charges: The Imam (ruler) of the people is a guardian and is responsible for his subjects; a man is the guardian of his family (household) and is responsible for his subjects; a woman is the guardian of her husband's home and of his children and is responsible for them; and the slave of a man is a guardian of his master's property and is responsible for it. Surely, everyone of you is a guardian and responsible for his charges." (Sahih Al-Bukhari: 9.252)

"The Jews say: "Uzair (Azra) is the son of Allah," and the Christians say: "Messiah (Christ) is the son of Allah." That is what they say with their mouths, imitating the sayings of the former unbelievers. May Allah destroy them! How perverted they are! They (Jews and Christians) have taken their rabbis and priests to be their Lords beside Allah and so they did with Messiah (Jesus) the son of Maryam (Mary), although they were commanded in the Torah and the Gospel to worship none but One Ilah (Allah); besides Whom there is none worthy of worship. Exalted be He above those whom they associate with Him. They desire to extinguish the light of Allah with their mouths but Allah will not allow it to happen, for He seeks to perfect His light even though the disbelievers may dislike it. It is He Who has sent His Rasool with guidance and true Deen (faith) to make it prevail over all other deens (faiths) even though the mushrikin may hate it." (At-Tauba: 9.30-33)23

**(23) Narrated by Ibn Abbas (r.a.a.):**

"The Prophet said, "Allah said, 'The son of Adam tells a lie against me though he has no right to do so, and he abuses Me though he has no right to do so. As for his telling a lie against Me, it is that he claims that I cannot recreate him as I created him before; and as for his abusing Me, it is his statement that I have offspring. No! Glorified be Me! I am far from taking a wife or offspring.' "(Sahih Al-Bukhari: 6.9)

"O Muhammad, relate to them the story of Maryam in the Book (The Qur'an) when she withdrew from her family to a place in the East. She chose to be secluded from them. We sent to her Our angel and he appeared before her as a grown up man. She said: "I seek Rahman's (Allah's) protection against you, leave me alone if you are Godfearing". He said: "Don't be afraid, I am merely a messenger from your Rabb to tell you about the gift of a holy son." She said: "How shall I bear a son, no man has ever touched me nor am I unchaste?" The angel replied: "So shall it be - Your Rabb says: `It is easy for Me. We wish to make him a Sign for mankind and a blessing from Us' - and this matter has already been decreed." So she conceived the child and she retired with him to a remote place. The pains of childbirth drove her to the trunk of a palm-tree. She cried in her anguish: "Ah! Would that I had died before this, and been long forgotten!" An angel from beneath the palm-tree consoled her, saying: "Do not grieve! Your Rabb has provided a brook at your feet. If you shake the trunk of this palm-tree, it will drop fresh ripe dates in your lap. So eat, drink and refresh yourself. If you see anyone, tell him: `I have vowed a fast to Rahman (Allah), so I will not speak to anyone today'." Carrying the baby, she came back to her people. They said: "O Maryam! You have brought something hard to believe! O sister (a woman from the noble family) of Haroon! Your father was not a bad man nor your mother an unchaste woman". In response she merely pointed towards the baby. They said: "How can we talk to a babe in the cradle?" Whereupon the baby spoke out: "I am indeed a servant of Allah. He has given me the Book and made me a Prophet. His blessing is with me wherever I go. He has commanded me to establish Salah and give Zakah as long as I shall live. He has exhorted me to honor my mother and has not made me domineering, hard to deal with. Peace be upon me the day I was born, the day I shall die and the Day I shall be raised to life again". Such was Isa (Jesus) the son of Maryam, and this is the True statement about him concerning which they are in doubt." (Maryam: 19.16-34)24

### (24) Narrated by Ubaida (r.a.a.):

"The Prophet said, "If anyone testifies that none has the right to be worshipped but Allah Alone Who has no partners, and that Muhammad is His Slave and His Apostle, and that Jesus is Allah's Slave and His Apostle and His Word which He bestowed on Mary and a Spirit created by Him, and that Paradise is true, and Hell is true, Allah will admit him into Paradise with the deeds which he had done even if those deeds were few." (Junada, the sub-narrator said, " 'Ubaida added, 'Such a person can enter Paradise through any of its eight gates he likes.' ") (Sahih Al-Bukhari: 4.644)

"It is not befitting to the majesty of Allah that He Himself should beget a son! He is far above this (weakness to get a son for name, fame, help or continuity of race); for when He decrees a matter He need only say: "Be" and it is. Isa declared, "Verily Allah is my Rabb and your Rabb: therefore serve Him. This is a Right Way." Inspite of this, the sects from among them are divided concerning Jesus. So woe to the disbelievers who shall be punished after witnessing this Truth on the Great Day of Judgement. They will be able to see and hear very clearly on that Day when they will appear before Us! But today these wrong doers, neither want to hear nor see the Truth and, are in manifest error. O Muhammad, forewarn them about the Day of intense regret when this matter will be decided, even though at present they are paying no heed and do not believe. Ultimately, all things will perish and it is We, Who will inherit the earth and all that is on it, and to Us shall they return." (Maryam: 19.35-40)25

## (25) Narrated by Abu Sa'id Al Khudri (r.a.a.):

"During the lifetime of the Prophet some people said, "O Allah's Apostle! Shall we see our Lord on the Day of Resurrection?" The Prophet said, "Yes; do you have any difficulty in seeing the sun at midday when it is bright and there is no cloud in the sky?" They replied, "No." He said, "Do you have any difficulty in seeing the moon on a full moon night when it is bright and there is no cloud in the sky?" They replied, "No." The Prophet said, "(Similarly) you will have no difficulty in seeing Allah on the Day of Resurrection as you have no difficulty in seeing either of them. On the Day of Resurrection, a call-maker will announce, 'Let every nation follow that which they used to worship.' Then none of those who used to worship anything other than Allah like idols and other deities but will fall in Hell (Fire), till there will remain none but those who used to worship Allah, both those who were obedient (i.e. good) and those who were disobedient (i.e. bad) and the remaining party of the people of the Scripture. Then the Jews will be called upon and it will be said to them, 'Who did you use to worship?' They will say, 'We used to worship Ezra, the son of Allah.' It will be said to them, 'You are liars, for Allah has never taken anyone as a wife or a son. What do you want now?' They will say, 'O our Lord! We are thirsty, so give us something to drink.' They will be directed and addressed thus, 'Will you drink,' whereupon they will be gathered unto Hell (Fire) which will look like a mirage whose different sides will be destroying each other. Then they will fall into the Fire. Afterwards the Christians will be called upon and it will be said to them, 'Who did you use to worship?' They will say, 'We used to worship Jesus, the son of Allah.' It will be said to them, 'You are liars, for Allah has never taken anyone as a wife or a son,' Then it will be said to them, 'What do you want?' They will say what the former people have said. Then, when there remain (in the gathering) none but those who used to worship Allah (Alone, the real Lord of the Worlds) whether they were obedient or disobedient. Then (Allah) the Lord of the worlds will come to them in a shape nearest to the picture they had in their minds about Him. It will be said, 'What are you waiting for?' Every nation have followed what they used to worship.' They will reply, 'We left the people in the world when we were in great need of them and we did not take them as friends. Now we are waiting for our Lord Whom we used to worship.' Allah will say, 'I am your Lord.' They will say twice or thrice, 'We do not worship any besides Allah.' "(Sahih Al-Bukhari: 6.105)

"And remember when Isa (Jesus) the son of Maryam said: "O children of Israel! I am the Rasool of Allah towards you, confirming the Torah which came before me, and to give you good news of a Rasool that will come after me whose name shall be Ahmed (another name of Muhammad, meaning 'The praised one')." But when he (Muhammad) came to them with clear signs, they said "This is plain magic." Who could be more wrong than the one who invents falsehoods against Allah while he is being called towards Islam? Allah does not guide those who are wrongdoers. They seek to extinguish the Light of Allah with their mouths, but Allah will perfect His Light, much as the unbelievers may dislike it. It is He Who has sent His Rasool with the guidance and the religion of truth so that he may proclaim it over all religions, much as the Mushrikin may dislike it." (As-Saff: 61.6-9.)26

**(26) a. Narrated by Jubair bin Mu'tim (r.a.a.):**
"Allah's Apostle said, "I have five names: I am Muhammad and Ahmad; I am Al-Mahi through whom Allah will eliminate infidelity; I am Al-Hashir who will be the first to be resurrected,

the people being resurrected there after; and I am also Al-'Aqib (i.e. There will be no prophet after me)." (Sahih Al-Bukhari: 4.732)

## b. Narrated by Abu Huraira (r.a.a.):

"Allah's Apostle said, "By Him in Whose Hands my soul is, son of Mary (Jesus) will shortly descend amongst you people (Muslims) as a just ruler and will break the cross and kill the pig and abolish the Jizya (a tax taken from the non-Muslims who are in the protection of the Muslim government). Then there will be abundance of money and nobody will accept charitable gifts. (Sahih Al-Bukhari: 3.425)

"These are the revelations of Allah; We recite them to you in truth. Surely you, O Muhammad, are one of Our Rasools. These are the Rasools (which We have sent for the guidance of mankind). We have exalted some above others. To some Allah spoke directly; others He raised high in ranks; to Isa (Jesus) the son of Maryem (Mary) We gave clear Signs and supported him with the Holy Spirit. If Allah wished the people who received the clear signswould not have fought against each other; but they disputed as a result, there were some who believed while others rejected. Yet If Allah wanted, they would not have fought each other; but Allah does what He intends." (Al-Baqara: 2.252-253)27

## (27) Narrated by Abu Huraira (r.a.a.):

The Prophet said, "The Israelis used to be ruled and guided by prophets: Whenever a prophet died, another would take over his place. There will be no prophet after me, but there will be Caliphs who will increase in number." The people asked, "O Allah's Apostle! What do you order us (to do)?" He said, "Obey the one who will be given the pledge of allegiance first. Fulfil their (i.e., the Caliphs) rights, for Allah will ask them about (any shortcoming) in ruling those Allah has put under their guardianship." (Sahih Al-Bukhari: 4.661)

"O Muhammad, We have not sent you but as a blessing for all the worlds. Tell them: "It has been revealed to me that your God is One God - will you then become Muslims?" If they give no heed, tell them: "I have warned you all alike in complete fairness; now I do not know whether what you are threatened with is near or far. It is He Who knows your spoken words and hidden thoughts. I do not know whether this delay is a trial for you or you are being given respite for an appointed time."Finally the Prophet said: "O Rabb! Pass Your Judgment with fairness. And O People! Our Rabb is most Compassionate, Whose help we seek against the blasphemies you utter."" (Al-Anbiyaa: 21.107-112)28

## (28) Narrated by Ibn Umar (r.a.a.):

"Allah's Apostle said: "I have been ordered (by Allah) to fight against the people until they testify that none has the right to be worshipped but Allah and that Muhammad is Allah's Apostle, and offer the prayers perfectly and give the obligatory charity, so if they perform that, then they save their lives and property from me except for Islamic laws and then their reckoning (accounts) will be done by Allah." (Sahih Al-Bukhari: 1.24)

"By the star when it set, your companion (Muhammad) is neither astray, nor misguided, nor does he speak out of his own desire. This Qur'an is but an inspired revelation. He is being taught by one who is mighty, powerful (angel Gabriel); the one free from defects who became stable in the view. He stood poised at the uppermost horizon, then he drew near, coming closer within the length of two bows or even closer, and revealed to Allah's servant that what he was supposed to reveal. His (Muhammad's) own heart did not deny that which he saw. How can you, O unbelievers then, question what he saw? And he (Muhammad) saw him once again near Sidra-tul-

Muntaha (the Lot-tree at the farthest end of the seven heavens, beyond which none can pass). Near it is Janna-tul-M'awa (the rest-house of paradise). When that Lot-tree was covered with what covered it, his eyes did not turn aside nor did it exceed the limit: and he did indeed see some of his Rabb's greatest signs." (An-Najm: 53.1-18)29

**(29) Narrated by Malik bin Sasaa (r.a.a.):**

The Prophet said, "While I was at the House in a state midway between sleep and wakefulness, (an angel recognized me) as the man lying between two men. A golden tray full of wisdom and belief was brought to me and my body was cut open from the throat to the lower part of the abdomen and then my abdomen was washed with Zam-zam water and (my heart was) filled with wisdom and belief. Al-Buraq, a white animal, smaller than a mule and bigger than a donkey was brought to me and I set out with Gabriel. When I reachedthe nearest heaven. Gabriel said to the heavens gatekeeper, 'Open the gate.' The gatekeeper asked, 'Who is it?' He said, 'Gabriel.' The gatekeeper asked, 'Who is accompanying you?' Gabriel said, 'Muhammad.' The gatekeeper said, 'Has he been called?' Gabriel said, 'Yes.' Then it was said, 'He is welcomed. What a wonderful visit his is!' Then I met Adam and greeted him and he said, 'You are welcomed O son and a Prophet.' Then we ascended to the second heaven. It was asked, 'Who is it?' Gabriel said, 'Gabriel.' It was said, 'Who is with you?' He said, 'Muhammad' It was asked, 'Has he been sent for?' He said, 'Yes.' It was said, 'He is welcomed. What a wonderful visit his is!" Then I met Jesus and Yahya (John) who said, 'You are welcomed, O brother and a Prophet.' Then we ascended to the third heaven. It was asked, 'Who is it?' Gabriel said, 'Gabriel.' It was asked, 'Who is with you? Gabriel said, 'Muhammad.' It was asked, 'Has he been sent for?' 'Yes,' said Gabriel. 'He is welcomed. What a wonderful visit his is!' - (The Prophet added:). -There I met Joseph and greeted him, and he replied, 'You are welcomed, O brother and a Prophet!' Then we ascended to the 4th heaven and again the same questions and answers were exchanged as in the previous heavens. There I met Idris and greeted him. He said, 'You are welcomed O brother and Prophet.' Then we ascended to the 5th heaven and again the same questions and answers were exchanged as in previous heavens. There I met and greeted Aaron who said, 'You are welcomed O brother and a Prophet". Then we ascended to the 6th heaven and again the same questions and answers were exchanged as in the previous heavens. There I met and greeted Moses who said, 'You are welcomed O brother and a Prophet.' When I proceeded on, he started weeping and on being asked why he was weeping, he said, 'O Lord! Followers of this youth who was sent after me will enter Paradise in greater number than my followers.' Then we ascended to the seventh heaven and again the same questions and answers were exchanged as in the previous heavens. There I met and greeted Abraham who said, 'You are welcomed O son and a Prophet.' Then I was shown Al-Bait-al-Ma'mur (i.e., Allah's House). I asked Gabriel about it and he said, 'This is Al Bait-ul-Ma'mur where 70,000 angels perform prayers daily and when they leave they never return to it (but always a fresh batch comes into it daily).' Then I was shown Sidrat-ul-Muntaha (i.e., a tree in the seventh heaven) and I saw its Nabk fruits which resembled the clay jugs of Hajr (i.e. a town in Arabia), and its leaves were like the ears of elephants, and four rivers originated at its root, two of them were apparent and two were hidden. I asked Gabriel about those rivers and he said, 'The two hidden rivers are in Paradise, and the apparent ones are the Nile and the Euphrates.' Then fifty prayers were enjoined on me. I descended till I met Moses who asked me, 'What have you done?' I said, 'Fifty prayers have been enjoined on me.' He said, 'I know the people better than you, because I had the hardest experience to bring Bani Israel to obedience. Your followers cannot put up with such obligation. So, return to your Lord and request Him (to reduce the number of prayers.' I returned and requested Allah (for reduction) and He made it forty. I returned and (met Moses) and had a similar discussion, and then returned again to Allah for reduction and He made it thirty, then twenty, then ten, and then I came to Moses who repeated the same advice. Ultimately Allah reduced it to five. When I came to Moses again, he said, 'What have you done?' I said, 'Allah has made it five only.' He repeated the same advice but I said that I surrendered (to Allah's Final Order)' " Allah's Apostle was addressed by Allah, "I have decreed My obligation and have reduced the burden on My slaves, and I shall reward a single good deed as if it were ten good deeds." (Sahih Al-Bukhari: 4.429)

"Muhammad is not the father of any of your men (he is not going to leave any male heirs). He is the Rasool of Allah and the Seal of the Prophets. Allah has the knowledge of all things. O believers! Remember Allah as a frequent remembrance, and glorify Him morning and evening. It is He Who sends His blessings on you (believers) and so do His angels, that He may bring you out of darkness into light, for He is Merciful to the believers. On the Day of their meeting with Him, their greeting shall be: "Salaam (peace)!": and He has prepared for them a generous reward. O Prophet! Surely We have sent you as a witness, as a bearer of good news and as a Warner, and to call the people towards Allah by His leave and a lamp spreading light (guidance). Give good news to the believers that they shall have great blessings from Allah. Do not obey the unbelievers and the hypocrites, disregard their annoyances and put your trust in Allah; for Allah is sufficient as a disposer of affairs." (Al-Ahzab: 33.40-48)30

**(30) a. Narrated by Abu Huraira: (r.a.a.)**

"Allah's Apostle said, "My similitude in comparison with the other prophets before me, is that of a man who has built a house nicely and beautifully, except for a place of one brick in a corner. The people go about it and wonder at its beauty, but say: 'Would that this brick be put in its place!' So I am that brick, and I am the last of the Prophets." (Sahih Al-Bukhari: 4.735)

### b. Narrated by Jabir bin Abdullah (r.a.a.):

"Some angels came to the Prophet while he was sleeping. Some of them said, "He is sleeping." Others said, "His eyes are sleeping but his heart is awake." Then they said, "There is an example for this companion of yours." One of them said, "Then set forth an example for him." Some of them said, "He is sleeping." The others said, "His eyes are sleeping but his heart is awake." Then they said, "His example is that of a man who has built a house and then offered therein a banquet and sent an inviter (messenger) to invite the people. So whoever accepted the invitation of the inviter, entered the house and ate of the banquet, and whoever did not accept the invitation of the inviter, did not enter the house, nor did he eat of the banquet." Then the angels said, "Interpret this example to him so that he may understand it." Some of them said, "He is sleeping." The others said, "His eyes are sleeping but his heart is awake." And then they said, "The houses stands for Paradise and the call maker is Muhammad; and whoever obeys Muhammad, obeys Allah; and whoever disobeys Muhammad, disobeys Allah. Muhammad separated the people (i.e., through his message, the good is distinguished from the bad, and the believers from the disbelievers)." (Sahih Al-Bukhari: 9.385)

### c. Narrated by Abu Musa (r.a.a.):

"The Prophet said, "My example and the example of what I have been sent with is that of a man who came to some people and said, 'O people! I have seen the enemy's army with my own eyes, and I am the naked warner; so protect yourselves!' Then a group of his people obeyed him and fled at night proceeding stealthily till they were safe, while another group of them disbelieved him and stayed at their places till morning when the army came upon them, and killed and ruined them completely So this is the example of that person who obeys me and follows what I have brought (the Qur'an and the Sunna), and the example of the one who disobeys me and disbelieves the truth I have brought." (Sahih Al-Bukhari: 9.387)

"Indeed Allah and His angels send blessings on the Prophet. O believers, call for Allah's blessings on him and salute him with all respect." (Al-Ahzab: 33.56)31

## (31) Narrated by Abdur Rahman bin Abi Laila (r.a.a.):

Ka'b bin Ujrah met me and said, "Shall I not give you a present I got from the Prophet?" 'Abdur-Rahman said, "Yes, give it to me." I said, "We asked Allah's Apostle saying, 'O Allah's Apostle! How should one (ask Allah to) send blessings on you, the members of the family, for Allah has taught us how to salute you (in the prayer)?' He said, 'Say: O Allah! Send Your Mercy on Muhammad and on the family of Muhammad, as You sent Your Mercy on Abraham and on the family of Abraham, for You are the Most Praiseworthy, the Most Glorious. O Allah! Send Your Blessings on Muhammad and the family of Muhammad, as You sent your Blessings on Abraham and on the family of Abraham, for You are the Most Praiseworthy, the Most Glorious.' "(Sahih Al-Bukhari: 4.589)

"A questioner asked you about the punishment which is bound to happen. It is for the disbelievers and there is none to avert it. It will come from Allah, the Owner of the Ways of Ascent. The angels and the Spirit ascend to Him in a Day the measure of which is fifty thousand years. Therefore, endure with graceful patience. They see it (Day of Judgement) to be far-off: but We see it quite near. On that Day, the sky shall become like molten brass and the mountains like tufts of wool; even a close friend will not ask of his friend, though they will see each other. To save himself from the punishment of that Day, the culprit (disbeliever) will wish to give his children, his wife, his brother, his relatives - who gave him shelter - and all that is in the earth, in ransom to save himself. By no means! It will be the fire of hell, eager to pluck out his skull, it will be calling all those who try to escape and turn their back, who collected wealth and withheld it. Indeed, man has been created impatient, when evil befalls him, he becomes despondent; but when blessed with good fortune, he becomes stingy; with the exception of those who offer the Salah (prayer), remain steadfast in their Salaah (prayer), set aside a due share in their wealth for the beggars and the deprived, accept the truth of the Day of Judgment, dread the punishment of their Rabb - for none is secure from the punishment of their Rabb - and guard their private parts, except from their wives and those whom their right hands possess, for in their case they are not blameworthy. As for those who seek to go beyond this, they are transgressors. Those who keep their trusts and honor their promises, who stand firm in their testimonies and strictly guard their Salah (prayers). It is they who shall live with honor in paradise." (Al-Ma'arij: 70.1-35)32

## (32) a. Narrated by Jarir bin Abdullah (r.a.a.):

- "gave the pledge of allegiance to Allah's Apostle for the following:
- Offer prayers perfectly
- Pay the Zakat (obligatory charity)
- And be sincere and true to every Muslim." (Sahih Al-Bukhari: 1.54)

## b. Narrated by Ibn Umar:

"Allah's Apostle said, "Whoever misses the 'Asr prayer (intentionally) then it is as if he lost his family and property." (Sahih Al-Bukhari: 1.527)

"About what are they asking? About the mighty event - the theme of their disputes. Very soon they shall come to know; We repeat, very soon they shall come to know. Is it not true that We have spread the earth like a bed, and the mountains as pegs, created you in pairs, provided you rest in sleep, made the night a mantle, made the day to work for earning your livelihood, built above you seven firmaments, placed therein a shining lamp, sent down abundant water from the clouds, bringing forth grain, vegetation and gardens of luxurious growth? The Day of decision is already fixed. On that Day, the Trumpet shall be sounded and you shall come forth in multitude. The sky shall be opened as if there were doors. The mountains shall vanish as if they were a mirage. For sure, the hell shall lie in ambush, to become a home for the transgressors. There they shall live for ages, in it they shall taste neither refreshment nor drink, except scalding water and decaying filth: a fitting recompense for their deeds. For they never expected to be accountable, and wittingly rejected Our revelations. But We had recorded everything in a Book. It will be said: "Taste the fruits of your deeds! You shall have nothing but increase in punishment." On that Day, the righteous will certainly achieve their Heart's desires: beautiful gardens, vineyards; and young women of their own age, and overflowing cups; they shall hear no vanity, nor any falsehood; - a recompense from your Rabb and a gift beyond their account from the Compassionate, Who is the Rabb of the heavens, the earth and all that lies between them; before Whom no one shall be able to speak. On that Day, the Spirit (Gabriel) and the angels shall stand in their ranks; none shall speak except the one to whom the Compassionate (Allah) shall grant permission to speak, and he will speak straight to the point. That Day is a sure reality. Let him who desires, seek a way back to his Rabb. Indeed We have forewarned you of an imminent punishment which lies close-at-hand, on the Day when man shall see what his hands have sent forth and the unbeliever will cry: "I wish! I could remain merely dust."" (Al-Nabaa: 78.1-40)33

**(33) Narrated by Abu Huraira (r.a.a.):**
"Allah's Apostle said, "If any one of you improve (follows strictly) his Islamic religion then his good deeds will be rewarded ten times to seven hundred times for each good deed and a bad deed will be recorded as it is." (Sahih Al-Bukhari: 1.40)

"I swear by the Day of Resurrection, and I swear by the self reproaching soul! Does man think that We shall not be able to put his bones together? Why not? We are able to put together, in perfect order, the very tips of his fingers. But man wishes to keep on doing evil in the future as well. He questions: "When will this Day of Resurrection be?" Well, it will come when the sight shall be dazed, the moon will be eclipsed, and the sun and the moon will be brought together on that Day man will ask: "Is there any way to escape?" Nay! There will be no refuge. On that Day, the refuge will only be towards your Rabb. On that Day man shall be told about all his deeds, from the first to the last. Indeed, man shall bear witness against himself, even though he shall plead with excuses." (Al-Qiyamat: 75.1-15)34

**(34) a. Narrated by Abu Huraira (r.a.a.):**
"The Prophet said, "The sun and the moon will be folded up (deprived of their light) on the Day of Resurrection." (Sahih Al-Bukhari: 4.422)

**b. Narrated by Ibn Umar (r.a.a.):**
"On the Day of Resurrection the people will fall on their knees and every nation will follow their prophet and they will say, "O so-and-so! Intercede (for us with Allah)," till (the right) intercession is given to the Prophet (Muhammad) and that will be the day when Allah will raise him into a station of praise and glory (i.e. Al-Maqam-al-Mahmud). (Sahih Al-Bukhari: 6.242)

"When the Trumpet will be sounded, that Day will be a very difficult Day, not easy for the disbelievers. Leave Me and the one (Walid bin Mughirah, a staunch opponent of the Prophet) whom I created, alone. I gave him abundant resources, thriving sons, and made his life smooth and comfortable. Yet he hopes that I shall give him more. By no means! Because he has stubbornly denied Our revelations. Soon I shall make him suffer mounting calamities, surely he pondered and devised a plot. May he perish, how he plotted! Again, may he perish, how he plotted! He looked around, frowned and scowled, then he turned his back in scornful pride and said: "This is nothing but counterfeited magic, this is nothing but the word of a human being." Soon I shall cast him into Saqar. What will make you understand, what Saqar is? It is burning fire which leaves nothing and spares none. It shrivels human flesh. It is guarded by nineteen guards. We have appointed none but angels as wardens of the fire; and We have made their number a trial for the unbelievers, so that the People of the Book may be convinced and the faith of the true believers may be increased, and that no doubts will be left for the People of the Book and the believers, and that those in whose hearts there is a disease and the disbelievers may say: "What could Allah mean by this parable?" Thus, Allah leaves to stray whom He wills and guides whom He pleases. No one knows the forces of your Rabb except Himself, and this (Qur'an) is nothing but a reminder to mankind." (Al-Muddaththir: 74.8-31)35

## (35) Narrated by Anas bin Malik (r.a.a.):

"A man said, "O Allah's Prophet! Will Allah gather the non-believers on their faces on the Day of Resurrection?" He said, "Will not the One Who made him walk on his feet in this world, be able to make him walk on his face on the Day of Resurrection?" (Qatada, a subnarrator, said: Yes, By the Power of Our Lord!) (Sahih Al-Bukhari: 6.283)

"Many of them will be from the former and many from the later generations. As for those of the left hand - how unfortunate will be the people of the left hand! They will be in the midst of scorching winds and in boiling water: in the shade of a pitch-black smoke, neither cool nor refreshing. For they lived in comfort before meeting this fate. They persisted in heinous sins and used to say: "When we are dead and turned to dust and bones, shall we then be raised to life again? And our fore fathers, too?" Tell them: "Surely those of old and those of present age shall certainly be brought together on an appointed time of a known Day. Then, "O the mistaken rejecters, you shall eat of the Zaqqum tree, and fill your bellies with it; and drink on top of it scalding water; yet you shall drink it like a thirsty camel." Such will be their entertainment on the Day of Reckoning." (Al-Waqi'a: 56.39-56)36

## (36) a. Narrated by Anas (r.a.a.):

"The Prophet said, "Allah will say to that person of the (Hell) Fire who will receive the least punishment, 'If you had everything on the earth, would you give it as a ransom to free yourself (i.e. save yourself from this Fire)?' He will say, 'Yes.' Then Allah will say, 'While you were in the backbone of Adam, I asked you much less than this, i.e. not to worship others besides Me, but you insisted on worshipping others besides me.' "(Sahih Al-Bukhari: 4.551)

## b. Narrated by Abu Said Al Khudri (r.a.a.):

"Allah's Apostle said, "On the Day of Resurrection Death will be brought forward in the shape of a black and white ram. Then a call maker will call, 'O people of Paradise!' Thereupon they will stretch their necks and look carefully. The caller will say, 'Do you know this?' They will say, 'Yes, this is Death.' By then all of them will have seen it. Then it will be announced again, 'O people of Hell !' They will stretch their necks and look carefully. The caller will say, 'Do you know this?' They will say, 'Yes, this is Death.' And by then all of them will have seen it.

Then it (that ram) will be slaughtered and the caller will say, 'O people of Paradise! Eternity for you and no death. O people of Hell! Eternity foryou and no death.' " Then the Prophet recited: "And warn them of the Day of distress when the case has been decided, while (now) they are in a state of carelessness (i.e. the people of the world) and they do not believe." (19.39) (Sahih Al-Bukhari: 6.254)

"When the inevitable event will come to pass - no one will be able to deny its coming to pass - then some shall be abased and some exalted. The earth shall be shaken with severe shaking and the mountains shall be made to crumble with awful crumbling and become like scattered dust. Then you shall be divided into three groups: those on the right hand - how blessed shall be the people of the right hand; hose on the left hand - how damned shall be the people of the left hand; and foremost shall be the foremost. They will be nearest to Allah, in the gardens of bliss. Most of them will be from the former and a few from the later generations. They shall have the jeweled couches, reclining on them facing each other, and there shall wait on them the eternal youths with goblets, shining beakers and cups of pure wine, - which will neither pain their heads nor take away their senses. They shall have fruits of their own choice and flesh of fowls that they may desire, and dark eyed hurs (damsels), as lovely as well guarded pearls as a reward for their good deeds that they had done. There they shall not hear any vain talk nor sinful words, but only the greetings of "Peace be upon you! Peace be upon you!"" (Al-Waqi'a: 56.1-26)37

## (37) Narrated by Abu Huraira (r.a.a.):

"Allah's Apostle said, "The first group (of people) who will enter Paradise will be (glittering) like the moon when it is full. They will not spit or blow their noses or relieve nature. Their utensils will be of gold and their combs of gold and silver; in their centers the aloe wood will be used, and their sweat will smell like musk. Everyone of them will have two wives; the marrow of the bones of the wives' legs will be seen through the flesh out of excessive beauty. They, i.e., the people of Paradise) will neither have differences nor hatred amongst themselves; their hearts will be as if one heart and they will be glorifying Allah in the morning and in the evening." (Sahih Al-Bukhari: 4.468)

"Allah has the most excellent names (over ninety-nine attributes); call on Him by them; and shun those people who use profanity in His Names, such people shall be requited for their misdeeds." (Al-A'raf:7.180)38

## (38) a. Narrated by Abu Huraira (r.a.a.):

"Allah has ninety-nine Names, i.e., one hundred minus one, and whoever believes in their meanings and acts accordingly, will enter Paradise; and Allah is Witr (one) and loves 'the Witr' (i.e., odd numbers)." (Sahih Al-Bukhari: 8.419)

## b. Narrated by Abu Huraira (r.a.a.):

"Allah's Apostle said, "Whoever says: 'La ilaha illal-lah wahdahu la sharika lahu, lahu-l-mulk wa lahu-l-hamd wa huwa 'ala kulli shai'in qadir,' one hundred times will get the same reward as given for manumitting ten slaves; and one hundred good deeds will be written in his accounts, and one hundred sins will be deducted from his accounts, and it (his saying) will be a shield for him from Satan on that day till night, and nobody will be able to do a better deed except the one who does more than he." (Sahih Al-Bukhari: 8.412)

"O believers! When you rise up for Salaah (prayer), wash your faces and your hands as far as the elbows, wipe your heads with wet hands and wash your feet to the ankles. If you had an emission of semen, then take a full bath. However, if you are sick or on a journey or you have used the toilet or you had intercourse with your women (your wife) and you do not find any water then resort to Tayammum - find clean soil and rub your faces and hands with it. Allah does not wish to burden you; He only wishes to purify you and to perfect His favor upon you, so that you may be thankful." (Al-Maida: 5.6)39

## (39) Narrated by Abu Musa (r.a.a.):

"The Prophet said, "The example of the one who celebrates the Praises of his Lord (Allah) in comparison to the one who does not celebrate the Praises of his Lord, is that of a living creature compared to a dead one." (Sahih Al-Bukhari: 8.416)

""Establish Salah from the decline of the sun till the darkness of the night (Zuhr, Asr, Maghrib and Isha) and read at Fajr (dawn); for the reading at Fajr is witnessed (by the angels). During a part of the night, pray Tahajjud, an additional prayer for you (O Muhammad), very soon your Rabb may exalt you to 'Maqam-e-Mahmood' (a station of great glory)." " (Al-Israa: 17.78-79)40

## (40) a. Narrated by Ibn Masud (r.a.a.):

A man kissed a woman and then came to Allah's Apostle and told him of that, so this Divine Inspiration was revealed to the Prophet: "And offer Prayers perfectly at the two ends of the day, and in some hours of the night; (i.e. (five) compulsory prayers). Verily, the good deeds remove the evil deeds (small sins). That is a reminder for the mindful." (11.114) The man said, Is this instruction for me only?" The Prophet said, "It is for all those of my followers who encounter a similar situation." (Sahih Al-Bukhari: 6.209)

## b. Narrated by Ubaida bin As -Samit (r.a.a.):

"Allah's Apostle said, "Whoever does not recite Al-Fatiha in his prayer, his prayer is invalid." (Sahih Al-Bukhari: 1.723)

## c. Narrated by Abu Huraira (r.a.a.):

"The Prophet said, "No prayer is harder for the hypocrites than the Fajr and the 'Isha' prayers and if they knew the reward for these prayers at their respective times, they would certainly present themselves (in the mosques) even if they had to crawl." The Prophet added, "Certainly I decided to order the Mu'adhdhin (call-maker) to pronounce Iqama and order a man to lead the prayer and then take a fire flame to burn all those who had not left their houses so far for the prayer along with their houses." (Sahih Al-Bukhari: 1.626)

### d. Narrated by Abu Salama bin Abdur Rahman (r.a.a.):

"Abu Huraira said, "I heard Allah's Apostle saying, 'The reward of a prayer in congregation is twenty five times greater than that of a prayer offered by a person alone. The angels of the night and the angels of the day gather at the time of Fajr prayer.' " Abu Huraira then added, "Recite the Holy Book if you wish, for indeed, the recitation of the Qur'an in the early dawn (Fajr prayer) is ever witnessed."

### e. Narrated by 'Abdullah bin 'Umar (r.a.a.):

"The reward of the congregational prayer is twenty seven times greater (than that of the prayer offered by a person alone)." (Sahih Al-Bukhari: 1.621)

### f. Narrated by Jabir bin Abdullah (r.a.a.):

"Allah's Apostle said, "Whoever, after listening to the Azaan (for the prayer) says, 'O Allah, the Lord of this complete call and of this prayer, which is going to be established! Give Muhammad Al-Wasila and Al-Fazila and raise him to Al-Maqam-al-Mahmud which You have promised him,' will be granted my intercession for him on the Day of Resurrection." (Sahih Al-Bukhari: 6.243)

### g. Narrated by Abu Huraira (r.a.a.):

"Allah's Apostle said, "Whoever says, 'Subhan Allahi wa bihamdihi,' one hundred times a day, will be forgiven all his sins even if they were as much as the foam of the sea." (Sahih Al-Bukhari: 8.414)

"Therefore, O Prophet, bear with them in patience whatever they say, and keep on glorifying your Rabb before sunrise and before sunset. And glorify Him during a part of the night and after the prostration (prayers)." (Qaf: 50.39-40) 41

### (41) Narrated by Qais (r.a.a.):

"Jarir said, "We were with the Prophet and he looked at the moon--full-moon--and said, 'Certainly you will see your Lord as you see this moon and you will have no trouble in seeing Him. So if you can avoid missing (through sleep or business, etc.) a prayer before the sunrise (Fajr) and a prayer before sunset ('Asr), you must do so.' He then recited Allah's statement: And celebrate the praises of your Lord before The rising of the sun And before (its) setting." (50.39) Isma'il said, "Offer those prayers and do not miss them." (Sahih Al-Bukhari: 1.529)

"Guard your Salaah (obligatory regular prayers) especially the middle Salah and stand up with true devotion to Allah. If you are in danger, pray on foot or while riding; and when you are safe, remember Allah in the manner that He has taught you which you did not know before" (Al-Baqara: 2.238-239)42

### (42) a. Narrated by Ibn Umar (r.a.a.):

"Allah's Apostle said, "Whoever misses the 'Asr prayer (intentionally) then it is as if he lost his family and property." (Sahih Al-Bukhari: 1.527)

### b. Narrated by Abu Al Mahh (r.a.a.):

"We were with Buraida in a battle on a cloudy day and he said, "Offer the 'Asr prayer early as the Prophet said, "Whoever leaves the 'Asr prayer, all his (good) deeds will be annulled." (Sahih Al-Bukhari: 1.528)

### c. Narrated by Salih bin Khawwat (r.a.a.):

"Concerning those who witnessed the Fajr Prayer that was performed in the battle of Dhat-ur-Riqa' in the company of

Allah's Apostle: one batch lined up behind him while another batch (lined up) facing the enemy. The Prophet led the batch that was with him in one Rak'a, and he stayed in the standing posture while that batch completed their (two Rakat) prayer by themselves and went away, lining in the face of the enemy, while the other batch came and he (i.e. the Prophet) offered his remaining Rak'a with them, and then, kept on sitting till they completed their prayer by themselves, and he then finished his prayer with Taslim along with them."

Narrated Ibn Az-Zubair: Jabir said, "We were with the Prophet at Nakhl," and then he mentioned the Fajr prayer.

Narrated Al-Qasim bin Muhammad: The Prophet offered the Fajr prayer in the Ghazwa of Banu Anmar.(Sahih Al-Bukhari: 5.451)

"The reasons which prevent their contributions from being accepted are: that they disbelieve in Allah and His Rasool, that they come to offer Salah but reluctantly, and that they offer contributions but unwillingly." (At-Tauba: 9.54)43

## (43) Narrated by Abu Huraira (r.a.a.):

"The Prophet said, "No prayer is harder for the hypocrites than the Fajr and the 'Isha' prayers and if they knew the reward for these prayers at their respective times, they would certainly present themselves (in the mosques) even if they had to crawl." The Prophet added, "Certainly I decided to order the Mu'adhdhin (call-maker) to pronounce Iqama and order a man to lead the prayer and then take a fire flame to burn all those who had not left their houses so far for the prayer along with their houses." (Sahih Al-Bukhari: 1.626)

"His Light is found in those houses which Allah has sanctioned to be built for the remembrance of His name; where His praise is sung, in the mornings and in the evenings again and again, by such people whom neither business nor business profit can divert from the remembrance of Allah, nor from establishing Salah and nor from paying Zakah, for they fear the Day of Judgement when hearts will be overturned and eyes will be petrified." (An-Nur: 24.36-37)44

### (44) a. Narrated by Abu Qatada Al Aslami (r.a.a.):

"Allah's Apostle said, "If anyone of you enters a mosque, he should pray two Rakat before sitting." (Sahih Al-Bukhari: 1.435)

### b. Narrated by Abu Huraira (r.a.a.):

"Allah's Apostle said, "The reward of the prayer offered by a person in congregation is twenty five times greater than that of the prayer offered in one's house or in the market (alone). And this is because if he performs ablution and does it perfectly and then proceeds to the mosque with the sole intention of praying, then for every step he takes towards the mosque, he is upgraded one degree in reward and his one sin is taken off (crossed out) from his accounts (of deeds). When he offers his prayer, the angels keep on asking Allah's blessings and Allah's forgiveness for him as long as he is (staying) at his Musalla. They say, 'O Allah! Bestow Your blessings upon him, be Merciful and kind to him.' And one is regarded in prayer as long as one is waiting for the prayer." (Sahih Al-Bukhari: 1.620)

"It is the month of Ramadhan in which the Qur'an was revealed, a guidance for mankind with clear teachings showing the right way and a criterion of truth and falsehood. Therefore, anyone of you who witnesses that month should fast therein, and whoever is ill or upon a journey shall fast a similar number of days later on. Allah intends your well-being and does not want to put you to hardship. He wants you to complete the prescribed period so that you should glorify His Greatness and render thanks to Him for giving you guidance." (Al-Baqara: 2.185)45

**(45) a. Narrated by Talha bin Ubaidullah (r.a.a.):**

"A bedouin with unkempt hair came to Allah's Apostle and said, "O Allah's Apostle! Inform me what Allah has made compulsory for me as regards the prayers." He replied: "You have to offer perfectly the five compulsory prayers in a day and night (24 hours), unless you want to pray Nawafil." The bedouin further asked, "Inform me what Allah has made compulsory for me as regards fasting." He replied, "You have to fast during the whole month of Ramadan, unless you want to fast more as Nawafil." The bedouin further asked, "Tell me how much Zakat Allah has enjoined on me." Thus, Allah's Apostle informed him about all the rules (i.e. fundamentals) of Islam. The bedouin then said, "By Him Who has honored you, I will neither perform any Nawafil nor will I decrease what Allah has enjoined on me. Allah's Apostle said, "If he is saying the truth, he will succeed (or he will be granted Paradise)." (Sahih Al-Bukhari: 3.115)

**b. Narrated by Abu Huraira (r.a.a.):**

"Allah's Apostle said, "Fasting is a shield (or a screen or a shelter). So, the person observing fasting should avoid sexual relation with his wife and should not behave foolishly and impudently, and if somebody fights with him or abuses him, he should tell him twice, 'I am fasting." The Prophet added, "By Him in Whose Hands my soul is, the smell coming out from the mouth of a fasting person is better in the sight of Allah than the smell of musk. (Allah says about the fasting person), 'He has left his food, drink and desires for My sake. The fast is for Me. So I will reward (the fasting person) for it and the reward of good deeds is multiplied ten times." (Sahih Al-Bukhari: 3.118)

"When my servants question you about Me, tell them that I am very close to them. I answer the prayer of every suppliant when he calls Me; therefore, they should respond to Me and put their trust in Me, so that they may be rightly guided." (Al-Baqara: 2.186)46

## (46) Narrated by Abu Huraira (r.a.a.):

"Allah's Apostle said, "Allah said, 'I will declare war against him who shows hostility to a pious worshipper of Mine. And the most beloved things with which My slave comes nearer to Me, is what I have enjoined upon him; and My slave keeps on coming closer to Me through performing Nawafil (praying or doing extra deeds besides what is obligatory) till I love him, so I become his sense of hearing with which he hears, and his sense of sight with which he sees, and his hand with which he grips, and his leg with which he walks; and if he asks Me, I will give him, and if he asks My protection (Refuge), I will protect him; (i.e., give him My Refuge) and I do not hesitate to do anything as I hesitate to take the soul of the believer, for he hates death, and I hate to disappoint him." (Sahih Al-Bukhari: 8.509)

"Yet they were commanded nothing but to worship Allah, with their sincere devotion to Him, being True in their faith; to establish Salah (prayers); and to pay Zakah (poor due); and that is the infallible true Religion." (Al-Baiyina: 98.5)47

## (47) Narrated by Abu Sa'id Al-Khudri (r.a.a.):

"Allah's Apostle said, "There is no Zakat on less than five camels and also there is no Zakat on less than five Awaq (of silver). (5 Awaq = 22 Fransa Riyals of Yamen or 200 Dirhams.) And there is no Zakat on less than five Awsuq. (A special measure of food-grains, and one Wasq equals 60 Sa's.) (For gold 20, Dinars i.e. equal to 12 Guinea English. No Zakat for less than 12 Guinea (English) of gold or for silver less than 22 Fransa Riyals of Yamen.) (Sahih Al-Bukhari: 2.526)

"Whatever you spend in charity or whatever vow you make, surely Allah knows it. The wrongdoers shall have no helpers. To give charity in public is good, but to gives the poor in private is better and will remove from you some of your sins. Allah is aware of your actions. Charity is for those needy people who are engaged so much in the cause of Allah that they cannot move about in the land to earn their livelihood: the ignorant think that they are wealthy on account of their modest behavior. You can recognize them by their look because they do not make insistent demands on people. Whatever you spend on them, surely Allah knows it. Those who spend their wealth in charity by night and day, secretly and openly, they will have their reward from their Rabb. They shall have nothing to fear or to regret." (Al-Baqara: 2.270-271, 273-274)48

## (48) Narrated by Abu Zar (r.a.a.):

"Once I went to him (the Prophet) and he said, "By Allah in Whose Hands my life is," (or probably said, "By Allah, except Whom none has the right to be worshipped") "whoever had camels or cows or sheep and did not pay their Zakat, those animals will be brought on the Day of Resurrection far bigger and fatter than before and they will tread him under their hooves, and will butt him with their horns, and (those animals will come in circle): When the last does its turn, the first will start again, and this punishment will go on till Allah has finished the judgments amongst the people." (Sahih Al-Bukhari: 2.539)

"In fact the Sadaqat (Zakaah) collection is for the poor, the helpless, those employed to administer the funds, those whose hearts need to be won over to the truth, ransoming the captives, helping the destitute, in the Way of Allah and for the wayfarer. That is a duty enjoined by Allah; and Allah is All-Knowledgeable, Wise." (At-Tauba: 9.60)49

## (49) Narrated by Abu Huraira (r.a.a.):

"Allah's Apostle said, "The poor person is not the one who goes round the people and ask them for a mouthful or two (of meals) or a date or two but the poor is that who has not enough (money) to satisfy his needs and whose condition is not known to others, that others may give him something in charity, and who does not beg of people." (Sahih Al-Bukhari: 2.557)

"It is He who has created all kinds of plants, trellised and untrellised, the palm trees, the field crops with produce of different kinds, the olives and pomegranates, similar in kind yet different in taste. Eat of their fruit in their season and give away their Zakah on the harvest day. Do not be spend thrift, surely He does not love the spend thrifts." (Al-An'am: 6.141)50

## (50) Narrated by Anas (r.a.a.):

"When Abu Bakr sent me to (collect the Zakat from) Bahrein, he wrote to me the following :- (In the name of Allah, the Beneficent, the Merciful). These are the orders for compulsory charity (Zakat) which Allah's Apostle had made obligatory for every Muslim, and which Allah had ordered His Apostle to observe: Whoever amongst the Muslims is asked to pay Zakat accordingly, he should pay it (to the Zakat-collector) and whoever is asked more than that (what is specified in this script) he should not pay it; for twenty-four camels or less, sheep are to be paid as Zakat; for every five camels one sheep is to be paid, and if there are between twenty-five to thirty-five camels, one Bint Makhad is to be paid; and if they are between thirty-six to forty-five (camels), one Bint Labun is to be paid; and if they are between forty-six to sixty (camels), one Hiqqa is to be paid; and if the number is between sixty-one to seventy-five (camels), one Jadh'a is to be paid; and if the number is between seventy-six to ninety (camels), two Bint Labuns are to be paid; and if they are from ninety-one to one-hundred-and twenty (camels), two Hiqqas are to be paid; and if they are over one-hundred and-twenty (camels), for every forty (over one-hundred-and-twenty) one Bint Labun is to be paid, and for every fifty camels (over one-hundred-and-twenty) one Hiqqa is to be paid; and who ever has got only four camels, has to pay nothing as Zakat, but if the owner of these four camels wants to give something, he can. If the number of camels increases to five, the owner has to pay one sheep as Zakat. As regards the Zakat for the (flock) of sheep; if they are between forty and one-hundred-and-twenty sheep, one sheep is to be paid; and if they are between one-hundred-and-twenty to two hundred (sheep), two sheep are to be paid; and if they are between two-hundred to three-hundred (sheep), three sheep are to be paid; and for over three-hundred sheep, for every extra hundred sheep, one sheep is to be paid as Zakat. And if somebody has got less than forty sheep, no Zakat is required, but if he wants to give, he can. For silver the Zakat is one-fortieth of the lot (i.e. 2.5%), and if its value is less than two-hundred Dirhams, Zakat is not required, but if the owner wants to pay he can.'(Sahih Al-Bukhari: 2.534)

"Rather seek, by means of what Allah has given you, to attain the abode of the hereafter, while not neglecting your share in this world. Be good to others as Allah has been good to you, and do not seek mischief in the land, for Allah does not love the mischief makers." One day he came out before his people in his worldly glitter. Those who sought the life of this world said: "Would that we had the like of Qarun's fortune! He is indeed a very lucky man." Then We caused the earth to swallow him, together with his dwelling, and he had no host to help him against Allah; nor was he able to defend himself." (Al-Qasas: 28.77, 79, 81)51

## (51) Narrated by Abu Huraira (r.a.a.):

"Allah's Apostle, "Allah will not look, on the Day of Resurrection, at a person who drags his Izar (behind him) out of pride and arrogance." (Sahih Al-Bukhari: 7.679)

"Undoubtedly the first House for the worship of Allah ever built for mankind is the one at Bakka (Makkah), a blessed site and a guidance for all the worlds. In it are clear signs and the Station of Ibrahim (Abraham) where he used to worship. Whoever enters it is safe. Performance of Hajj (pilgrimage) to this House is a duty to Allah for all who can afford the journey to it; and the one who disobeys this commandment should know that Allah is Self-sufficient, beyond the need of anyone from the worlds." (Al-i'Imran: 3.96-97)52

### (52) Narrated by Aisha (r.a.a.):

(That she said), "O Allah's Apostle! We consider Jihad as the best deed. Should we not fight in Allah's cause?" He said, "The best Jihad (for women) is Hajj-mabrur (i.e. Hajj which is done according to the Prophet's tradition and is accepted by Allah)." (Sahih Al -Bukhari: 4.43)

"Complete the Hajj (obligatory pilgrimage to Makkah) and the Umrah (optional visit to Makkah) for the sake of Allah. If you are prevented from proceeding then send such offering for sacrifice as you can afford and do not shave your head until the offerings have reached their destination. But if any of you is ill or has an ailment in his scalp which necessitates shaving, he must pay ransom either by fasting or feeding the poor or offering a sacrifice. If in peacetime anyone wants to take the advantage of performing Umrah and Hajj together, he should make an offering which he can afford; but if he lack the means, let him fast three days during the Hajj and seven days on his return making ten days in all. This order is for the one whose household is not in the precincts of the Sacred Mosque. Fear Allah and know that Allah is strict in retribution. Hajj is in the well known months. He who undertakes to perform it must abstain from husband-wife relationship, obscene language, and wrangling during Hajj. Whatever good you do, Allah knows it. Take necessary provisions with you for the journey, and piety is the best provision of all. Fear Me, O people endowed with understanding. There is no blame on you if you seek the bounty of your Rabb during this journey. When you return from Arafat (stop at Muzdalifah and) praise Allah near Mash'ar-il-Haram. Praise Him as He has guided you, for before this you were from the people who had lost the Right Way. Then return from where the others return and ask Allah's forgiveness; surely Allah is

Forgiving, Merciful. When you have fulfilled your sacred duties, praise Allah as you used to praise your forefathers or with deeper reverence. There are some who say: "Our Rabb! Give us abundance in this world." Such people will not have any share in the hereafter. Celebrate the praises of Allah during these appointed days. If anyone hastens to leave Mina after two days or stays there a day longer there is no blame on him provided he spends these days in piety. Fear Allah and remember that you will surely be gathered before Him." (Al-Baqara: 2.196-203)53

## (53) Narrated by Abu Huraira (r.a.a.):

"Allah's Apostle said, "(The performance of) 'Umra is an expiation for the sins committed (between it and the previous one). And the reward of Hajj Mabrur (the one accepted by Allah) is nothing except Paradise." (Sahih Al-Bukhari: 3.1)

"Behold! Safa and Marwah (two hills in the Sacred Mosque) are among the symbols of Allah. So anyone who performs Hajj or Umrah (pilgrimage) to the House, there is no blame if one goes around both of them; and anyone who does good voluntarily should know that surely Allah knows the grateful." (Al-Baqara: 2.158)54

## (54) Narrated by Ibn Abbas (r.a.a.):

"The first lady(Hajira) to use a girdle was the mother of Ismael. She used a girdle so that she might hide her tracks from Sarah. Abraham brought her and her son Ismael while she was suckling him, to a place near the Ka'ba under a tree on the spot of Zam-zam, at the highest place in the mosque. During those days there was nobody in Mecca, nor was there any water. So he made them sit over there and placed near them a leather bag containing some dates, and a small water-skin containing some water, and set out homeward. Ishmael's mother followed him saying, "O Abraham! Where are you going, leaving us in this valley where there is no person whose company we may enjoy, nor is there anything (to enjoy)?" She repeated that to him many times, but he did not look back at her. Then she asked him, "Has Allah ordered you to do so?" He said, "Yes." She said, "Then He will not neglect us," and returned while Abraham proceeded onwards, and on reaching the Thaniya where they could not see him, he faced the Ka'ba, and raising both hands, invoked Allah saying the following prayers: "O our Lord! I have made some of my offspring dwell in a valley without cultivation, by Your Sacred House (Kaba at Mecca) in order, O our Lord, that they may offer prayer perfectly. So fill some hearts among men with love towards them, and (O Allah) provide them with fruits, so that they may give thanks." (14.37) Ishmael's mother went on suckling Ishmael and drinking from the water (she had). When the water in the water-skin had all been used up, she became thirsty and her child also became thirsty. She started looking at him, i.e., Ishmael) tossing in agony. She left him, for she could not endure looking at him, and found that the mountain of Safa was the nearest mountain to her on that land. She stood on it and started looking at the valley keenly so that she might see somebody, but she could not see anybody. Then she descended from Safa and when she reached the valley, she tucked up her robe and ran in the valley like a person in distress and trouble, till she crossed the valley and reached the Marwa mountain where she stood and started looking, expecting to see somebody, but she could not see anybody. She repeated that (running between Safa and Marwah) seven times. The Prophet said, "This is the source of the tradition of the walking of people between them (i.e., Safa and Marwah). When she reached the Marwah (for the last time) she heard a voice and she asked herself to be quiet and listened attentively. She heard the voice again and said, 'O, (whoever you may be)! You have made me hear your voice; have you got something to help me?" And behold! She saw an angel at the place of Zam-zam, digging the earth with his heel (or his wing), till water flowed from that place. She started to make something like a basin around it, using her hand in this way, and started filling her water-skin with water with her hands, and the water was flowing out after she had scooped some of it." The Prophet added, "May Allah bestow Mercy on Ishmael's mother! Had she let the Zam-zam (flow without trying to control it) (or had she not scooped from that water) (to fill her water-skin), Zam-zam would have been a stream flowing on the surface of the earth." The Prophet further added, "Then she drank (water) and suckled her child. The angel said to her, 'Don't be afraid of being neglected, for this is the House of Allah which will be built by this boy and his father, and Allah never neglects His people.' The House (i.e., Kaba) at that time was on a high place resembling a hillock, and when torrents came, they flowed to its right and left. She lived in that way till som people from the tribe of Jurhum or a family from Jurhum passed by her and her child, as they (i.e., the Jurhum people) were coming through the way of Kada'. They landed in the lower part of Mecca where they saw a bird that had the habit of flying around water and not leaving it. They said, 'This bird must be flying around water, though we know that there is no water in this valley.' They sent one or two messengers who discovered the source of water, and returned to inform them of the water. So, they all came (towards the water)." The Prophet added, "Ishmael's mother was sitting near the water. They asked her, 'Do you allow us to stay with you?' She replied, 'Yes, but you will have no right to possess the water.' They agreed to that." The Prophet further said, "Ishmael's mother was pleased with the whole situation as she used to love to enjoy the company of the people. So, they settled there, and later on they sent for their families who came and settled with them so that some families became permanent residents there. The child (i.e., Ishmael) grew up and learnt Arabic from them and (his virtues) caused them to love and admire him as he grew up, and when he reached the age of puberty they made him marry a woman from amongst them. After Ishmael's mother had died, Abraham came after Ishmael's marriage in order to see his family that he had left before, but he did not find Ishmael there. When he asked Ishmael's wife about him, she replied, 'He has gone in search of our livelihood.' Then he asked her about their way of living and their condition, and she replied, 'We are living in misery; we are living in hardship and destitution,' complaining to him. He said, 'When your husband returns, convey my salutation to him and tell him to change the threshold of the gate (of his house).' When Ishmael came, he seemed to have felt something unusual, so he asked his wife, 'Has anyone visited you?' She replied, 'Yes, an old man of so-and-so description came and asked me about you and I informed him, and he asked about our state of living, and I told him that we were living in a hardship and poverty.' On that Ishmael said, 'Did he advise you anything?' She replied, 'Yes, he told me to convey his salutation to you and to tell you to change the threshold of your gate.' Ishmael said, 'It was my father, and he has ordered me to divorce you. Go back to your family.' So, Ishmael divorced her and married another woman from amongst them (i.e. Jurhum). Then Abraham stayed away from them for a period as long as Allah wished and called on them again but did not find Ishmael. So he came to Ishmael's wife and asked her about Ishmael. She said, 'He has gone in search of our livelihood.' Abraham asked her, 'How are you getting on?' asking her about their sustenance and living. She replied, 'We are prosperous and well-off (i.e., we have everything in abundance).' Then she thanked Allah. Abraham said, 'What kind of food do you eat?' She said. 'Meat.' He said, 'What do you drink?' She said, 'Water." He said, "O Allah! Bless their meat and water." The Prophet added, "At that time they did not have grain, and if they had grain, he would have also invoked Allah to bless it." The Prophet added, "If somebody has only these two things as his sustenance, his health and disposition will be badly affected, unless he lives in Mecca."

The Prophet added," Then Abraham said Ishmael's wife, "When your husband comes, give my regards to him and tell him that he should keep firm the threshold of his gate.' When Ishmael came back, he asked his wife, 'Did anyone call on you?' She replied, 'Yes, a good-looking old man came to me,' so she praised him and added. 'He asked about you, and I informed him, and he asked about our livelihood and I told him that we were in a good condition.' Ishmael asked her, 'Did he give you any piece of advice?' She said, 'Yes, he told me to give his regards to you and ordered that you should keep firm the threshold of your gate.' On that Ishmael said, 'It was my father, and you are the threshold (of the gate). He has ordered me to keep you with me.' Then Abraham stayed away from them for a period as long as Allah wished, and called on them afterwards. He saw Ishmael under a tree near Zam-zam, sharpening his arrows. When he saw Abraham, he rose up to welcome him (and they greeted each other as a father does with his son or a son does with his father). Abraham said, 'O Ishmael! Allah has given me an order.' Ishmael said, 'Do what your Lord has ordered you to do.' Abraham asked, 'Will you help me?' Ishmael said, 'I will help you.' Abraham said, Allah has ordered me to build a house here,' pointing to a hillock higher than the land surrounding it." The Prophet added, "Then they raised the foundations of the House (i.e., the Ka'ba). Ishmael brought the stones and Abraham was building, and when the walls became high, Ishmael brought this stone and put it for Abraham who stood over it and carried on building, while Ishmael was handing him the stones, and both of them were saying, 'O our Lord! Accept (this service) from us, Verily, You are the All-Hearing, the All-Knowing.' The Prophet added, "Then both of them went on building and going round the Ka'ba saying: O our Lord Accept (this service) from us, Verily, You are the All-Hearing, the All-Knowing." (2.127) (Sahih Al-Bukhari: 4.583)

"For every nation We prescribed a way of sacrifice so that they may pronounce the name of Allah over the cattle which He has given them for food, but the object is one and the same: to remember that your God is one God; so submit yourselves to Him as a Muslim, and O Prophet, give good news to the humble, whose hearts tremble at the mention of Allah; who endure adversity with patience, who establish Salaah and spend in charity out of what we have given them. We have included the sacrificial camels among the Symbols of Allah, for there is much good for you in them. Therefore, pronounce the name of Allah over them while standing, and when they fall down on their sides after slaughter, when their movement completely stops, then eat of their meat, feed the contented (poor who do not ask) and the beggars (poor who ask). Thus We have subjected these animals to you so that you may be grateful. It is neither their meat nor their blood that reaches Allah; it is your piety that reaches Him. Thus, He has subjected these animals to you so that you may glorify Allah for giving you guidance, and O Prophet, give good news to those who do good to others." (Al-Hajj: 22.31-37)55

## (55) Narrated by Abu Bakr (r.a.a.):

"The Prophet delivered to us a sermon on the Day of Nahr. He said, "Do you know what is the day today?" We said, "Allah and His Apostle know better." He remained silent till we thought that he might give that day another name. He said, "Isn't it the Day of Nahr?" We said, "It is." He further asked, "Which month is this?" We said, "Allah and His Apostle know better." He remained silent till we thought that he might give it another name. He then said, "Isn't it the month of Dhul-Hijja?" We replied: "Yes! It is." He further asked, "What town is this?" We replied, "Allah and His Apostle know it better." He remained silent till we thought that he might give it another name. He then said, "Isn't it the forbidden (sacred) town (of Mecca)?" We said, "Yes. It is." He said, "No doubt, your blood and your properties are sacred to one another like the sanctity of this day of yours, in this month of yours, in this town of yours, till the day you meet your Lord. No doubt! Haven't I conveyed Allah's message to you?" They said, "Yes." He said, "O Allah! Be witness. So it is incumbent upon those who are present to convey it (this information) to those who are absent because the informed one might comprehend it (what I have said) better than the present audience, who will convey it to him. Beware! Do not renegade (as) disbelievers after me by striking the necks (cutting the throats) of one another." (Sahih Al- Bukhari: 2.797)

"It is not fitting for a believing man or a believing woman to have an option in their affairs when a matter has been decided by Allah and His Rasool; and whoever disobeys Allah and His Rasool has indeed strayed into a clearly wrong path." (Al-Ahzab: 33.36)56

### (56) a. Narrated by Anas bin Malik (r.a.a.):

"While the Prophet and I were coming out of the mosque, a man met us outside the gate. The man said, "O Allah's Apostle! When will be the Hour?" The Prophet asked him, "What have you prepared for it?" The man became afraid and ashamed and then said, "O Allah's Apostle! I haven't prepared for it much of fasts, prayers or charitable gifts but I love Allah and His Apostle." The Prophet said, "You will be with the one whom you love." (Sahih Al-Bukhari: 9.267)

### b. Narrated by Abu Huraira (r.a.a.):

"The Prophet (p.b.u.h) said, "Seven people will be shaded by Allah under His shade on the day when there will be no shade except His. They are:

(1) A just ruler;

(2) A young man who has been brought up in the worship of Allah, (i.e. worship Allah (Alone) sincerely from his childhood),

(3) A man whose heart is attached to the mosque (who offers the five compulsory congregational prayers in the mosque);

(4) Two persons who love each other only for Allah's sake and they meet and part in Allah's cause only;

(5) A man who refuses the call of a charming woman of noble birth for an illegal sexual intercourse with her and says: I am afraid of Allah;

(6) A person who practices charity so secretly that his left hand does not know what his right hand has given (i.e. nobody knows how much he has given in charity).

(7) A person who remembers Allah in seclusion and his eyes get flooded with tears." (Sahih Al-Bukhari: 2.504)

"and taught him how to convey his feelings and thoughts." (Ar-Rahman: 55.4)57

## (57) Narrated by Abu Burda's father (r.a.a.):

"Allah's Apostle said, -Any man who has a slave girl whom he educates properly, teaches good manners, manumits and marries her, will get a double reward. And if any man of the people of the Scriptures believes in his own prophet and then believes in me too, he will (also) get a double reward. And any slave who fulfills his duty to his master and to his Lord, will (also) get a double reward." (Sahih Al-Bukhari: 7.20)

"O Children of Adam! Put on your adornment (decent proper dress) when you attend your Masjid at the time of every prayer. Eat and drink, but do not be extravagant; surely He does not love the extravagant." (Al-A'raf: 7.31)58

## (58) Narrated by Aisha (r.a.a.):

"Allah's Apostle used to offer the Fajr prayer and some believing women covered with their veiling sheets used to attend the Fajr prayer with him and then they would return to their homes unrecognized. (Sahih Al -Bukhari: 1.368)

"When anyone greets you in a courteous manner, let your greetings be better than his - or at least return the same. Allah keeps account of everything." (An-Nisaa: 4.86)59

## (59) Narrated by Abu Huraira (r.a.a.):

"The Prophet said, "Allah created Adam in His picture, sixty cubits (about 30 meters) in height. When He created him, He said (to him), 'Go and greet that group of angels sitting there, and listen what they will say in reply to you, for that will be your greeting and the greeting of your offspring.' Adam (went and) said, 'As-Salamu alaikum (Peace be upon you).' They replied, 'As-Salamu-'Alaika wa Rahmatullah (Peace and Allah's Mercy be on you).' So they increased 'Wa Rahmatullah.' " The Prophet added: So whoever will enter Paradise, will be of the shape and picture of Adam. Since then the creation of Adam's (offspring) (i.e. stature of human beings is being diminished continuously) to the present time." (Sahih Al- Bukhari: 8.246)

"O Prophet! Enjoin your wives, daughters and the believing women that they should draw their outer garments over their persons. That is more proper, so that they may be recognized and not bothered." (Al-Ahzab: 33.59)60

## (60) Narrated by Safiya bint Shaiba (r.a.a.):

"Aisha used to say: "When (the Verse): 'They should draw their veils over their necks and bosoms,' was revealed, (the ladies) cut their waist sheets at the edges and covered their faces with the cut pieces." (Sahih Al- Bukhari: 6.282)

"We have enjoined man concerning his parents - his mother carries him in her womb while suffering weakness upon weakness and then weans him for two years - That's why We commanded him: "Give thanks to Me and to your parents, and keep in mind that, to Me is your final goal.. If they argue with you to commit shirk, of which you have no knowledge, then do not obey them; however you should still treat them kindly in this world, but follow the way of that individual who has turned to Me. After all, to Me is your return; then I will inform you about the reality of all that you have done." " (Luqman: 31.14-15)61

## (61) Narrated by Ibn Masud (r.a.a.):

"A man asked the Prophet "What deeds are the best?" The Prophet said: (1) To perform the (daily compulsory) prayers at their (early) stated fixed times, (2) To be good and dutiful to one's own parents. (3) and to participate in Jihad in Allah's Cause." (Sahih Al- Bukhari: 9.625)

"O believers! Stand firm for justice and bear true witness for the sake of Allah, even though it be against yourselves, your parents or your relatives. It does not matter whether the party is rich or poor - Allah is well wisher of both. So let not your selfish desires swerve you from justice. If you distort your testimony or decline to give it, then you should remember that Allah is fully aware of your actions." (An-Nisaa: 4.135)62

## (62) Narrated by Abdullah (r.a.a.):

"Allah's Apostle, thc true and truly inspired said, "(as regards your creation), every one of you is collected in the womb of his mother for the first forty days, and then he becomes a clot for an other forty days, and then a piece of flesh for an other forty days. Then Allah sends an angel to write four words: He writes his deeds, time of his death, means of his livelihood, and whether he will be wretched or blessed (in religion). Then the soul is breathed into his body. So a man may do deeds characteristic of the people of the (Hell) Fire, so much so that there is only the distance of a cubit between him and it, and then what has been written (by the angel) surpasses, and so he starts doing deeds characteristic of the people of Paradise and enters Paradise. Similarly, a person may do deeds characteristic of the people of Paradise, so much so that there is only the distance of a cubit between him and it, and then what has been written (by the angel) surpasses, and he starts doing deeds of the people of the (Hell) Fire and enters the (Hell) Fire." (Sahih Al-Bukhari: 4.549)

"You are the best nation which has ever been raised for the guidance of mankind. You enjoin good, forbid evil, and believe in Allah. Had the People of the Book (Jews and Christians) believed, it would surely have been better for them; among them some are believers but most of them are transgressors. Anyhow, they can do no harm to you except a trifling annoyance; if they do fight against you, they will turn their backs and run, getting no help from anywhere. Disgrace will be branded on them wherever they are found except when they get refuge under the favor of Allah or the patronage of other people; they have incurred the wrath of Allah and have been branded with misery because they disbelieved Allah's revelations and slew His prophets unjustly and because they disobeyed and transgressed the limits. Yet they are not all alike: there are some among the People of the Book who are upright, who recite the revelations of Allah all night long and then prostrate before Him; they believe in Allah and the Last Day they enjoin good and forbid evil and rush in emulating each other in good deeds. These are the righteous people. Whatever good they do, its reward will not be denied to them; Allah knows the righteous." (Al-i'Imran: 3.110-115)63

## (63) Narrated by Abu Huraira (r.a.a.):

"The Verse: "You (true Muslims) are the best of peoples ever raised up for mankind," means, the best of peoples for the people, as you bring them with chains on their necks till they embrace Islam. (Sahih Al- Bukhari: 6.80)

"If you avoid the heinous sins which you have been forbidden, We will do away with your small sins and cause you to enter a place of great honor (paradise). Do not envy that Allah has given some of you more than the others. Men will be rewarded according to their deeds and women will be rewarded according to theirs. Ask Allah for His grace. Surely Allah has perfect knowledge of everything." (An-Nisaa: 4.31-32)64

## (64) Narrated by Abu Huraira (r.a.a.):

"The Prophet said, "Avoid the seven great destructive sins." They (the people) asked, "O Allah's Apostle! What are they?" He said, "To join partners in worship with Allah; to practice sorcery; to kill the life which Allah has forbidden except for a just cause (according to Islamic law); to eat up usury (Riba), to eat up the property of an orphan; to give one's back to the enemy and fleeing from the battlefield at the time of fighting and to accuse chaste women who never even think of anything touching chastity and are good believers." (Sahih Al- Bukhari: 8.840)

"O believers! Let no men laugh at other men who may perhaps be better than themselves; and let no woman laugh at another woman, who may perhaps be better than herself. Do not defame through sarcastic remarks about one another, nor call one another by offensive nicknames. It is an evil thing to be called by a bad name after being a believer, and those who do not repent are the ones who are the wrongdoers. O believers! Avoid immoderate suspicion, for in some cases suspicion is a sin. Do not spy on one another, nor backbite one another (to say something about another behind ones back that if one hears it, dislikes it). Would any of you like to eat the flesh of his dead brother? Surely you would abhor it. Fear Allah; for Allah is the Accepter of repentance, Merciful." (Al-Hujurat: 49.11-12)65

## (65) Narrated by Abu Huraira (r.a.a.):

"Allah's Apostle said, "Beware of suspicion, for suspicion is the worst of false tales. And do not look for the others' faults, and do not do spying on one another, and do not practice Najsh, and do not be jealous of one another and do not hate one another, and do not desert (stop talking to) one another. And O, Allah's worshipers! Be brothers!" (Sahih Al- Bukhari: 8.92)

"Say to the believing men that they should lower their gaze and guard their modesty: that will make for greater purity for them: and Allah is well acquainted with all that they do. And say to the believing women that they should lower their gaze and guard their modesty; that they should not display their beauty and ornaments except what (must ordinarily) appear thereof; that they should draw their veils over their bosoms and not display their beauty except to their husbands their fathers their husbands' fathers their sons their husbands' sons their brothers or their brothers' sons or their sisters' sons or their women or the slaves whom their right hands possess or male servants free of physical needs or small children who have no sense of the shame of sex; and that they should not strike their feet in order to draw attention to their hidden ornaments. And O ye Believers! turn ye all together towards Allah that ye may attain Bliss." (An – Nur: 24.30-31)66

### (66) Narrated by Safiya bint Shaiba (r.a.a.):

"Aisha used to say: "When (the Verse): 'They should draw their veils over their necks and bosoms,' was revealed, (the ladies) cut their waist sheets at the edges and covered their faces with the cut pieces." (Sahih Al- Bukhari: 6.282)

"Have We not given him two eyes to observe? One tongue and two lips to control it? Then shown him the two high ways (good leading towards paradise and evil leading towards hell)? Yet he does not attempt to tackle the Aqabah (steep path)! And what will explain to you what the Aqabah is? It is the freeing of a neck (slave) from bondage; or the giving of food in a day of famine to an orphan relative, or to a needy in distress; besides this, he should be of those who believe, enjoin fortitude, encourage kindness and compassion. Such are the people of the right hand (going towards paradise)." (Al-Balad: 90.8 -18)67

**(67) Narrated by Abu Huraira (r.a.a.):**

"The Prophet said, "Whoever frees a Muslim slave, Allah will save all the parts of his body from the (Hell) Fire as he has freed the body-parts of the slave." Said bin Marjana said that he narrated that Hadith to 'Ali bin Al-Husain and he freed his slave for whom 'Abdullah bin Ja'far had offered him ten thousand Dirhams or one-thousand Dinars. (Sahih Al -Bukhari: 3.693)

"You are forbidden to eat the meat of any animal that dies by itself (dead body), blood, the flesh of swine (pork) and that on which any name other than Allah has been invoked; also that which is strangled to death, killed by a violent blow, killed by a headlong fall and of those beaten or gored to death; and that which has been partly eaten by a wild animal unless you are able to slaughter it before its death; also that which is sacrificed on altars or is divided by raffling of arrows. All these are sinful acts." (Al-Maida: 5.3)68

**(68) a. Narrated by Tarif Abi Tamima (r.a.a.):**

"I saw Safwan and Jundab and Safwan's companions when Jundab was advising. They said, "Did you hear something from Allah's Apostle?" Jundab said, "I heard him saying, 'Whoever does a good deed in order to show off, Allah will expose his intentions on the Day of Resurrection (before the people), and whoever puts the people into difficulties, Allah will put him into difficulties on the Day of Resurrection.' " The people said (to Jundab), "Advise us." He said, "The first thing of the human body to purify is the abdomen, so he who can eat nothing but good food (Halal and earned lawfully) should do so, and he who does as much as he can that nothing intervene between him and Paradise by not shedding even a handful of blood, (i.e., murdering) should do so." (Sahih Al-Bukhari: 9.266)

**b. Narrated by Abdullah bin Umar (r.a.a.):**

"The Prophet met Zaid bin 'Amr bin Naufil in the bottom of (the valley of) Baldah before any Divine Inspiration came to the

Prophet. A meal was presented to the Prophet but he refused to eat from it. (Then it was presented to Zaid) who said, "I do not eat anything which you slaughter in the name of your stone idols. I eat none but those things on which Allah's Name has been mentioned at the time of slaughtering." Zaid bin 'Amr used to criticize the way Quraish used to slaughter their animals, and used to say, "Allah has created the sheep and He has sent the water for it from the sky, and He has grown the grass for it from the earth; yet you slaughter it in other than the Name of Allah. He used to say so, for he rejected that practice and considered it as something abominable." (Sahih Al-Bukhari: 5.169)

"They ask you about drinking and gambling. Tell them: "There is great sin in both, although they may have some benefit for men; but the sin is greater than the benefit." They ask you what they should spend; tell them: "Whatever you can." Thus Allah makes His revelations clear to you, so that you may reflect upon." (Al-Baqara: 2.219)69

## (69) Narrated by Abu Amir or Abu Malik Al Ash'ari (r.a.a.):

"That he heard the Prophet saying, "From among my followers there will be some people who will consider illegal sexual intercourse, the wearing of silk, the drinking of alcoholic drinks and the use of musical instruments, as lawful. And there will be some people who will stay near the side of a mountain and in the evening their shepherd will come to them with their sheep and ask them for something, but they will say to him, 'Return to us tomorrow.' Allah will destroy them during the night and will let the mountain fall on them, and He will transform the rest of them into monkeys and pigs and they will remain so till the Day of Resurrection." (Sahih Al- Bukhari: 7.494b)

"If the debtor is in a difficulty, grant him time till it is easy for him to repay; but if you waive the sum by way of charity it will be better for you, if you understand it." (Al-Baqara: 2.280)70

**(70) Narrated by Abu Huraira (r.a.a.):**
"Allah's Apostle said, "A man used to give loans to the people and used to say to his servant, 'If the debtor is poor, forgive him, so that Allah may forgive us.' So when he met Allah (after his death), Allah forgave him." (Sahih Al -Bukhari: 4.687)

"O You who believe! Fear Allah and waive what is still due to you from usury if you are indeed believers." (Al-Baqara: 2.278)71

**(71) a. Narrated by Aun bin Abu Huzaifa (r.a.a.):**
"My father bought a slave who practiced the profession of cupping. (My father broke the slave's instruments of cupping). I asked my father why he had done so. He replied, "The Prophet forbade the acceptance of the price of a dog or blood, and also forbade the profession of tattooing, getting tattooed and receiving or giving Riba, (usury), and cursed the picture-makers."(Sahih Al- Bukhari: 3.299)

**b. Narrated by Abu Huzaifa (r.a.a.):**
"That he had bought a slave whose profession was cupping. The Prophet forbade taking the price of blood and the price of a dog and the earnings of a prostitute, and cursed the one who took or gave (Riba') usury, and the lady who tattooed others or got herself tattooed, and the picture-maker. ( Sahih Al- Bukhari: 7.845)

**c. Narrated by Abu Sa'id al Khudri (r.a.a.):**
"Once Bilal brought Barni (i.e. a kind of dates) to the Prophet and the Prophet asked him, "From where have you brought these?" Bilal replied, "I had some inferior type of dates and exchanged two Sas of it for one Sa of Barni dates in order to give it to the Prophet to eat." Thereupon the Prophet said, "Beware! Beware! This is definitely Riba (usury)! This is definitely Riba (Usury)! Don't do so, but if you want to buy (a superior kind of dates)

sell the inferior dates for money and then buy the superior kind of dates with that money." (Sahih Al- Bukhari: 3.506)

"If you are on a journey and cannot find a scribe to write down the transaction, then transect your business by taking possession of a pledge. If one of you entrust another with a pledge, let the trustee deliver the pledged property to its owner, and let him fear Allah, his Rabb. Do not conceal testimony, and whoever conceals it, his heart is surely sinful. Allah is aware of all your actions." (Al-Baqara: 2.283) 72

## (72) Narrated by Aisha (r.a.a.):

"The Prophet bought some foodstuff on credit for a limited period and mortgaged his armor for it." (Sahih Al- Bukhari: 3.686)

"O Prophet! If you and the believers divorce your wives, divorce them at the end of their prescribed periods, and count their prescribed periods accurately. Fear Allah, your Rabb. Do not expel them from their homes during their waiting period, nor they themselves should leave, unless they have committed an open lewdness. These are limits set by Allah; he that transgresses the limits of Allah will wrong his own soul. You never know, Allah may, thereafter, bring about some new situation of reconciliation. Then when their waiting period ends, either keep them honorably or part with them in an honorable way. Call to witness two honest persons among you, and O witnesses, bear witness equitably for the sake of Allah. This advice is being given to all who believe in Allah and the last Day. He that fears Allah may be provided a way out by Him, and given sustenance from the sources he could never imagine: for Allah is all sufficient for the person who puts his trust in Him. Surely Allah brings about what He pleases, and Allah has set a measure for all things. If you have any doubt concerning those of your wives who have ceased menstruating, then you should know that their waiting period will be three months, and the same will apply to those who have no menstruation due to young age or a disease. As for those who are pregnant, their waiting period will end with delivery. Allah will ease the hardship of those who fear Him. This is the command of Allah which He has sent down to you. He that fears Allah, will have his sins removed and his reward enlarged. Let those women, during their waiting period (Iddat), live where you yourselves live according to your means. You shall not harass them so as to make life intolerable for them. If they are pregnant, maintain them until their delivery: and if, after that, they suckle your offspring, compensate them and settle the matter of compensation with mutual consultation and in all fairness. But if you cannot bear with each other then let another woman suckle the baby for you. Let the rich man give according to his means, and the poor man give according to what Allah has given him. Allah does not charge a man with more than He has given him; soon Allah may bring ease after hardship." (At-Talaq: 65.1-7)73

### (73) Narrated by Abdullah bin Umar (r.a.a.):

"That he had divorced his wife while she was menstruating during the lifetime of Allah's Apostle. 'Umar bin Al-Khattab asked Allah's Apostle about that. Allah's Apostle said, "Order him (your son) to take her back and keep her till she is clean and then to wait till she gets her next period and becomes clean again, whereupon, if he wishes to keep her, he can do so, and if he wishes to divorce her he can divorce her before having sexual intercourse with her; and that is the prescribed period which Allah has fixed for the women meant to be divorced." (Sahih Al- Bukhari: 7.178)

"If any of your women are guilty of fornication, ask for four reliable witnesses from among yourselves against them; and if they testify and their guilt is proved, confine them to their houses until they die or Allah opens some other way out for them. And the two, whether married or unmarried, who are guilty of this offense, punish them both. If they repent and mend their ways, leave them alone. Surely Allah is the Acceptor of Repentance, Merciful." (An-Nisaa: 4.15-16)74

## (74) a. Narrated by Abu Huraira (r.a.a.):

"Allah's Apostle judged that the unmarried person who was guilty of illegal sexual intercourse be exiled for one year and receive the legal punishment (i.e., be flogged with one-hundred stripes). (Sahih Al- Bukhari: 8.819)

## b. Narrated by Jabir bin Abdullah Al Ansari (r.a.a.):

"A man from the tribe of Bani Aslam came to Allah's Apostle and informed him that he had committed illegal sexual intercourse and bore witness four times against himself. Allah's Apostle ordered him to be stoned to death as he was a married person. (Sahih Al-Bukhari: 8.805)

"Do not entrust your property which Allah has made a means of support for your family, to feebleminded people for investment in business, however, provide such people with food and clothing and speak to them nicely and give them good advice." (An-Nisaa: 4.5)75

## (75) Narrated by Al Mughira bin Shuba (r.a.a.):

"The Prophet said, "Allah has forbidden for you,

a. To be undutiful to your mothers,

b. To bury your daughters alive,

c. To not to pay the rights of the others (e.g., charity, etc.) and

d. To beg of men (begging). And Allah has hated for you

e. Vain, useless talk or that you talk too much about others,

f. To ask too many questions, (in disputed religious matters) and

g. To waste the wealth (by extravagance). (Sahih Al-Bukhari: 3.591)

"Whenever the news of a female child is announced to any one of them, his face darkens and he chokes with inward gloom. He hides himself from his people because of the bad news he has heard, asking himself whether he should retain her with disgrace or bury her in the dust. Beware! Evil is the judgement they make about Allah" (An-Nahal: 16.58-59)76.

## (76) a. Narrated by Asma bint Abi Bakr (r.a.a.):

"I saw Zaid bin Amr bin Naufil standing with his back against the Ka'ba and saying, "O people of Quraish! By Allah, none amongst you is on the religion of Abraham except me." He used to preserve the lives of little girls: If somebody wanted to kill his daughter he would say to him, "Do not kill her for I will feed her on your behalf." So he would take her, and when she grew up nicely, he would say to her father, "Now if you want her, I will give her to you, and if you wish, I will feed her on your behalf." (Sahih- Al-Bukhari: 5.169)

## b. Narrated by Warrad (r.a.a.):

"The clerk of Al-Mughira) Muawiya wrote to Al-Mughira: "Write to me what you have heard from Allah's Apostle." So he (Al-Mughira) wrote to him: Allah's Prophet used to say at the end of each prayer: "La ilaha illalla-h wahdahu la sharika lahu, lahul Mulku, wa lahul Hamdu wa hula ala kulli shai'in qadir. 'Allahumma la mani' a lima a'taita, wala mu'tiya lima mana'ta, wala yanfa'u dhuljadd minkal-jadd." He also wrote to him that the Prophet used to forbid

- Qil and Qal (idle useless talk or that you talk too much about others),
- Asking too many questions (in disputed religious matters);

- And wasting one's wealth by extravagance;
- And to be undutiful to one's mother
- And to bury the daughters alive
- And to prevent your favors (benevolence) to others (i.e. not to pay the rights of others)
- And asking others for something (except when it is unavoidable)." (Sahih Al-Bukhari: 9.395)

"Carrying the baby, she came back to her people. They said: "O Maryam! You have brought something hard to believe! O sister (a woman from the noble family) of Haroon! Your father was not a bad man nor your mother an unchaste woman". In response she merely pointed towards the baby. They said: "How can we talk to a baby in the cradle?" Whereupon the baby spoke out: "I am indeed a servant of Allah. He has given me the Book and made me a Prophet. His blessing is with me wherever I go. He has commanded me to establish Salah and give Zakah as long as I shall live. He has exhorted me to honor my mother and has not made me domineering, hard to deal with. Peace be upon me the day I was born, the day I shall die and the Day I shall be raised to life again". Such was Isa (Jesus) the son of Maryam, and this is the True statement about him concerning which they are in doubt." (Maryam: 19. 27-34)77

## (77) Narrated by Abu Huraira (r.a.a.):

"The Prophet said, "None spoke in cradle but three: (The first was) Jesus, (the second was) a man from Bani Israel called Juraij. While he was offering his prayers, his mother came and called him. He said (to himself), 'Shall I answer her or keep on praying?' (He went on praying) and did not answer her, his mother said, 'O Allah! Do not let him die till he sees the faces of prostitutes.' So while he was in his hermitage, a lady came and sought to seduce him, but he refused. So she went to a shepherd and presented herself to him to commit illegal sexual intercourse with her and then later she gave birth to a child and claimed that it belonged to Juraij. The people, therefore, came to him and dismantled his hermitage and expelled him out of it and abused him. Juraij performed the ablution and offered prayer, and then came to the child and said, 'O child! Who is your father?' The child replied, 'The shepherd.' (After hearing this) the people said, 'We shall rebuild your hermitage of gold,' but he said, 'No, of nothing but mud.'(The third was the hero of the following story) A lady from Bani Israel was nursing her child at her breast when a handsome rider passed by her. She said, 'O Allah! Make my child like him.' On that the child left her breast, and facing the rider said, 'O Allah! Do not make me like him.' The child then started to suck her breast again. (Abu Huraira further said, "As if I were now looking at the Prophet sucking his finger (in way of demonstration.") After a while the people passed by, with a lady slave and she (i.e. the child's mother) said, 'O Allah! Do not make my child like this (slave girl)! , On that the child left her breast and said, 'O Allah! Make me like her.' When she asked why, the child replied, 'The rider is one of the tyrants while this slave girl is falsely accused of theft and illegal sexual intercourse.' " (Sahih Al-Bukhari: 4.645)

# References:

Site - http://www.iiu.edu.my/deed/hadith/bukhari/index.html

**Translation of Sahih Bukhari** by **M. Muhsin Khan**

| Volume & Hadis No. | Page No |
|---|---|
| Sahih Al-Bukhari: 1.24 | 196 |
| Sahih Al-Bukhari: 1.331 | 180 |
| Sahih Al-Bukhari: 1.368 | 227 |
| Sahih Al-Bukhari: 1.40 | 203 |
| Sahih Al-Bukhari: 1.47 | 175 |
| Sahih Al-Bukhari: 1.47 | 179 |
| Sahih Al-Bukhari: 1.47 | 177 |
| Sahih Al-Bukhari: 1.47 | 179 |
| Sahih Al-Bukhari: 1.50 | 183 |
| Sahih Al-Bukhari: 1.54 | 202 |
| Sahih Al-Bukhari: 1.435 | 213 |
| Sahih Al-Bukhari: 1.527 | 202 |
| Sahih Al-Bukhari: 1.527 | 211 |
| Sahih Al-Bukhari: 1.528 | 211 |
| Sahih Al-Bukhari: 1.529 | 211 |
| Sahih Al-Bukhari: 1.620 | 213 |
| Sahih Al-Bukhari: 1.621 | 210 |
| Sahih Al-Bukhari: 1.626 | 212 |
| Sahih Al-Bukhari: 1.626 | 210 |
| Sahih Al-Bukhari: 1.723 | 174 |
| Sahih Al-Bukhari: 1.723 | 209 |
| Sahih Al-Bukhari: 2.504 | 227 |
| Sahih Al-Bukhari: 2.526 | 216 |
| Sahih Al-Bukhari: 2.534 | 218 |
| Sahih Al-Bukhari: 2.539 | 216 |
| Sahih Al-Bukhari: 2.557 | 217 |

| Volume & Hadis No. | Page No |
|---|---|
| Sahih Al-Bukhari: 2.797 | 226 |
| Sahih Al-Bukhari: 3.1 | 220 |
| Sahih Al-Bukhari: 3.115 | 214 |
| Sahih Al-Bukhari: 3.118 | 215 |
| Sahih Al-Bukhari: 3.234 | 184 |
| Sahih Al-Bukhari: 3.299 | 235 |
| Sahih Al-Bukhari: 3.425 | 194 |
| Sahih Al-Bukhari: 3.506 | 236 |
| Sahih Al-Bukhari: 3.591 | 239 |
| Sahih Al-Bukhari: 3.693 | 233 |
| Sahih Al-Bukhari: 4.43 | 219 |
| Sahih Al-Bukhari: 4.66 | 183 |
| Sahih Al-Bukhari: 4.422 | 204 |
| Sahih Al-Bukhari: 4.429 | 198 |
| Sahih Al-Bukhari: 4.446 | 182 |
| Sahih Al-Bukhari: 4.468 | 207 |
| Sahih Al-Bukhari: 4.549 | 230 |
| Sahih Al-Bukhari: 4.551 | 206 |
| Sahih Al-Bukhari: 4.583 | 224 |
| Sahih Al-Bukhari: 4.589 | 201 |
| Sahih Al-Bukhari: 4.644 | 192 |
| Sahih Al-Bukhari: 4.645 | 241 |
| Sahih Al Bukhari: 4.651 | 184 |
| Sahih Al-Bukhari: 4.661 | 195 |
| Sahih Al-Bukhari: 4.687 | 235 |
| Sahih Al-Bukhari: 4.732 | 194 |

# 10.
# The Life of Hazrat Muhammad (Sallallahu Alaihi Wasallam)

## Muhammad's (s.a.w.) family

Muhammad (s.a.w.) was born in Mecca (Makkah), Arabia, on Monday, 12 Rabi' Al-Awwal (2 August A.D. 570). His mother, Aminah, was the daughter of Wahb Ibn 'Abdu Manaf of the Zahrah family. His father, Abdullah, was the son of Abdul Muttalib. His genealogy has been traced to the noble house of Ismaeel, the son of Prophet Abraham in about the fortieth descent.

Muhammad's (s.a.w.) father died before his birth. When he was six years old his mother died and the doubly orphaned Muhammad (s.a.w.) was put under the charge of his grandfather Abdul Muttalib who took tender care of him. But the old chief died two years afterwards. On his deathbed he confided to his son Abu Talib the charge of the little orphan.

When Muhammad (s.a.w.) was twelve years old, he accompanied his uncle Abu Talib on a mercantile journey to Syria, and they proceeded as far as Basra. The journey lasted for some months. It was at Basra that the Christian monk Bahirah met Muhammad (s.a.w.). He is related to have said to Abu Talib: "Return with this boy and guard him against the hatred of the Jews, for a great career awaits your nephew." After this journey, the youth of Muhammad (s.a.w.) seems to have been passed uneventfully, but all authorities agree in ascribing to him such correctness of manners and purity of morals as were rare among the people of Mecca. The fair character and the honorable bearing of the unobtrusive youth won the approbation of the citizens of Mecca, and by common consent he received the title of "Al Ameen," (The Faithful).

In his early years, Muhammad (s.a.w.) was not free from the cares of life. He had to watch the flocks of his uncle, who, like the rest of the Bani Hashim, had lost the greater part of his wealth. From youth to manhood he led an almost solitary life. The lawlessness rife among the Meccans, the sudden outbursts of causeless and bloody quarrels among the tribes frequenting the Fair of Ohadh (the Arabian Olympia) and the immorality and skepticism of the Quraish, naturally caused feelings of pity and sorrow in the heart of the sensitive youth. Such scenes of social misery and religious degradation were characteristic of a depraved age.

These are nearly all the public acts related by historians in which Muhammad (s.a.w.) took part in the first fifteen years of his marriage to Khadijah. As for his private life he is described to have been ever helpful to the needy and the helpless. His uncle, Abu Talib, had fallen into distress through his endeavors to maintain the old position of his family. Muhammad (s.a.w.) being rather rich at this time by his alliance with Khadijah, tried to discharge part of the debt of gratitude and obligation which he owed to his uncle by undertaking the bringing up and education of his son Ali. A year later he adopted Aqeel, another of his uncle's sons. Khadijah had three sons and four daughters before marrying Muhammad (s.a.w). All the males died in childhood, but in loving Ali he found much consolation.

## Muhammad (s.a.w.) Settled Meccan Disputes:

When Muhammad (s.a.w.) reached thirty-five years, he settled by his judgement a grave dispute which threatened to plunge the whole of Arabia into a fresh series of her oft-recurring wars. In rebuilding the Sacred House of the Ka'ba in A.D. 605, the question arose as to who should have the honor of raising the black stone (Hajr-e-aswad) , the most holy relic of that House, into its proper place. Each tribe claimed that honor. The senior citizen advised the disputants to accept for their arbitrator the first man to enter from a certain gate. The proposal was agreed upon, and the first man who entered the gate was Muhammad (s.a.w.) "Al-Ameen." His advice satisfied all the contending parties. He ordered the stone to be placed on a piece of cloth and each tribe to share the honor of lifting it up by taking hold of a part of the cloth. The stone was thus deposited in its place, and the rebuilding of the House was completed without further interruption.

It is related that, about this time, a certain Usman, Ibn Huwairith (Haris), supported by Byzantine gold, made an attempt to convert the territory of Hijaz into a Roman dependency, but the attempt failed, chiefly through the instrumentality of Muhammad (s.a.w.).

## Muhammad (s.a.w.) and Meditation

Muhammad (s.a.w.) was now approaching his fortieth year, and his mind was ever engaged in profound contemplation and reflection. Before him lay his country, bleeding and torn by fratricidal wars and intolerable dissensions; his people, sunk in barbarism, addicted to the observation of rites and superstitions, were, with all their desert virtues, lawless and cruel. His two visits to Syria had opened to him a scene of unutterable moral and social desolation, rival creeds and sects tearing each other to pieces, carrying their hatred to the valleys and deserts of Hijaz, and rending the townships of Arabia with their quarrels and bitterness.

For years after his marriage, Muhammad (s.a.w.) had been accustomed to secluding himself in a cave in Mount Hira, a few miles from Mecca. To this cave he used to go for prayer and meditation, sometimes alone and sometimes with his family. There, he often spent whole nights in deep thought and profound communion with the Unseen yet All-Knowing Allah of the Universe. It was during one of those retirements and in the still hours of the night, when no human sympathy was near, that an angel came to him to tell him that he was the Messenger of Allah sent to reclaim a fallen people to the knowledge and service of their Lord.

## Muhammad's (s.a.w.) First Revelation

Renowned compilers of authentic traditions of Islam agree on the following account of the first revelations received by the Prophet. Muhammad (s.a.w.) would seclude himself in the cave of Mount Hira and worship three days and nights. He would, whenever he wished, return to his family at Mecca and then go back again, taking with him the necessities of life. Thus he continued to return to Khadijah from time to time until one day the revelation came down to him and the Angel Gabriel (Jibraeel) appeared to him and said: "Read!" But as Muhammad (s.a.w.) was illiterate, having never received any instruction in reading or writing, he said to the angel: "I am not a reader." The angel took hold of him and squeezed him as much as he could bear, and then said again: "Read!" The Prophet said: "I am not a reader." The Angel again seized the Prophet and squeezed him and said: "Read! In the Name of your Lord, Who has created (all that exists), has created man from something that clings. Read! And your Lord is the Most Generous, Who has taught (the writing) by the pen, has taught man that which he knew not." (Surah 96: 1-5)

## Early Years of Prophethood: Muhammad (s.a.w.) Speaks with Khadijah and Waraqah

Then the Prophet repeated the words with a trembling heart. He returned to Khadijah from Mount Hira and said: "Wrap me up! Wrap me up!" She wrapped him in a garment until his fear was dispelled. He told Khadijah what had occurred and that he was becoming either a soothsayer or one smitten with madness.

She replied: "Allah forbid! He will surely not let such a thing happen, for you speak the truth, you are faithful in trust, you bear the afflictions of the people, you spend in good works what you gain in trade, you are hospitable and you assist your fellow men. Have you seen anything terrible?" Muhammad (s.a.w.) replied: 'Yes," and told her what he had seen. Whereupon, Khadijah said: "Rejoice, O dear husband and be cheerful. He in Whose hands stands Khadijah's life bears witness to the truth of this fact, that you will be the prophet to this people."

Then she arose and went to her cousin Waraqah Ibn Naufil, who was old and blind and who knew the Scriptures of the Jews and the Christians, and is stated to have translated them into Arabic. When she told him of what she had heard, he cried out: "Holy! Holy! Verily, this is the Namus (The Holy Spirit) who came to Moses. He will be the prophet of his people. Tell him this and bid him be brave of heart." When the two men met subsequently in the street, the blind old student of the Jewish and Christian Scriptures spoke of his faith and trust: "I swear by Him in Whose hand Waraqah's life is, Allah has chosen you to be the prophet of this people. They will call you a liar, they will persecute you, they will banish you, they will fight against you. Oh, that I could live to those days., I would fight for these." And he kissed him on his forehead.

## Muhammad (s.a.w.) Begins Preaching

The first vision was followed by a considerable period, during which Muhammad (s.a.w.) suffered much mental depression. The angel spoke to the grieved heart of hope and trust and of the bright future when he would see the people of the earth crowding into the one true faith. His destiny was unfolded to him when, wrapped in profound meditation, melancholy and sad, he felt himself called by a voice from heaven to arise and preach. O you (Muhammad) (s.a.w.) enveloped (in garments)! Arise and warn! And your Lord (Allah) magnify! (Surah 74: 1-3) He arose and engaged himself in the work to which he was called. Khadijah was the first to accept his mission. She was to believe in the revelations, to abandon the idolatry of her people and to join him in purity of heart and in offering up prayers to Allah the Almighty.

## Muhammad (s.a.w.) Speaks with Abu Talib

At the beginning of his mission, Muhammad (s.a.w.) - hereinafter called the Prophet - opened his soul only to those who were attached to him and tried to free them from the gross practices of their forefathers. After Khadijah, his cousin Ali was the next companion. The Prophet used often to go into the desert around Mecca with his wife and young cousin that they might together offer their heart felt thanks to the Lord of all nations for His manifold blessings.

Once they were surprised by Abu Talib, the father of Ali. He said to the Prophet: "O son of my brother, what is this religion you are following?" "It is the religion of Allah of His Angels, of His Messengers and of our ancestor Abraham," answered the Prophet. "Allah has sent me to His servants, to direct them towards the truth, and you, O my uncle, are the most worthy of all. It is meet that I should thus call upon you and it is meet that you should accept the truth and help in spreading it." Abu Talib replied: "Son of my brother, I cannot abjure the religion of my fathers; but by the Supreme Lord, while I am alive, none shall dare to injure you." Then turning towards Ali, the venerable chief asked what religion was his. Ali answered: "O father, "I believe in Allah and His Prophet and go with him." Abu Talib replied: "Well my son, he will not call you to anything except what is good, therefore you are free to go with him."

After Ali, Muhammad's (s.a.w.) adopted son Zaid became a convert to the new faith. He was followed by Abu Bakr, a leading member of the Quraish tribe and an honest, wealthy merchant who enjoyed great consideration among his compatriots. He was but two years younger than the Prophet. His adoption of the new faith was of great moral effect. Soon after, five notables presented themselves before the Prophet and accepted Islam. Several converts also came from lower classes of the Arabs to adopt the new religion.

For three weary long years, the Prophet labored very quietly to deliver his people from the worship of idols. Polytheism was deeply rooted among the people. It offered attractions which the new faith in its purity did not possess. The Quraish had personal material interests in the old worship, and their prestige was dependent upon its maintenance. The Prophet had to contend with the idolatrous worship of its followers and to oppose the ruling oligarchy which governed its destinies.

## Muhammad's (s.a.w.) First Address to the Public

After three years of constant but quiet struggle, only thirty followers were secured. An important change now occurred in the relations of the Prophet with the citizens of Mecca. His compatriots had begun to doubt his sanity, thinking him crazy or possessed by an evil spirit. Hitherto he had preached quietly and unobtrusively. He now decided to appeal publicly to the Meccans, requesting them to abandon their idolatry. For this he arranged a gathering on a neighbouring hill and there spoke to them of their folly in the sight of Allah in worshipping pieces of stone which they called their gods. He invited them to abandon their old impious worship and adopt the faith of love, truth, and purity. He warned them of the fate that had overtaken past races who had not heeded the preaching of former prophets. But the gathering departed without listening to the warning given them by the Prophet.

## Muhammad's (s.a.w.) Address to Foreigners

Having thus failed to induce his fellow citizens to listen to him, he turned his attention to the strangers arriving in the city on commerce or pilgrimage. But the Quraish made attempts to frustrate his efforts. They hastened themselves to meet the strangers first on the different routes, to warn them against holding any communication with the Prophet, whom they represented as a dangerous magician. When the pilgrims or traders returned to their homes, they carried with them the news of the advent of the bold preacher who was inviting the Arabs loudly - at the risk of his own life - to abandon the worship of their dear idols.

## Muhammad's (s.a.w.) Message to the Meccans

The Prophet continued preaching to the Arabs in a most gentle and reasonable manner. He called the people, so accustomed to inequality and wrong doings, to abandon their abominations. In burning words which excited the hearts of his hearers, he warned them of the punishment which Allah had inflicted upon the ancient tribes of 'Ad (Aad) and Thamud (Samud) who had obstinately disobeyed the teachings of Allah's messengers to them. He adjured them by the wonderful sights of nature, by the noonday brightness, by the night when it spreads its veil, by the day when it appears in glory to listen to his warning before a similar destruction befell them. He spoke to them of the Day of Reckoning, when their deeds in this world will be weighed before the Eternal Judge, when the children who had been buried alive will be asked for what crime they were put to death.

## The First Hijrah (migration)

Persecution by the Quraish grew fiercer every day and the sufferings of the Prophet's disciples became unbearable. He had heard of the righteousness, tolerance, and hospitality of the neighbouring Christian king of Abyssinia. He recommended such of his companions who were without protection to seek refuge in the kingdom of that pious king, Al Najashi (Negus). Some fifteen of the unprotected adherents of Islam promptly availed themselves of the advice and sailed to Abyssinia. Here they met with a very kind reception from the Negus. This is called the first hijrah (migration) in the history of Islam and occurred in the fifth year of the Prophet Muhammad's (s.a.w.) mission, A.D. 615. These emigrants were soon followed by many of their fellow sufferers, until the number reached eighty-three men and eighteen women.

## Muhammad (s.a.w.) Continues Preaching to the Quraish

While the followers of the Prophet sought safety in foreign lands against the persecution of their people, he continued his warnings to the Quraish more strenuously than ever. Again they came to him with offers of riches and honor, which he firmly and utterly refused. But they mocked at him and urged him for miracles to prove his mission. He used to answer: "Allah has not sent me to work wonders; He has sent me to preach to you." Thus disclaiming all power of wonder-working, the Prophet ever rested the truth of his divine mission upon his wise teachings. He addressed himself to the inner consciousness of man, to his common sense and to his own better judgment. Say (O Muhammad (s.a.w.): 'I am only a human being like you. It is inspired in me that your Ilah (God) is One Ilah (God - Allah), therefore take the Straight Path to Him (with true Faith - Islamic Monotheism) and obedience to Him, and seek forgiveness of Him. And woe to Al-Mushrikeen: polytheists, pagans, idolaters, and disbelievers in the Oneness of Allah etc., those who worship others along with Allah or set up rivals or partners to Allah etc., (Surah 41: 6)

## Muhammad (s.a.w.) Preaches in Ta'if

Prophet, weighed down by the loss of his amiable protector and his beloved wife, without hope of turning the Quraish from idolatry, with a saddened heart, yet full of trust, resolved to exercise his ministry in some other field. He chose Ta'if, a town about sixty miles east of Mecca, where he went accompanied by his faithful servant Zaid. The tribe of Thakif (Saqif), who were the inhabitants of Ta'if, received Muhammad (s.a.w.) very coldly. However, he stayed there for one month. Though the more considerate and better sort of men treated him with a little respect, the slaves and common people refused to listen to his teachings; they were outrageously indignant at his invitation to abandon the gods they worshipped with such freedom of morals and lightness of heart. At length they rose against him, and bringing him to the wall of the city, obliged him to depart and return to Mecca.

## Muhammad (s.a.w.) Converts some Jews:

The repulse greatly discouraged his followers; however, the Prophet boldly continued to preach to the public assemblies at the pilgrimage and gained several new converts, among whom were six of the city of Yathrib (Yasrib - later called Madinah) and of the Jewish tribe of Khazraj. When these Yathribites returned home, they spread the news among their people that a prophet had arisen among the Arabs who was to call them to Allah and put an end to their iniquities.

## The Miraj:

Abbas Ibn Malik (r.a.a.) reported that Malik Ibn Sasaa said that Allah's Messenger described to them his Night Journey saying: "While I was lying in Al-Hateem or Al-Hijr, suddenly someone came to me and cut my body open from here to here." I asked Al-Jarud, who was by my side, "What does he mean?" He said: "It means from his throat to his pubic area," or said, "From the top of the chest." The Prophet further said, "He then took out my heart. Then a gold tray of Belief was brought to me and my heart was washed and was filled (with Belief) and then returned to its original place. Then a white animal which was smaller than a mule and bigger than a donkey was brought to me." (On this Al-Jarud asked: "Was it the Buraq, O Abu Hamza?" I (i.e., Anas) replied in the affirmative. The Prophet said: 'The animal's step (was so wide that it) reached the farthest point within the reach of the animal's sight. I was carried on it, and Gabriel set out with me till we reached the nearest heaven. "When he asked for the gate to be opened, it was asked, 'Who is it?' Gabriel answered, 'Gabriel.' It was asked, 'Who is accompanying you?' Gabriel replied, 'Muhammad (s.a.w.).' It was asked, 'Has Muhammad (s.a.w.) been called?' Gabriel replied in the affirmative. Then it was said, 'He is welcomed. What an excellent visit his is!' The gate was opened, and when I went over the first heaven, I saw Adam (a.s.) there. Gabriel said (to me): 'This is your father, Adam (a.s.); pay him your greetings.' So I greeted him and he returned the greeting to me and said: 'You are welcomed, O pious son and pious Prophet.' Then Gabriel ascended with me till we reached the second heaven. Gabriel asked for the gate to be opened. It was asked: 'Who is it?' Gabriel answered: 'Gabriel.' It was asked: 'Who is accompanying you?' Gabriel replied, 'Muhammad (s.a.w.).' It was asked: 'Has he been called?' Gabriel answered in the affirmative. Then it was said: 'He is welcomed. What an excellent visit his is!' The gate was opened. "When I went over the second heaven, there I saw John (Yahya, a.s.) and Jesus (Isa, a.s.), who were cousins of each other. Gabriel said (to me): 'These are John and Jesus; pay them your greetings.' So I greeted them and both of them returned my greetings to me and said, 'You are welcomed, O pious brother and pious Prophet.'

Then Gabriel ascended with me to the third heaven and asked for its gate to be opened. It was asked: 'Who is it?' Gabriel replied: 'Gabriel.' It was asked: 'Who is accompanying you?' Gabriel replied, 'Muhammad (s.a.w.).' It was asked: 'Has he been called?' Gabriel replied in the affirmative. Then it was said: 'He is welcomed, what an excellent visit his is!' The gate was opened, and when I went over the third heaven there I saw Joseph (Yusuf, a.s.)). Gabriel said (to me): 'This is Joseph; pay him your greetings.' So I greeted him and he returned the greeting to me and said: 'You are welcomed, O pious brother and pious Prophet.' Then Gabriel ascended with me to the fourth heaven and asked for its gate to be opened. It was asked: 'Who is it?'

Gabriel replied, 'Gabriel' It was asked: 'Who is accompanying you?' Gabriel replied: 'Muhammad (s.a.w.).' It was asked: 'Has he been called?' Gabriel replied in the affirmative. Then it was said: 'He is welcomed, what an excellent visit his is!' "The gate was opened, and when I went over the fourth heaven, there I saw Enoch (Idris, a.s.). Gabriel said (to me): This is Enoch; pay him your greetings.' So I greeted him and he returned the greeting to me and said: 'You are welcomed, O pious brother and pious Prophet.' Then Gabriel ascended with me to the fifth heaven and asked for its gate to be opened. It was asked: 'Who is it?' Gabriel replied: 'Gabriel.' It was asked: 'Who is accompanying you?' Gabriel replied: 'Muhammad (s.a.w.).' It was asked: 'Has he been called?' Gabriel replied in the affirmative. Then it was said: "He is welcomed, what an excellent visit his is! So when I went over the fifth heaven, there I saw Aaron (Harun, a.s.), Gabriel said (to me): 'This is Aaron; pay him your greetings.' I greeted him and he returned the greeting to me and said: 'You are welcomed, O pious brother and pious Prophet.' Then Gabriel ascended with me to the sixth heaven and asked for its gate to be opened. It was asked: 'Who is it?' Gabriel replied, 'Gabriel.' It was asked: 'Who is accompanying you?' Gabriel replied: 'Muhammad (s.a.w.).' It was asked: 'Has he been called?' Gabriel replied in the affirmative. It was said: 'He is welcomed. What an excellent visit his is!' "When I went (over the sixth heaven), there I saw Moses (Musa,a.s.). Gabriel said (to me): 'This is Moses; pay him your greeting. So I greeted him and he returned the greetings to me and said: 'You are welcomed, O pious brother and pious Prophet.' When I left him (i.e. Moses) he wept. Someone asked him: 'What makes you weep?' Moses said: 'I weep because after me there has been sent (as Prophet) a young man whose followers will enter Paradise in greater numbers than my followers.' Then Gabriel ascended with me to the seventh heaven and asked for its gate to be opened. It was asked: 'Who is it?' Gabriel replied: 'Gabriel.' It was asked: 'Who is accompanying you?' Gabriel replied: 'Muhammad (s.a.w.).' It was asked: 'Has he been called?' Gabriel replied in the affirmative. Then it was said: 'He is welcomed. What an excellent visit his is!' "So when I went (over the seventh heaven), there I saw Abraham (Ibrahim,a. s.). Gabriel said (to me): This is your father; pay your greetings to him.' So I greeted him and he returned the greetings to me and said: 'You are welcomed, O pious son and pious Prophet.' Then I was made to ascend to Sidrat-ul-Muntaha (i.e. the Lote Tree of the utmost boundary). Behold! Its fruits were like the jars of Hajr (i.e. a place near Medina) and its leaves were as big as the ears of elephants. Gabriel said: 'This is the Lote Tree of the utmost boundary.' Behold! There ran four rivers; two were hidden and two were visible, I asked: 'What are these two kinds of rivers, O Gabriel?' He replied: 'As for the hidden rivers, they are two rivers in Paradise and the visible rivers are the Nile and the Euphrates.'

'Then Al-Bait-ul-Ma'mur (i.e., the Sacred House) was shown to me and a container full of wine and another full of milk and a third full of honey were brought to me. I took the milk. Gabriel remarked: 'This is the Islamic religion which you and your followers are following.' Then the prayers were enjoined on me: they were fifty prayers a day. When I returned, I passed by Moses, who asked (me): 'What have you been ordered to do?' I replied: 'I have been ordered to offer fifty prayers a day.' Moses said: 'Your followers cannot bear fifty prayers a day, and by Allah I have tested people before you, and I have tried my level best with Bani Israeel (in vain). Go back to your Lord and ask for reduction to lessen your followers' burden.' So I went back, and Allah reduced ten prayers for me. Then again I came to Moses, but he repeated the same as he had said before. Then again I went back to Allah, and He reduced ten more prayers. When I came back to Moses he said the same. I went back to Allah, and He ordered me to observe ten prayers a day. When I came back to Moses, he repeated the same advice, so I went back to Allah and was ordered to observe five prayers a day. "When

I came back to Moses, he said: 'What have you been ordered?' I replied: 'I have been ordered to observe five prayers a day.' He said: 'Your followers cannot bear five prayers a day, and no doubt, I have got an experience of the people before you, and I have tried my level best with Bani Israeel, so go back to your Lord and ask for reduction to lessen your followers' burden.' I said: 'I have requested so much of my Lord that I feel ashamed, but I am satisfied now and surrender to Allah's Order.' When I left, I heard a voice saying: 'I have passed My order and have lessened the burden of My worshippers."'

## Muhammad (s.a.w.) Converts Jews of Yathrib (Madina)

In this year, twelve men of Yathrib, of whom ten were of the Jewish tribe of Khazraj and the other two of Aws, came to Mecca and took an oath of fidelity to the Prophet at Al Aqaba, a hill on the north of that city. This oath was called the Women's Oath, not that any women were present at this time, but because a man was not thereby obliged to take up arms in defense of the Prophet or his religion, it being the same oath that was afterwards exacted of the women. This oath was as follows: "We will not associate anything with Allah; we will not steal nor commit adultery or fornication, nor kill our children (as the pagan Arabs used to do when they apprehended that they would not be able to maintain them), nor forge calumnies; we will obey the Prophet in everything that is reasonable, and we will be faithful to him in well and sorrow." When they had solemnly engaged to do all this, the Prophet sent one of his disciples, Mus'ab Ibn Umair, home with them to teach them the fundamental doctrines and ceremonies of the religion. Mus'ab, having arrived at Yathrib by the assistance of those who had been formerly converted, gained several new converts, particulary Uz'aid Ibn Khuzair, a chief man of the city, and Saad Ibn Mu'adh (Mua'z), prince of the tribe of Aws. Islam spread so fast that there was scarcely a house that did not have some Muslims in it.

## Muslims Find Refuge in Yathrib (Medina)

The next year, being the thirteenth of the mission (A.D. 622) Mus'ab returned from Yathrib accompanied by seventy-three men and two women of that city who had adopted Islam, besides others who were as yet unbelievers. On their arrival, these Yathribites immediately sent to the Prophet and invited him to their city. The Prophet was now in great need of such assistance, for his opponents had by this time grown so powerful in Mecca that he could not stay there much longer without imminent danger. He therefore accepted their proposal and met them one night by appointment at Al-Aqaba attended by his uncle Al Abbas, who, though he was not then a convert, wished his nephew well.

Al Abbas made a speech to those of Yathrib wherein he told them that, as the Prophet Muhammad (s.a.w.) was obliged to quit his native city and seek shelter elsewhere, and they had offered him their protection, they would do well not to deceive him; and that if they were not firmly resolved to defend and not to betray him, they had better declare their minds and let him provide for his safety in some other manner. Upon their professing their sincerity, the Prophet swore to be faithful to them, on condition that they should worship none but Allah, observe the precepts of Islam, obey the Prophet in all that was right, and protect him against all insults as heartily as they would their wives and families. They then asked him what would be their return, if they should happen to be killed in the cause of Allah; he answered:' "Paradise," whereupon they pledged their faith to him and his cause. The Prophet then selected twelve men out of their number to act as his delegates. Thus was concluded the second covenant of Al Aqaba.

The Yathribites returned home leaving the Prophet to arrange for the journey to their city. The Prophet directed his followers to seek immediate safety at Yathrib, which they accordingly did. About one hundred families silently disappeared from

Mecca and proceeded to Yathrib, where they were received with enthusiasm and much hospitality. Finally, all the disciples had gone to Yathrib. The Prophet alone remained at Mecca, keeping with him only his young cousin Ali, and his devoted friend Abu Bakr.

## Muhammad (s.a.w.) in Medina

Narrated Urwa Ibn Az-Zubair: "Allah's Messenger met Az-Zubair in a caravan of Muslim merchants who were returning from Sham. Az-Zubair provided Allah's Messenger and Abu Bakr with white clothes to wear. When the Muslims of Medina heard the news of the departure of Allah's Messenger from Mecca (towards Medina), they started going to the Ha'rra every morning. They would wait for him till the heat of the noon forced them to return. One day, after waiting for a long while, they returned home, and when they went into their houses, a Jew climbed up to the roof of one of the forts of his people to look for something, and he saw Allah's Messenger and his companions, dressed in white clothes, emerging out of the desert mirage. "The Jew could not help shouting at the top of his voice: 'O you Arabs! Here is your great man whom you have been waiting for!' So all the Muslims rushed to their arms and received Allah's Messenger on the summit of Ha'rra.

The Prophet turned with them to the right and alighted at the quarters of Bani Amr Ibn 'Auf, and this was on Monday in the month of Rabi-ul-Awwal. Abu Bakr stood up, receiving the people, while Allah's Messenger sat down and kept silent. Some of the Ansar who came and had not seen Allah's Messenger before began greeting Abu Bakr, but when the sunshine fell on Allah's Messenger and Abu Bakr came forward and shaded him with his sheet, only then the people came to know Allah's Messenger. Allah's Messenger stayed with Bani Amr Ibn Auf for ten nights and established the mosque (Mosque of Quba) which was founded on piety. Allah's Messenger prayed in it and then mounted his she-camel and proceeded on, accompanied by the people till his she-camel knelt down at (the place of) the Mosque of Allah's Messenger at Medina.

Some Muslims used to pray there in those days, and that place was a yard for drying dates belonging to Suhail and Sahl, the orphan boys who were under the guardianship of Asad Ibn Zurara. When his she-camel knelt down, Allah's Messenger said: 'This place, Allah willing, will be our abiding place.' Allah's Messenger then called the two boys and told them to suggest a price for that yard so that he might take it as a mosque. The two boys said: 'No, but we will give it as a gift, O Allah's Messenger!" Allah's Messenger then built a mosque there. The Prophet himself started carrying unburnt bricks for its building and while doing so, he was saying: 'This load is better than the load of Khaibar, for it is more pious in the Sight of Allah and purer and better rewardable.' He was also saying: 'O Allah! The actual reward is the reward in the Hereafter, so bestow Your Mercy on the Ansar and the Emigrants.' Thus the Prophet recited (by way of proverb) the poem of some Muslim poet whose name is unknown to me." (Ibn Shihab said, "In the Hadiths it does not occur that Allah's Messenger recited a complete poetic verse other than this one)." Thus was accomplished the hijrah, or the flight of Muhammad (s.a.w.) as called in European annals, from which the Islamic calendar dates.

## Yathrib Becomes Medina

When the Prophet Muhammad (s.a.w.) and his companions settled at Yathrib, this city changed its name, and henceforth was called, Al-Medina Al-Munawwara, The Illuminated City, or more shortly, Medina, The City. It is situated about eleven day's journey to the north of Mecca. At that time it was ruled by two Kahtanite tribes, Aws and Khazraj. These two tribes, however, were constantly quarreling among themselves. It was only about the time when the Prophet announced his mission at Mecca that these tribes, after long years of continuous warfare, entered on a period of comparative peace.

When the Prophet settled at Medina, the tribes of Aws and Khazraj forgot entirely their old feuds and were united together in the bond of Islam. Their old divisions were soon effaced and the "Ansaar", the Helpers of the Prophet, became the common designation of all Medinites who had helped the Prophet in his cause. Those who emigrated with him from Mecca received the title of "Muhajereen" or The Emigrants. The Prophet, in order to unite both classes in closer bonds, established between them a brotherhood which linked them together as children of the same parents, with the Prophet as their guardian.

## Muhammad (s.a.w.) Makes a Contract in Medina:

The first step the Prophet took, after his settlement at Medina, was to build a mosque for the worship of Allah according to the principles of Islam. Also, houses for the accommodation of the emigrants were soon erected. Medina and its suburbs were at this time inhabited by three distinct parties, the Emigrants, the Helpers, and the Jews. In order to weld them together into an orderly federation, the Prophet granted a charter to the people, clearly defining their rights and obligations. This charter represented the framework of the first commonwealth organized by the Prophet. It started thus: "In the name of the Most Merciful and Compassionate Lord, this charter is given by Muhammad (s.a.w.), the Messenger of Allah to all believers, whether of Quraish or Medina, and all individuals of whatever origin who have made common cause with them, who shall all constitute one nation."

The following are some extracts from the charter: The state of peace and war shall be common to all Muslims; no one among them shall have the right of concluding peace with, or declaring war against, the enemies of his co-religionists. The Jews who attach themselves to our commonwealth shall be protected from all insults and vexations; they shall have an equal right with our own people to our assistance and good offices. The Jews of the various branches and all others domiciled in Medina shall form with the Muslims one composite nation; they shall practise their religion as freely as the Muslims. The allies of the Jews shall enjoy the same security and freedom. The guilty shall be pursued and punished. The Jews shall join the Muslims in defending Medina against all enemies. The interior of Medina shall be a sacred place for all who accept this charter. All true Muslims shall hold in abhorrence every man guilty of crime, injustice or disorder; no one shall uphold the culpable, though he be his nearest kin. After dealing with the interior management of the State, the charter concluded as follows: "All future disputes arising among those who accept this charter shall be referred, under Allah, to the Prophet." Thus this charter put an end to the state of anarchy that prevailed among the Arabs. It constituted the Prophet Muhammad (s.a.w.) as chief magistrate of the nation.

## Muhammad (s.a.w.) Establishes a Contract with the Christians

It was about this time that the Prophet granted to the monks of the Monastery of St. Catherine, near Mount Sinai, his liberal charter by which they secured for the Christians noble and generous privileges and immunities. He undertook himself, and enjoined his followers, to protect the Christians, to defend their churches and the residences of their priests and to guard them from all injuries. They were not to be unfairly taxed; no bishop was to be driven out of his diocese; no Christian was to be forced to reject his religion; no monk was to be expelled from his monastery; no pilgrim was to be stopped from his pilgrimage; nor were the Christian churches to be pulled down for the sake of building mosques or houses for the Muslims. Christian women married to Muslims were to enjoy their own religion and not to be subjected to compulsion or annoyance of any kind. If the Christians should stand in need of assistance for the repair of their churches or monasteries, or any other matter pertaining to their religion, the Muslims were to assist them. This was not to be considered as supporting their religion, but as simply rendering them assistance in special circumstances. Should the Muslims be engaged in hostilities with outside Christians, no Christian resident among the Muslims should be treated with contempt on account of his creed. The Prophet declared that any Muslim violating any clause of the charter should be regarded as a transgressor of Allah's commandments, a violator of His testament and neglectful of His faith.

## The Treaty of Hudaibiya

Six years had already elapsed since the Prophet and his Meccan followers had fled from their birthplace. Their hearts began to yearn for their homes and for their Sacred House, the Kaba. As the season of the pilgrimage approached, the Prophet announced his intention to visit the holy center, and numerous voices of his disciples responded to the call. Preparations were soon made for the journey to Mecca. The Prophet, accompanied by seven or eight hundred Muslims, Emigrants and Ansaars, all totally unarmed, set out on the pilgrimage. The Quraish, who were still full of animosity towards the Muslims, gathered a large army to prevent them from entering Mecca and maltreated the envoy whom the Prophet had sent to ask their permission to visit the holy places. After much difficulty, a treaty was concluded by which it was agreed that all hostilities should cease for ten years; that any one coming from the Quraish to the Prophet without the permission of the guardian or chief should be given back to the idolaters; that any Muslim persons going over to the Meccans should not be surrendered; that any tribe desirous of entering into alliance, either with the Quraish or with the Muslims, should be at liberty to do so without disputes; that the Muslims should go back to Medina on the present occasion and stop advancing further; that they should be permitted in the following year to visit Mecca and to remain there for three days with the arms they used on journeys, namely, their scimitars in sheaths. The Treaty of Hudaibiya thus ended, the Prophet returned with his people to Medina.

## Muhammad (s.a.w.)'s Preaching through Letters

About this time it was revealed to the Prophet that his mission should be universal. He dispatched several envoys to invite the neighboring sovereigns to Islam. The embassy to the king of Persia, Khusro Parvez, received him with disdain and contumely. He was haughtily amazed at the boldness of the Meccan fugitive in addressing him on terms of equality. He was so enraged that he tore into pieces the Prophet's letter of invitation to Islam and dismissed the envoy from his presence with great contempt. When the Prophet received information on this treatment, he calmly observed: 'Thus will the Empire of Khusro be torn to pieces."

The embassy to Heracles Caesar, the Emperor of the Romans, received much more politely and reverentially. He treated the ambassador with great respect and sent the Prophet a gracious reply to his message. Another envoy was sent to an Arab prince of the Ghassanite tribe, a Christian feudatory of Heracles. This prince, instead of receiving the envoy with any respect, cruelly murdered him. This act caused great consternation among the Muslims, who considered it as an outrage of international obligations.

## Letters to Emperors, Vicegerents, Kings, Rulers, Governors, etc.

### 1. Letter to Khusro Pervez, King of Persia

*In the name of Allah, the most Compassionate, the most Merciful.*

From Muhammad (s.a.w.), Prophet of Allah to Kisra, King of Fars (Persia).

May peace be on him who follows the guidance, believes in Allah and his Prophet. I testify that there is non worthy of worship except Allah, Who is alone and without an associate and Muhammad (s.a.w.) is His servant and prophet. Allah has made me a prophet and sent me for the entire world, in order that I may infuse the fear of Allah in every living person. Accept

Islam and be secure. If you refuse, the sins of all the Zoroastrians shall be your responsibility.

Seal:

Allah's Prophet

Muhammad (s.a.w.)

(Tabari's History, vol. 3, p.-90)

## 2. Letter to Roman Emperor (Heracles Caesar)

*In the name of Allah, the most Compassionate, the most Merciful.*
From Muhammad (s.a.w.), Prophet of Allah to Heracles Caesar.

May peace be on him, who follows the right path. After this, I invite you to the fold of Islam. Therefore, if you desire security, accept Islam. If you accept Islam, Allah shall reward you doubly and if you refuse to do so, the responsibility for the transgression of the entire nation shall be yours.

O people of the book! Leaving aside all matters of differences and disputes, agree on a thing, which is equally incontrovertible both as you and we are concerned and it is that we should not worship anyone else with Him, nor regard anyone else except Allah as our sustainer.

If you deny this, you must know that we believe in oneness of Allah, in all circumstances.

Seal:

Allah's Prophet

Muhammad (s.a.w.)

(Sahih Bukhari, vol.1, p.-5, Delhi, Asahul Matabe.)

## 3. Letter to Haris Ghassani, King of Damishq (Damascus)

*In the name of Allah, the most Compassionate, the most Merciful.*
From Muhammad (s.a.w.), Prophet of Allah to Haris bin Abi Shimr.

Peace be on him who follows the right path, believes in it and regards it as true. I invite you to believe in one Allah, Who has no associate.

Your country would remain with you.

Seal:

Allah's Prophet

Muhammad (s.a.w.)

(Tabaqat-e-Ibn S'ad, vol. 3, p.-17)

## 4. Letter to Negus, the King of Ethiopia

*In the name of Allah, the most compassionate, the merciful.*

From Muhammad (s.a.w.) prophet of Allah to Negus (the king of Ethiopia)

I praise Allah, except Whom there is none to be worshiped, Who is the Ruler of the world. He is innocent and pure (free from all blemishes, defects, flaws, or shortcomings). He gives refuge and sustains all.

I do admit that Isa (Jesus, A.S.) son of Mariyam (Mary), was the soul from Allah and His word (order), he was infused to Mariyam, who was clean and proof against evil. And Isa (A.S.) was born of Mariyam. Allah created him from His soul and breath in the same manner as He created Adam (a.s.) (A.S.) with His own hand. I invite you towards Allah the One Who has no associate. Believe in Him and join me in obedience to Him. Follow me and accept my prophethood because I am the Messenger of Allah. I have wished you well in conveying the message of Allah in all sincerity. It is upto you to accept my sympathetic advice. Extend the same invitation to your subjects. I am sending my cousin Jaffer (R.A.A.) with the other Muslims. When they reach you, treat them hospitably, by setting aside the vanity and pride of the ruler. Peace be on him who followed the right path.

Seal:

Allah's Prophet

Muhammad (s.a.w.)

(Tabari's History, vol.3:789)

## 5. Letter to the Vicegerent of Egypt

*In the name of Allah, the most compassionate, the merciful.*

From Muhammad (s.a.w.), prophet of Allah to Muqawuis, Vicegerent of Egypt.

Peace be on him who has taken the right course. Therefore, I invite you to accept Islam. Therefore if you want security, accept Islam. If you accept Islam, Allah, the Sublime, shall reward you doubly. But if you refuse to do so, responsibility for transgression of the entire nation will be yours.

O people of the book! Leaving aside all matters of difference and dispute, agree on a matter which is equally consistent between you and us and it is that we should not worship anyone except Allah and that we should neither associate anyone with Him, nor make anyone else as our god.

If you refuse it, you must know that we, in all circumstances believe in oneness of Allah.

Seal:

Allah's Prophet

Muhammad (s.a.w.).

(Zadul Ma'ad, vol.3, p.- 61)

## Pilgrimage to Mecca

Before the end of the year, it being the seventh year of the hijrah, the Prophet and his adherents availed themselves of their armistice with the Quraish to visit the holy Kaba. The Prophet, accompanied by two hundred Muslims, went to Mecca to perform the rites of pilgrimage. On this occasion the Quraish evacuated the city during the three days which the ceremonies lasted.

## Islam Continues to Spread Universally

During his stay at Mecca, the Prophet dispatched his principal disciples in every direction to preach Islam among the wild tribes of the desert and call them to the true religion of Allah. He sent small detachments of his troops into the suburbs who destroyed the temples of Al 'Uzza, Suwaa and Mana't, the three famous idols in the temples of the neighboring tribes. The Prophet gave strict orders that these expeditions should be carried out in a peaceable manner. These injunctions were obeyed in all cases, with one exception. The troops under Khalid Ibn Al-Waleed, the fierce newly-converted warrior, killed a few of the Bani Jazima. When the news of this wanton bloodshed reached the Prophet, he was deeply grieved and exclaimed: "Oh, my Lord, I am innocent of what Khalid has done." He dispatched a large sum of money for the widows and orphans of the slain and severely rebuked Khalid.

## Muhammad (s.a.w.)'s Last Sermon

On the return of the sacred month of pilgrimage, the Prophet, under the presentiment of his approaching end, determined to make a farewell pilgrimage to Mecca. In February 632, he left Medina with a very considerable concourse of Muslims. It is stated that from ninety thousand to one hundred and forty thousand persons accompanied the Prophet. Before completing all rites of the pilgrimage, he addressed the assembled multitude from the top of Mount Arafat in the following words: "O people! Listen to my words, for I know not whether another year will be vouchsafed to me after this year to find myself among you. Your lives and property are sacred and inviolable among one another until you appear before the Lord, as this day and this month are sacred for all; and remember; you will have to appear before your Lord Who will demand from you an account for all your actions. O people, you have rights over your wives, and your wives have rights over you. Verily you have taken them on the security of Allah and have made their persons lawful unto you by the words of Allah. And your slaves, see that you feed them with such food as you eat yourselves, and clothe them with the stuff you wear, and if they commit a fault which you are not inclined to forgive, then part with them; for they are the servants of the Lord and are not to be harshly treated. O people, listen to my words and understand them. Know that all Muslims are brothers. You are one brotherhood; but no man shall take aught from his brother, unless by his free consent. Keep yourselves from injustice. Let him who is present tell this to him who is absent. It may be that he who is told this afterward may remember better than he who has now heard it.

"The Prophet concluded his sermon by exclaiming: "O Lord, I have fulfilled my message and accomplished my work." The assembled multitude, all in one voice, cried: "Yea, verily you have." The Prophet again exclaimed: "O Lord, I beseech You, bear witness to it." Having rigorously performed all the ceremonies of the pilgrimage, that his example might be followed by all Muslims for all succeeding ages, the Prophet returned with his followers to Medina.

## Muhammad (s.a.w.)'s Last Prayer

The health of the Prophet grew worse. His last days were remarkable for the calmness and serenity of his mind. He was able, though weak and feeble, to lead the public prayers until within three days of his death. He requested that he might be permitted to stay at Aisha's house close to the mosque during his illness, an arrangement to which his other wives assented. As long as his strength lasted, he took part in the public prayers. The last time he appeared in the mosque he addressed the congregation, after the usual prayers were over, in the following words: "O Muslims, if I have wronged anyone of you, here I am to answer for it; if I owe anything to anyone, all I may happen to possess belongs to you."

A man in the crowd rose and claimed three dirhams which he had given to a poor man at the request of the Prophet. They were immediately paid back with these words: "Better to blush in this world than in the next."

The Prophet then prayed and implored Allah's mercy for those who had fallen in the persecution of their enemies. He recommended to all his followers the observance of religious duties and the leading of a life of peace and goodwill. Then he spoke with emotion and with a voice still so powerful as to reach beyond the outer doors of the mosque: "By the Lord in Whose hand lies the soul of Muhammad (s.a.w.) as to myself, no man can lay hold on me in any matter; I have not made lawful anything excepting what Allah has made lawful; nor have I prohibited anything but that which Allah in His Book has prohibited."

Then turning to the women who sat close by, he exclaimed: "O Fatimah, my daughter, and Safia, my aunt, work you both that which will procure your acceptance with the Lord, for verily I have no power to save you in any wise." He then rose and re-entered the house of Aisha.

## Death of Prophet Muhammad (s.a.w.)

After this, the Prophet never appeared at public prayers. A few hours after he returned from the mosque, the Prophet died while laying his head on the bosom of Aisha. As soon as the Prophet's death was announced, a crowd of people gathered at the door of the house of Aisha, exclaiming: "How can our messenger be dead?" Umar said: "No, he is not dead; he will be restored to us, and those are traitors to the cause of Islam who say he is dead. If they say so let them be cut into pieces."

But Abu Bakr entered the house at this moment, and after he had touched the body of the Prophet with a demonstration of profound affection, he appeared at the door and addressed the crowd with the following speech: "O Muslims, if any of you has been worshipping Muhammad (s.a.w.), then let me tell you that Muhammad (s.a.w.) is dead. But if you really do worship Allah then know that Allah is living and will never die. Do you forget the verse in the Qur'an: Muhammad (s.a.w.) is no more than a Messenger, and indeed (many) Messengers have passed a way before him. If he dies or is killed, will you then turn back on your heels (as disbelievers)? And he who turns back on his heels, not the least harm will he do to Allah, and Allah will give reward to those who are grateful." (Surah 3:144) Upon hearing this speech of Abu Bakr, Umar acknowledged his error, and the crowd was satisfied and dispersed.

"Sallallahu Alaihi Wasallam (may Allah bestow salaah and salaam on him)"

## Reference:

http://www.alim.org/Alim_-_Islamic_Knowledge_Platform/index.html

# Concluding Prayers

We seek refuge with Allah from all evils and from slinking whispers:

*"We seek refuge with the Rabb of the dawn from the mischief of all that He has created; and from the mischief of darkness when it overspreads; from the mischief of those who blow on knots (black magic); and from the mischief of the envier when he envies."* (Al-Falaq: 113.1-5)

*"We seek refuge in the Rabb of the mankind, the King of mankind, the real God of mankind, from the mischief of the slinking whisperers (Shaitan and his workers) who whisper into the hearts of people, whether he be from among the jinn or from the mankind."* (An-Nas: 114.1-6)

Other Books on

## PHILOSOPHY, RELIGION & CULTURE

| | | |
|---|---|---|
| 21. | Culture India | 250/- |
| 22. | My Experiments With Truth | 250/- |
| 23. | Mahatma Gandhi The Bhagavadgita | 125/- |
| 24. | Shirdi Sai Baba | 80/- |
| 25. | The Ramayana For Every Home | 125/- |
| 26. | The Mahabharata For Every Home | 125/- |
| 27. | Sai The Age of Cosmic Family | 75/- |
| 28. | Sathya Sai and His Miraculous Powers | 95/- |
| 29. | To Bloom Like A Lotus | 150/- |
| 30. | The History of Sikh Gurus | 225/- |
| 31. | Intelligence Beyond Thought | 295/- |
| 32. | Indian Mythology | 195/- |

Lotus PRESS

Unit No. 220, Second Floor, 4735/22,
Prakash Deep Building,Ansari Road, Daryaganj,
New Delhi- 110002, Ph.: 32903912, 23280047, 09811838000
• E-mail : lotus_press@sify.com. www.lotuspress.co.in